Personal Property

Personal Property

Wives, White Slaves, and the Market in Women

Margit Stange

The Johns Hopkins University Press
BALTIMORE AND LONDON

© 1998 The Johns Hopkins University Press

All rights reserved. Published 1998
Printed in the United States of America on acid-free paper

07   06   05   04   03   02   01   00   99   98   5   4   3   2   1

The Johns Hopkins University Press
2715 North Charles Street
Baltimore, Maryland 21218-4363
The Johns Hopkins Press Ltd., London

Library of Congress Cataloging-in-Publication Data will be
found at the end of this book.

A catalog record for this book is available from the British Library.

ISBN 0-8018-5626-4

For my mother

CONTENTS

Acknowledgments   *ix*

Introduction   1

ONE   *The Woman of Exchange*

1   Exchange Value and the Female Self in *The Awakening*   21

2   Edith Wharton and the Problem of the Woman Author   36

3   Lily Bart at the Point of "Modification"   54

TWO   *The Great White Slavery Scare*

4   "No Girl Is Safe!"   75

5   Papa's Girl   104

Conclusion   128

Notes   *141*
Bibliography   *157*
Index   *165*

ACKNOWLEDGMENTS

This book reflects the inspiration and support of many people who have shaped its development since I first began to write about the exchange of woman. My work, like my career as a scholar, took form under the influence of my teachers, especially Walter Benn Michaels and Catherine Gallagher. The teaching of Julia Bader, Stephen Knapp, and Bonnie Isaac has left its imprint. The guidance of many colleagues and readers and the insights of students, both graduate and undergraduate, are reflected here.

My colleagues at Davis, particularly David Van Leer, Joanne Diehl, Tricia Moran, Phillip Barrish, Sandra Gilbert, and Linda Morris, have generously created an intellectual community for me and given freely of their time and expertise. I am grateful to the members of the Junior Faculty Reading Group, particularly Lynn Wardley and Susan Lurie, for careful, enlightening, and timely feedback. Inderpal Grewal and Lora Romero prompted me to elucidate crucial points, and the clarifying intelligence of the anonymous Johns Hopkins reader has been wonderfully helpful.

It is hard to separate my project from my life; both have benefited enormously from the instruction, companionship, and inspiration of friends and teachers, particularly the late Linda Arizona and the soul tribe she helped me find. Terrance Kelly and the Oakland Interfaith Gospel Choir, Renée Valentino, Bill Ganz, Donald Bender, Sandra Lee Goozée, and Estelle Rubenstein have been important to this process. And I have learned, with gratitude, to rely on the understanding and support of Eric Stange and Barbara Costa and Bob and Alida Stange.

Progress on this book was aided by a University of California at Davis Faculty Development Grant, University of California at Davis Faculty Research Grants, and a fellowship from the Davis Humanities Institute.

I am indebted to Dr. Willis Regier at the Johns Hopkins University Press for the careful guidance that has helped make this manuscript into a book. The final stages have been greatly facilitated by the expert help of Jennifer Trainor, Sue Smith, and Maria denBoer.

Chapter 1 originally appeared in slightly different form in *Genders* 5 (1989), and I thank the University of Texas Press for permission to reprint it here.

Personal Property

Introduction

A 1910 white slavery narrative, "The True Story of Estelle Ramon," tells of a young woman whose widowed mother has pressured her into marrying a flashy stranger from the city. The new husband turns out to be a white slave procurer who promptly sells Estelle into a life of forced prostitution and flees with the proceeds. Upon realizing her situation, Estelle falls into a faint; but the madam revives her, calmly informing the young woman that she "had bought her and paid for her" and therefore inexorably "was going to keep her." "Pretty girls like her," the madam adds, "usually go for $100"— a piece of information that implicitly ensures Estelle's bondage by demonstrating her incapacity ever to afford an item as costly as herself (Bell 1910, 92).

Texts published in the United States between 1899 and World War I tell many such stories of women who, like Estelle Ramon, find themselves defined as valuable and exchangeable property. Along with the hugely popular white slavery literature, of which Estelle's story is an instance, a variety of other textual forms, both fiction and nonfiction, awakened women to their status as commodities in a multileveled "market . . . where girls are sold and bought" (Roe, 169). This study groups together a selection of texts published in the United States during these years. Though they vary in generic form and in the specifics of their thematic focus, these texts all affirm a view of woman's social condition that derives from nineteenth-century anthropology.[1] Now known (since Lévi-Strauss's twentieth-century extrapolation) as "the exchange of woman," this account of the historical evolution of society asserts that male-dominated monogamous marriage, founded in tandem with the institution of private property, marks the turning point from barbarism to civilization. The wife, under this system of possessive monogamy, is acquired by the individual male through various means (including capture and more orderly modes of exchange) and serves as the fundamental and prototypical form of personal property.[2]

Despite their generic differences, the texts grouped together here all give voice to the period's near-obsession with the view that in the booming market economy of the early twentieth century, woman constituted a form of private property acquired through the market. The exchange of woman was not an accurate reflection of social reality; but, as its popularity indicates, it offered a timely response to the changes brought on by the growth of market capitalism. As a coherent (albeit vexed) view of contemporary society, it registered a protest against the coercive pressures of big business; it articulated anxieties over the destabilization of basic social structures, particularly the family; it gave voice to wishful visions of reform; and, in the painful situation of the woman treated as property, it provided a rich, paradoxical, and dramatic premise to the authors and readers of the day.

In the texts examined here, women are depicted as commodities; but the specifics of their commodity forms, and the particulars of the markets in which they circulate, vary according to the focus of the author's concerns. The white slavery market featured in stories like that of Estelle Ramon is an organized and rationalized commercial operation in which thousands of women's bodies are briskly bought and sold. With its lurid depictions of economic exploitation and its urgent calls for reform, white slavery literature is a nightmarish reflection of a social order overrun by business enterprise. The reforms it proposes, as chapters 4 and 5 discuss, imagine the renovation of the patriarchal family and the unification of a diversifying populace around the figure of a universally valuable "white" woman. In Kate Chopin's *The Awakening* (the subject of chapter 1), the interior life of the wife whose bourgeois husband sees her as "personal property" focuses the narrative. Chopin explores the possibilities for self-ownership—or even self-awareness—of a woman who, as a wife and mother, is defined by the claims of others. In Edith Wharton's fiction and nonfiction, the subject of chapters 2 and 3, the author depicts women who are exchanged and consumed both as prospective wives and as authors commodified through their published texts. Wharton's heroines negotiate the vexed relations among femininity, aesthetic fineness, and consumer demand. Consumer culture is also foremost in the feminist sociological writings of Charlotte Perkins Gilman and Jane Addams. These authors connect woman's sexual commodification to the material dependency that relegates her to the economic role of consumption. But in Gilman's *Women and Economics* (which I discuss later in this introduction) and in Addams' white slavery writings (which I explore in the conclusion), the authors argue, not that women should no longer be regarded as commodities and consumers, but that the vulnerability and debasement this status entails has earned them public powers and protections.

Some of the works studied here draw quite literally on the anthropological discourse. Gilman begins *Women and Economics* with a rehearsal of Herbert Spencer's synthesis of the evolutionary account of human social development. White slavery collections frequently open with an account of prostitution throughout the ages that derives from anthropological histories.[3] In white slavery writings, features of market society seem to be modeled on the bygone stages described in the anthropology. The barbaric bosses of the white slavery syndicates, the tyrannical, scheming, and irrationally greedy brothel madams, the dangerously acquisitive women who, like Estelle's mother, Amanda, come into possession of their daughters with disastrous consequences—and the relentless circulation of prostituted women among groups of men—figure a regression to the times before civilized monogamy, when horde or group marriage made paternity uncertain and lineage was traced through the mother (McLennan, Fee).

In other texts the anthropology is less literal. But each of the authors studied here works out a logic of productive sacrifice which reflects the premise that woman's reduction to property serves as the foundation of civilization. The subjugation that woman suffers as an object of exchange, the tragic losses and regrettable waste incurred by this system, are depicted with painful clarity; but the sacrifice always produces something valuable and necessary. Whether this is imagined as social reform, economic value, or aesthetic quality, this outcome of woman's subjection to the exchange system redeems her sacrifice and even argues its necessity.

The most fundamental sacrifice that the market inflicts on the exchanged woman is the loss of her freedom. For Wharton and Gilman, the property system, which has made woman dependent on man, has forced her to adapt to consumerism and rendered her helpless and unfit for survival in the modern-day industrial market. The white "slave" is the most extreme victim of the property system. She is the mirror opposite of the self-owning individual usually associated with market capitalism, the "possessive individual." A form of capitalist market selfhood that began to take shape in the seventeenth century, the possessive individual (as defined by C. B. MacPherson) is understood as having rights of ownership, his first such right being the right of property in himself. As John Locke writes, "every Man has a *Property* in his own *Person*. This no body has any Right to but himself." Owning his labor and capacities, this "man" is free to manage and alienate these and other properties as he sees fit. In effect, these rights do not merely inhere in the possessive individual but bring him into being as a self constituted through possessiveness.[4]

In the discourse of the exchange of woman, male possessive selfhood begins with the subjugation and bondage of woman through the property system.[5] The "woman question" that agitated the nineteenth century, when feminists claimed that women had rights to autonomy, equality, and self-possession, receives a very discouraging answer from the exchange of woman. In fact, in examining the late-nineteenth-century anthropological theory, scholar Elizabeth Fee concludes that the discourse of the exchange of woman was erected as an intellectual buttress to defend bourgeois male supremacy against the challenges posed both by liberalism in general, which unseated the "patriarchalisms" of monarchical governments, and by feminism in particular, which recruited liberal arguments to question the exclusion of woman from enjoyment of the "rights of man" (Fee, 86–88).

Strikingly, the theory that defines woman as the object of male ownership rose to cultural prominence at a time when women's opportunities for self-determination were conspicuously expanding. By the early years of the twentieth century, the "New Woman" who had begun to emerge in the 1880s and 1890s had staked her claim to public roles, rights, and powers that lay outside the traditional familial subjection of woman. Middle- and upper-class women increasingly took up careers, raised their public voices, and developed their own political and educational institutions. Lower-class women also entered the public sphere: as historian Paula Baker writes, "the growing number of women who worked for wages provided palpable examples of the limits of notions about a woman's place" (Baker, 80).[6]

The discourse of the exchange of woman, as it is articulated in the texts studied here, combines a reaction to the unsettling expansion of women's roles with a reaction to the great social changes brought by the growth of the market. Industrialization, by removing production from the home, had provided these new wage-earning jobs for women; and continuing rapid industrialization was supported by the development and consolidation of broad-ranging and integrated systems of finance, distribution, and marketing, as commodity capitalism rapidly transformed American society. But in the texts portraying the woman of exchange, the new roles for new women rehearse the old role of the chattel/wife—with a difference. Whereas the wife of old was exchanged in restricted, locally reciprocal markets (traded between kin groups, for example), in the texts studied here, woman is a commodity that circulates throughout a series of interlocking markets. Not only an item of trade, she is an opportunity for investment and profit, a speculative property passed from one agent to the next in a cycle of circulation that resembles the "generalized exchange" described by Lévi-Strauss.[7] Her status as a commodity is enforced and perpetuated by the new consumer culture, which creates ever-emerging demands for the value forms in which woman is traded and which supplies women for the market by translating the private dependency of the wife into the public neediness—and therefore the sexual accessibility—of the consumerist woman.[8]

The growth of the market means a life of perpetual exploitation for heroines like Estelle Ramon. Estelle has fallen into white slavery because of her mother's intemperate love for consumer luxuries (which the phony "husband" promises to provide). Under the tutelage of the brothel madam, Estelle learns that her value, and thus her subjection, does not begin and end with her $100 price tag. An elaborate system of overlapping and interdependent business operations, each one yielding profit for a number of different operatives, forces Estelle through a nightmarish trajectory of exploitation. First procured and sold for profit by the white slavery scout, Estelle then goes into circulation among the customers of the brothel, where she generates profit not only for the brothel keeper but also for its employees and co-contractors—the various landlords, the procurer who delivers her, the suppliers of clothing, drugs, liquor, entertainment, and abortions, the messengers, the police and municipal officials who must be paid off. Depreciated by her service in the brothel, Estelle moves on to the cheapened market of the street, where street pimps and (when she meets her inevitable early death) cadaver-suppliers extract their profits from her. In white slavery literature's "market in women," there are many opportunities to profit by exchanging the commodity for which, as Estelle finds to her horror, there is almost unlimited public demand: the female body.[9]

White slavery literature depicts the integrated workings of the Progressive Era market, with its commercial networks, its monopolies, and its paid-off officials. But in this vastly simplified dramatization, the oppressive power of the new economic and social order is absolute and clearly focused: it falls upon the enslaved woman. "The inmates of some houses in New York, Chicago, St. Louis and Denver do not own their own persons, and WHITE SLAVERY is a fact as true as ever black chattel slavery was in the South" (Regan, 22). In truth, the existence of white slavery was repeatedly disproved by well-publicized investigations. White slavery literature pushes the complex realities of oppression and inequality into the background. Its neo-abolitionist call to reform occludes race and class behind an outraged vision of the "white woman" exploited by the forces of commercialism. As chapter 4 explains, white slavery is a term that does not so much designate race as elide it: white slaves are undifferentiated "women" who, like the innocent young Estelle Ramon, might be the object of any bourgeois male's possessive aspirations. And, like the discourse of the exchange of "woman" in general, white slavery elides the differences of class and condition among women, overlooking both their agency and the diverse sources and forms of their actual oppression. The women who worked in the increasingly visible prostitution business were not exactly slaves—nor were they, like Estelle Ramon, gently reared young daughters suitable for respectable middle-class marriage. Most prostitution reflected the choices and constraints faced by lower-class women whose job options were few and whose wages (if they could get work) were not only depressed by the class system, but driven by gender exploitation far below even those of working-class men (see Rosen).

White slavery literature's nearly surreal depictions of interchangeable women reduced to commodities offer a strikingly literal response to the perplexing workings of the market. The economic changes of the time reflected not just growth in material output (production) but the transformative effects of developments in finance, distribution, and marketing as well. The importance of these nonproductive sectors of the economy raised questions about the nature of value. Exchange value is immaterial, socially created, and symbolic. It is endowed in, or on, the material object that is exchanged as a repository of value; but what is the relation between that object's attributes and the value that object represents? In the discourse of the exchange of woman, value is inextricable from the attribute of femaleness. An embodied condition—a "given" of the natural constitution of humans as sexed bodies—femaleness is also, in a system imagined as the exchange of woman, a conspicuously symbolic quality made, by social invention and agreement, to represent a variety of material and social desirables.[10]

The debates about women's roles and possibilities raised by the "woman question" had already demonstrated that femaleness is a protean and contested quality that could be held to signify a variety of conditions and consequences. The "woman question" and the value question (so to speak) converge in the textualizations of the woman of exchange—sometimes crudely, as in white slavery literature, and sometimes with complex subtlety, as in Wharton's explorations. In such texts, the woman of exchange affords a way to imagine and depict society's arbitrary and artificial yet absolutely powerful endowment of symbolic meaning in an object. It raises questions about the status of subjectivity—for example, the pleasurable outrage that white slavery literature seeks to incite stems partly from the clash between such objectification and the assumed subjective depth that the narrative conventions of the novel associate with women (Armstrong). And it foregrounds sexuality as the aspect of the body which, in the case of women in particular, makes the body constitutive of identity while it obliterates selfhood.

Estelle Ramon, for example, is told that her prettiness—that is, her body in its concrete specificity—makes her perfectly exchangeable with $100 (and therefore equivalent to many other commodities worth $100, including other female bodies). Estelle is thereby alienated from her body—whose high price makes her unable to purchase herself out of sexual bondage—and, because of that body, from herself (she is forced to live as a prostitute). A subject who is treated as an object—and who is internally split into subject and object—the woman of exchange is complexly textualized. In white slavery literature she is alternately titillating and melodramatic. She lends herself to Wharton's "tragic" dramas of debasement and to the ironic detachment of Wharton's examination of consumer culture. In Addams' narratives, the woman of exchange suffers the worker's unfulfilled, eroticized consumerist desire; in Gilman's tortuous rhetoric of redemption, she exemplifies the sacrifice of her own authentic nature. The contradictory relation between market value and selfhood these authors describe also applies to their published works and their own careers, for the public demand for narratives of the woman of exchange made some of these authors and texts (white slavery literature and Wharton's fiction, in particular) valuable commodities in themselves.

"The True Story of Estelle Ramon" presents itself as the vehicle that circulates and commodifies feminine innocence. "She was as pure as the air which she breathed in her humble home among the blue hills of the winding Cumberland," the narrative begins, as it offers up its story of the market's sexual debasement of this "pure" and "humble" woman whose innocent detachment from the status-seeking and venality of the marketplace will be so scandalously violated within the text (Bell 1910, 80). The white slavery narrative advertises itself within a textual economy in which what Barbara Welter has called the "True Woman"—woman imagined as domestic, altruistic, and chaste—is trafficked through texts that represent her debasement. Within the narrative frame, the True Woman is forced to render her commodity value; and within the textual economy in which white slavery texts circulate, she lends this commodity value to the value of the text itself (Welter).

Domestic ideology and market culture come together uneasily and productively in the discourse of the exchange of woman. Domestic ideology, the nineteenth century's cultural myth of woman and the family, places men and women in "separate spheres," installing woman in the private domain of the home, where bondedness, blood relation, and love oppose and compensate for the market, with its commodification, venality, objectification, and alien-

able relations. At the heart of the imagined domestic sphere is the domestic
woman—the cherished daughter, the loving and devoted wife, the altruistic
mother.

Recent critical work on domesticity has situated domesticity and the figure
of the domestic woman within market culture. Gillian Brown demonstrates
that domestic ideology is a mode of consumerism and a means of recreating
the individualism that undergirds capitalism's system of private ownership. For
turn-of-the-century social critics, the discourse of the exchange of woman, by
collapsing the family into the property system, provided a structural critique of
domesticity. Both Gilman and Olive Schreiner, for example, argued that bourgeois marriage is merely prostitution under less favorable circumstances—
from the point of view of the woman. But for Herbert Spencer, an influential
disseminator of the anthropological theory, the confluence of woman's domestic sanctity and her value as a sexual commodity strikes no dissonant chord. In
Spencer's social synthesis of the anthropological and Darwinian evolutionary
theories, the economic value endowed in the wife under civilized monogamy
makes her the love object of her husband. Protective possessiveness, conjugal
love, the desire for intimacy, the fostering of strong filial bonds—all the values
that animate domesticity—grow up, Spencer argues, under the property system that grounds ownership in the sanctity of individual and familial possessiveness (Spencer, 1:660 ff.).

In Thorstein Veblen's use of the discourse of the exchange of woman as a
critique of consumer culture, particularly his 1899 *Theory of the Leisure Class,*
the domestic woman and the evolutionary telos are sardonically exploded.
Veblen recounts the evolutionary progress of humankind, not to argue for the
perfection of its present state, but to explain how the property system has per-
verted man's instinctual endowment, causing him to admire wastefulness and
to desire, for purposes of prestigious display, property in its most useless and
extravagant form: the consuming woman. In Veblen's view of consumer culture, modern civilization, far from representing the perfected culmination of
successive stages, renovates and recirculates the harsh, arbitrary, and destruc-
tively inappropriate social codes of prior stages—particularly the barbarian
stage, with its superstitious and antiproductivist ethos.

Veblen subscribes to the work ethic. He posits a natural drive to produce
(accompanied by a repugnance for waste), which leads to a social "admiration
for efficiency" and for those who demonstrate it (29). But what counts as economic efficiency depends on the economic system; and this changes as humankind goes through its evolutionary stages. Under the prolonged stage of

barbarism, which, Veblen claims, has left its mark on modern civilization, survival depends not on productive labor but on "prowess" in "exploit"—that is,
proficiency in hunting, capturing, killing, and stealing. The barbarian who displays the evidence of his prowess attracts the admiration of others; and the
prototypical criterion of barbarian success is the display of a woman seized as a
"trophy" from the opposing tribe (30, 31, 34). Based on this first form of ownership, "the ownership of the woman by the man," other items are converted
from objects of possession into conventionalized private property through
which owners establish their social "reputability" (33, 36, 37).

Since the value of such property is symbolic rather than use-based, acquisitiveness has no built-in limit. But Veblen traces the striking wastefulness of
consumer culture, with its apparently limitless demand for more goods and
luxuries than necessity dictates, to the phase of economic organization in which
increased production allows for the accumulation of surplus wealth. During
this phase, rivals vie for relative superiority in "the game of ownership" (32,
36–37). Woman, once valued for her industrial utility as well as for the "reputability" she confers as a trophy, becomes most useful as a sign of the owner's
command of surplus wealth. Consigned to nonproductivity as a form of useless and expensive property in herself, she also displays her owner's exemption
from productivity and his capacity to waste wealth through consumption—
preferably, consumption so excessive as to require relegation to subordinates
in addition to herself (52, 53, 54ff.).

In the "latter-day outcome" of the archaic slavery of woman, Veblen writes,
the bourgeois wife "has become the ceremonial consumer" on behalf of the
husband. Assisting her husband in the "conspicuous consumption" that advertises his wealth, the housewife performs vicarious consumption and vicarious
leisure—not only by consumption of goods but also in elaborate and time-
wasting domestic and social rituals. Despite the apparent luxury of her consumerist privilege, Veblen emphasizes, the consuming wife is a slave: "she still
quite unmistakably remains [the husband's] chattel in theory; for the habitual
rendering of vicarious leisure and consumption is the abiding mark of the unfree servant" (55, 60, 69).

Veblen places woman's property value in the context of consumer society,
where value—a symbolic quality that exists in being perceived by others—is
rendered to the woman's owner through her performance of consumerism. To
own a woman, in short, is to "own" her consumerism—to be the designated
provider for, and the beneficiary of, her spending. Veblen's analysis emphasizes
that, within an imagined social system in which women are property, no self-

supporting woman can conceivably exist. The excessive need and desire that consumer culture incites in women intensify their dependency; and, unless already accommodated by a protector, this consumerism makes the woman available to be acquired as property. (We will see in chapters 4 and 5 that the white slavery narratives, in particular, portray the woman of exchange as subject to a consumerist desire that always exceeds her capacity for self-support and thus enforces her status as an object of ownership and exchange.)

In 1899, the year in which Veblen's *Theory of the Leisure Class* was published, Charlotte Perkins Gilman brought out her own critique of the exchange of woman. Like Veblen, Gilman embraces the social-evolutionary scheme developed by the anthropologists, and she sees in modern woman's excessive consumerism the effects of the commodity status of woman. In *Women and Economics,* Gilman attacks the system in which "he is the market, the demand; [s]he is the supply," indicting the commodification of woman and her enforced consumerism (86). But Gilman expands on Spencer's assertion that evolutionary progress culminating in possessive monogamy produces the familial sphere of love and altruism. In Gilman's argument, the bonds of altruistic love that the exchange of woman brings into the social order animate society at large. Without the transformation of woman into a form of property, as the anthropology explains, civilization could not exist: therefore, Gilman demonstrates, the very qualities that debase modern woman—her sexualization as a commodity, her greed and parasitism as a consumer—uphold market society, with its cooperative systems of production for exchange, and serve as the means through which original maternal altruism enters the social system.

Gilman is interested in showing how social arrangements are based in the physical constitution of the exchanged woman. Veblen's account begins with woman already constituted as sexual property: he traces the present-day ownership of woman back to the moment when a woman is seized, as a trophy, from the opposing tribe—that is, Veblen begins with woman already radically differentiated from man and defined as a form of property, available to be stolen (34). Gilman, in contrast, speculates on the underlying gender difference that makes woman a self-evident object of male acquisitiveness. As the symbol of male ownership rights and as the embodiment of the pleasures of possessive privilege, woman is defined through the attribute or quality that distinguishes her from the males who exchange her: embodied femaleness.

This quality, Gilman argues, is largely an evolutionary adaptation to commodification. Gilman imagines that monogamous marriage arose naturally out of sexual rivalry when "savage" man found it easier to "enslave" an individual

woman than to keep fighting other males for access to women. But to perpetuate this convenient innovation, man invented an economy that keeps woman
economically dependent. Woman's body and character respond to this "economic environment" through evolutionary modification (3). This means the
loss of a much more fulfilling, natural incarnation, for prior to her adaptation
to this "enforced condition" as a sexual property, a slave, and a dependent,
woman was productive and self-supporting. An efficient practitioner of the
"economic production [which] is the natural expression of human energy,"
the original woman was "tall, vigorous, beautiful" (116, 118, 45). More "human"
than woman, she was also an "individual" rather than a slave: befitted for
"great and varied exertion," "strong, free, active," she could energetically pursue her own good (46, 47).

Civilization destroys the natural woman by subjecting her to the exigencies of the "sexuo-economic" system in which "the female gets her food from
the male by virtue of her sex-relationship" to him (64). Adapting to maximize
her economic security, woman develops exaggerated versions of the feminine
traits that constitute value in the exchange system: as "[woman] has developed
in the lines of action to which she was confined," Gilman explains, she becomes the oversexed commodity of the sexual marketplace. "The body of
[modern] woman," in its adapted form, "manifests sex-distinction predominantly" in contrast to the less marked sexual differentiation of other female
mammals (44, 45).

Because for woman the "sex-relation" is not only the means of mating but
also the "means of getting her livelihood," the feminizing adaptations to commodification are accompanied by adaptations to her specific economic role,
consumption. Woman loses her natural instinct to produce under the pressure
of "the two great evolutionary forces"—sexual selection and natural selection—"acting together to the same end; namely, to develope sex-distinction in
the human female" (38). In the modern "consuming female," femininity and
consumerism produce and exhibit the same traits: the "feminine delicacy"
that makes woman sexually valuable comprises the "feebleness" and "clumsi-
ness" of the pampered dependent, while woman's "comparative smallness" and
rounded, "adipose" body contours are at once adaptations to consumerism
and marketable sexual attractants. "Psychic manifestation[s]" also evolve, as
woman's consuming role has "buil[t] into the constitution" "the habit and desire of taking" (45, 46, 47, 116).

In modern leisure-class woman, the instinctual human drive to produce is
superseded by an artificially enhanced instinct of "taking," which, "divorced

from its natural precursor and concomitant of making," exceeds all bounds. The consumerist woman is driven "to take and take and take forever," until she no longer resembles the original "human" (116, 118, 45). Deprived of the productive urge that characterizes humanity, she has also lost a natural endowment that is the particular birthright of females: the maternal capacity. The "tendency to protect and provide for," Gilman writes, "is a sex-distinction of females in general." But as a consuming female, woman is constitutionally self-indulgent, forever barred from experiencing her natural altruistic maternal nature. "To consume food, to consume clothes, to consume houses and furniture and decorations and ornaments and amusements, to take and take and take forever . . . this is the enforced condition of the mothers of the race" (41, 118).

As sexual commodities, women are forced to invest themselves in anti-maternal endeavors. "Maternity . . . low[ers] the personal charms and oc-cup[ies] the time of the mother," thus working against "the force of economic advantage"—that is, sexual attractiveness (46, 171). "Our civilized 'feminine delicacy,'" Gilman writes, "which appears somewhat less delicate when recognized as an expression of sexuality in excess—makes us no better mothers, but worse." No longer free to sacrifice themselves for their offspring, mothers are not only kept from nurturing their children but are forced to damage them. Both mothers and their children, in the modern regime of consumer culture, are "morbid, defective, irregular, diseased" because of the vitiation of women by feminizing modification to the market (181).

In this failure of the modern leisure-class mother, Gilman voices frank anxiety over the "racial good" (26). Often invoking the robust, unrefined maternity of peasants and other lower-class women, Gilman worries that the superior racial stock is dying out, for not only does the leisure-class wife reproduce less successfully and abundantly; she also passes down to succeeding generations her own biological vitiation while, in her parasitism, she contributes no productive improvements to the cultural environments of those who come after her.[11] But finally Gilman's discussion redeems the conventions of upper-middle-class white motherhood. The refined and specialized female roles, the exaggerated discourse of feminine delicacy and maternal sacrifice particular to leisure-class womanhood, Gilman goes on to show, constitute an exemplary feminine sacrifice, which gives rise to a civilization based on the emulation of genteel, maternalistic principles of altruism.

Along the tortuous route by which Gilman arrives at this argument, she deflates the culture's veneration for the sanctified figure of the self-giving mother. "Matriolatry" is Gilman's pejorative term for the popular worship of the mother as a figure of woman's ordained devotion to the larger interests of the human race. As voiced by one Mr. Grant Allen, who "very thoroughly states the general view on this subject," Gilman notes, the matriolatric view imagines that it is nature which has made "[woman] . . . a part of [the race] told specially off for the continuance of the species, just as truly as drones or male spiders are . . . told off. . . . She is the sex sacrificed to reproductive necessities" (172). But in fact, Gilman argues, this specialization is a social invention that works against nature's reproductive mandate: "the more absolutely woman is segregated to sex-functions only, cut off from all economic use and made wholly dependent on the sex-relation as a means of livelihood, the more pathological does her motherhood become. . . . Her excessive specialization in the secondary sexual characteristics is . . . detrimental." The suffering, frailty, and death of mother and child associated with modern motherhood—and held up as grounds for venerating maternal self-sacrifice—are seen by Gilman as objects of "shame" rather than pride (181, 182).

Matriolatry—the veneration of sacrificial motherhood—is, then, mistaken. But the mistake is not in seeing motherhood as a sacrifice, but in not seeing what it is a sacrifice of. Sacrificial motherhood is a sacrifice of natural motherhood. Natural motherhood, Gilman asserts, is not only less taxing to the woman but also much more successful. While natural motherhood is altruistic, it exacts minimal cost in woman's freedom, vigor, and range—and this is clearly nature's way, for healthy offspring require a vigorous and healthy mother. And the natural mother is not barred, by her maternal function, from free and fulfilling participation in the general productive and active functions of humankind.

To conform to the socially invented role of the modern, sacrificial mother, woman has made a sacrifice of her natural, nonsacrificial motherhood. But there is yet another twist: the venerated mother of "matriolatry" must relinquish even her socially invented, sanctified maternity. In the modern market, which treats women as commodities and dependents, women are forced to take economic provisions in return for their socially constituted status—that is, women are forced to *sell* their motherhood and, thus, to give up its sacrificial quality. "In treating of an economic exchange, asking what return in goods or labor women make for the goods and labor given them," Gilman writes, "we are told that the duties and services of the mother entitle her to support." But, Gilman expostulates, "are the cares and duties of the mother, her travail and her love, commodities to be exchanged for bread? It is revolting so to consider them" (15, 17). Revolting as Gilman shows this commodification of motherhood to be, it reflects the marketplace reality that as an aspect of exchanged womanhood, the modern version of motherhood (which represents the sacrifice of the natural mother) is reduced to an economic asset.

Women have had to give up all that is motherly in their mothering. But this means, not that motherhood has been destroyed by civilization, but that it has been relinquished by mothers in order to benefit the social order it thereby engenders. The exchange of women, as an economy in which "speaking collectively, men produce and distribute wealth; and women receive it at their hands has compelled [man] to . . . fulfill in his own person the thwarted uses of maternity. He became, and has remained, a sort of man-mother" (9). The subjection of woman has involved to an enormous degree the maternalizing of man. "Under its bonds he has been forced into new functions. . . . He has had to learn to work, to serve, to be human" (127). Although it is men who "work and serve," they do so as a reflex of female dependence, which is the form in which "maternal energy, working externally through our elaborate organism, is the source of productive industry, the main current of social life" (126).

The sacrifice of the mother is so thorough that it even sacrifices itself, allowing man to become the source of sacrifice; for the fact that "man was made part mother . . . should not be considered as an extreme maternal sacrifice, but as a novel and thorough system of paternal sacrifice" (125, 128, 126). Producing through sacrifice, what the sacrifice of motherhood produces is more motherhood—the entire system of the division of labor and exchange in which interdependence and mutual provisioning is the rule. Motherhood, sacrificed by mothers to become universalized, makes sacrifice universal.

Whether one lays an egg or a million eggs, whether one bears a cub, a kitten, or a baby, whether one broods its chickens, guards its litter, or tends a nursery full of children, these are but individual animal processes. But to serve each other more and more widely; . . . to [develop] special functions, so that we depend for our living on society's return. . . . This is civilization. (74)

Through the exchange of woman, which has caused woman to relinquish her maternity, "maternal energy" has become "the force through which have come into the world both love and industry," Gilman explains (118). Both the work ethic and the social bonds that hold society together ("love") are attributed to woman's sacrifice. And maternity, socialized through the sacrifice of woman, also provides the source and basis of exchange value. The great sacrifice of the mother is the original input which, represented in all its epiphenomenal social forms, still stands outside the social economy, exceeding all its representations within the market: "[Woman] . . . has been subjugated to the male for such enormous racial gain . . . that the sacrifice should never be mentioned nor thought of" (135). No equivalent in language, thought, or any other exchangeable currency—even matriolatry—can represent this transcendent, original, and perpetual source of value, for "nothing can ever exceed the truth as to the value of the mother" (176).

Gilman's sacrificial mother, then, does not sacrifice herself for mere motherhood; instead, as a mother, she sacrifices her motherhood so that its value—the value of original, undeformed womanhood transmuted into a social form by the debasing exchange of woman—will be injected into society. The mother's sexualized embodiment as a commodity and consumer is the form in which the original woman becomes a source of value; her subjection to exchange is at once her sacrifice itself and the means by which the value made available through her sacrifice is recirculated. For Gilman, the mother is the value form of exchanged woman who exists as such in the dual form of her commodified social manifestation and her original, sacrificial constitution. The natural and procreative mother enters the economy in the form of the sexual commodity that is the woman of exchange, refreshing the exchange system with a perpetual input of value that comes from "outside" the social system.[12]

Gilman's argument reconciles the woman of exchange—the sexual commodity, the bad mother, the selfish consumer—with the idealized domestic woman who engenders cherished offspring and provides a domain of love and bondedness to counter a venal market culture. In Gilman's argument, the woman of exchange not only redeems her maternal altruism through sacrificing herself as an item of exchange, thus saving the idealized realm of domesticity, but she gives up her title to domesticity to save the market. Indeed, the market itself, through the sacrifice of woman on which it is founded, becomes an expanded domestic domain animated by the maternalistic values of love, mutual service, and selflessness.

Gilman's argument moves from an account of the evolution of civilization to a projection of its future reform. Now that the universalization of motherhood—that is, the market society—has been put in place, she urges, women may reclaim their humanity. But Gilman's proposed reforms do not sweep away woman's dependency and exaggerated sexual differentiation. Rather than aiming to restore woman to her original, fully "human" incarnation, Gilman proposes that all parental care and domestic maintenance remain the province of women, but that woman's specialized role be collectivized. This socialization of child care and domestic maintenance would constitute society's recognition of the indispensable service of the mother, while it would mitigate each woman's individual dependency. In Gilman's collectivized society, the sacrifice woman has made to engender society will be patent and indisputable: disentangled from the private maintenance of woman as sexual chattel, collectivized and no longer parasitical, the universalized and incommensurate social value of mothers and mothering will emerge and demand acknowledgment, while the sacrifice that is motherhood will not be belied by the consumerism of each mother (21). As mothers of the social order, women will administer the domesticated market culture.

Gilman's reformism, like that of Jane Addams, exemplifies "Social Housekeeping": the collectivization and politicization of duties and functions socially ascribed to women under domestic ideology. (In the conclusion, I argue that Jane Addams' social housekeeping agenda reflects the politicization of a notion of domesticity based in the assumed embodiedness of female consumerism.)[13] In Gilman's argument, woman's deformation under the pressure of the exchange system makes possible her promotion to public power and political stature. As the sacrificial mother of the sexuo-economic marketplace—the woman whose sexual embodiment gives her to others—woman achieves, and is recognized for, her social contribution. And despite Gilman's productivist rhetoric, what woman brings into the market is not her labor but the value comprised by the form into which her productive instincts have been transmuted: the form of her commodified consumerist body, which circulates the value of presocial woman's sacrificial transformation in the debased forms of exchanged woman.

Lévi-Strauss ends his mid-twentieth-century exploration of the exchange of woman with a meditation on the inscription of social meaning on the natural world which the anthropologist sees in the exchange of "things"—primarily and paradigmatically, women (496). My study explores the rich literary and cultural discourse that anticipated Lévi-Strauss in asserting the centrality of the exchange of woman. Gayle Rubin, revisiting the discourse in the 1970s, delineated the various levels—social, economic, intrapsychic—at which the exchange of woman informs the ways "sex and gender are organized and produced" (177). This is feminist territory that Gilman, Chopin, Wharton, and Addams, in limited ways, have already occupied. For these turn-of-the-century writers, the exchange of woman is the central feature of the gender system. They indict its injustice and dramatize its injuriousness, but it serves as the lens through which they envision woman's possibilities and contributions as well.

Much of what these turn-of-the-century writers took for granted is now subject to question: the inevitability and unchanging basic structures of both gender difference and the capitalist market, the universal identity of "woman," the benefits to women of civil "equality"—yet we cannot claim to have found a way out of the discursive parameters of gender.[14] The narratives of the woman of exchange—particularly Wharton's and Chopin's much-taught and influential fictions—continue to fascinate us today, with their accounts of woman's marginal yet foundational status in market society, their narratives of the simultaneous emergence and effacement of female selfhood, and their dramatizations of the redemptive sacrifice that is woman's social and economic debasement.

PART One

The Woman of Exchange

Exchange Value and the
Female Self in *The Awakening*

For Charlotte Perkins Gilman, "the woman, the mother, the very source of sacrifice through love" embodies the tribute woman has paid to civilization in becoming a sexual commodity (Gilman 1898, 98). In the years prior to the appearance of Gilman's polemic, feminists had evoked this same sacrificial figure of the mother to argue for limited sexual independence. "Voluntary motherhood" was a reform proposal based on the view, which Gilman also expounds, that woman has relinquished her natural, autonomous selfhood in her self-giving role as "mother." This "sacrifice" (as Gilman calls it) earns certain rights: in the language of the feminists, women's service as mothers entitles them to "self-ownership." Defined as the perpetual freedom to refuse—and therefore willingly to accept—sexual relations with their husbands, self-ownership was framed as an acceptable kind of birth control and justified as a means to improve maternal care.

The heroine of *The Awakening* borrows the rhetoric of self-ownership when she vows she will "never again belong to another than herself" (100). But in Edna Pontellier's attempt to take possession of herself, Kate Chopin unpacks the paradoxical logic of self-ownership in all its contradiction and impossibility. It is through her role as the wife—and marital property—of Léonce Pontellier that Edna first looks for a self she might possess; and it is as a mother that Edna declares her resolve to withhold some part of that self from the claims of others. In her aspiration to self-ownership, Edna claims title to a self that exists only in relation to her status as the property of others.

As the novel opens, Edna's husband, a wealthy New Orleans stockbroker who has brought his family to an exclusive summer resort, surveys his wife like "property": "'You are burnt beyond recognition' [Léonce says], looking at his wife as one looks at a valuable piece of personal property which has suffered some damage" (21). Léonce's comment is both the reader's introduction to Edna and Edna's introduction to herself: for in response to Léonce's anxiety, Edna makes her first self-examination in this novel about a heroine who is "beginning to realize her position in the universe as a human being, and to recognize her relations as an individual to the world within and about her" (31–32).

Edna, having been told "you are burnt beyond recognition,"

held up her hands, strong, shapely hands, and surveyed them critically, drawing up her lawn sleeves above the wrists. Looking at them reminded her of her rings, which she had given to her husband before leaving for the beach. She silently reached out to him and he, understanding, took the rings from his vest pocket and dropped them into her open palm. She slipped them upon her fingers. (21)

In the context of the property system in which Edna exists as a sign of value, her body is detachable and alienable from her own viewpoint: the hands and wrists are part of the body yet can be objectified, held out and examined as if they belonged to someone else—as indeed, in some sense that Léonce insists on very literally, they do belong to someone else. Edna's perception of her own body is structured by the detachability of the hand and arm as signs of Léonce's ownership of her. Her hands also suggest the possibility of being an owner herself when they make the proprietary gesture of reaching out for the rings that Léonce obediently drops into the palm (this gesture of Edna's contrasts with a bride's conventional passive reception of the ring). The hands are the organs of appropriation: Elizabeth Cady Stanton, in a speech on female rights given in 1892, argued that "to deny [to woman] the rights of property is like cutting off the hands."[1] In having Edna put on the rings herself (a gesture she will again perform at a moment when she decisively turns away from her domestic role), Chopin suggests that the chief item of property owned by the proprietary Edna is Edna herself. Thus the opening scene foreshadows the turning point of the plot, when Edna, deciding to leave Léonce's house, resolves "never again to belong to another than herself" (100).

"Self-ownership," in the second half of the nineteenth century, signified a wife's right to refuse marital sex—a right feminists were demanding as the key to female autonomy. First popularized by Lucinda Chandler in the 1840s and widely promoted by the feminists who followed her, the practice of self-ownership, as Chandler saw it, would mean that the woman "has control over her own person, independent of the desires of her husband" (Chandler, 1–2). "By the 1870s," writes historian William Leach, "self-ownership . . . had become the stock in trade of feminist thinking on birth control," for it "meant that woman, not man, would decide when, where, and how the sexual act would be performed. It also meant that woman, not man, would determine when children would be conceived and how many" (Leach, 92, 89). "Voluntary motherhood"—woman's "right to choose when to be pregnant"—was usually evoked as the ground of self-ownership: "she should have pleasure or not allow access unless she wanted a child," explains advice writer Henry C. Wright. According to social historian Linda Gordon, by the mid-1870s, advocacy of voluntary motherhood was shared by "the whole feminist community" (Wright, 252; Gordon 1976, 109). Writing in 1881, reformer Dido Lewis demonstrates the central place of self-ownership/voluntary motherhood in the campaign for female autonomy when she evokes together the rights "of the wife to be her own person, and her sacred right to deny her husband if need be; and to decide how often and when she should become a mother" (18).

While the feminist community promoted voluntary motherhood, it unanimously opposed the use of birth control devices. This opposition, which contradicts the advocacy of choice and control for women, was shared by suffragists, moral reformers, and free love advocates alike. Various kinds of contraceptive technology were accessible to middle-class women. However, as Gordon notes, nineteenth-century birth control practice was determined by ideology rather than the availability of technology. In the prevailing ideology of even the most radical feminist reformers, motherhood was an inextricable part of female sexuality. Why did feminists, whose goal was to win for women the civil and proprietary rights that would make them equal to men, choose to deny women the freedom to have sex without pregnancy? As Gordon points out, the linkage of self-ownership with reproduction certainly reflects the reality of many women's lives, which were dominated by multiple births and the attendant realities of risk, disease, and pain. Some of the resistance to birth control technology, Gordon suggests, was motivated by material conditions: birth control devices, by separating sex from reproduction, appeared to threaten the family structure that provided most middle-class women their only social standing and economic security. But even among those reformers who were not concerned with upholding the family (free love advocates and nonmarrying career women, for example), there was a strong resistance to contraception—a resistance that amounts to a refusal to separate motherhood from female sexuality.

To put voluntary motherhood practiced without birth control devices at the center of self-ownership is to make motherhood central to a woman's life and identity. The capacity to bear children is the sexual function that most dramatically distinguishes the sexual lives—and the day-to-day lives—of women from those of men. The ban on contraceptive technology enforces a lived distinction between male and female sexuality: without effective contraception, sex for a woman always means sex as a woman because it means a potential pregnancy. The opposition to contraceptive technology (as well as the idealization of motherhood of which it is a part) reflects a commitment to the sexualization of female identity. This differentiated sexuality with motherhood at its core becomes the possession that a woman makes available or withholds in order to demonstrate self-ownership. To ask why the feminist reformers opposed contraceptive technology is, then, to ask how motherhood functions in the construction of the self-owning female self. In making motherhood a central possession of the self, the feminists were defining that self as sexual and as female. The possession of this sexualized self through self-ownership amounts to the exercise of a right to alienate (confirmed by a right to withhold). This selfhood, then, consists of the alienation of female sexuality in a market—a market about which Gilman writes, in the year Chopin's novel appeared, "he is . . . the demand . . . she is the supply" (86). The feminists' opposition to birth control technology reflects a commitment to this market: underlying their constructions of female selfhood is the ideology of woman's sexual value in exchange.

Chopin's dramatization of female self-ownership demonstrates the central importance of the ideology of woman's value in exchange to contemporary notions of female selfhood. If, as Stanton declares, "in discussing the rights of woman, we are to consider, first, what belongs to her as an individual" (247), what Edna Pontellier considers as her property is, first, her body. Her body is both what she owns and what she owns with. She begins to discover a self by uncovering her hands and "surveying them critically" with her eyes, thus making an appropriate visual assessment of herself as a proprietary being. Her hands and eyes will serve her in her "venture" into the "work" of sketching and painting (75). Thus her hands, by remaining attached (and not cut off like those of the woman who is denied the rights of property), serve her visual appropriation of the world and provide the first object of this appropriation: her own body.

Edna's hands appear in two states: naked and sunburned, and ringed. In the first state, they are conventionally "unrecognizable" as signs of her status as Léonce's wife. Sunburned hands, by indicating the performance of outdoor labor, would nullify Edna's "value" as a sign of Léonce's wealth. In the terminology of Thorstein Veblen's turn-of-the-century analysis of the ownership system, Edna is an item of "conspicuous consumption" that brings "reputability" (a degree of status) to Léonce. Such status-bearing wealth must be surplus wealth: useful articles do not serve to advertise the owner's luxurious freedom from need. Edna must, then, appear to be surplus—she must appear to perform no useful labor. The rings—showy, luxurious, useless items of conspicuous consumption par excellence—restore her status as surplus. Yet this status is also constituted by the sight of her hands without the rings: the significance of the sunburned hands quickly collapses into the significance of the ringed hands when the sunburned, naked hands "remind" both Léonce and Edna of the ringed, value-bearing hands. And Edna's sunburn is directly constitutive of her "value," for it results from her conspicuous, vicarious consumption of leisure on Léonce's behalf (what Veblen calls "vicarious leisure"): she has been enjoying a holiday at the respectable, luxurious resort frequented by Léonce's Creole circle.

Thus Edna's hands, in their naked and exposed state, serve as a reminder of Léonce's property interest while they also suggest an identity and proprietary interests of her own. The appropriative survey of the female body as a sign of male ownership continues to engage Edna: her visual fascination fastens on the hands and body of her friend, Adèle Ratignolle, whose "excessive physical charm" at first attracts Edna (32). Edna "like[s] to sit and gaze at her fair companion" (29). She watches Adèle at her domestic labors: "Never were hands more exquisite than [Adèle's], and it was joy to look at them when she threaded her needle or adjusted her gold thimble . . . as she sewed away on the little night-drawers" (27). Here, the hands are the organs of labor—but again, gender determines possessive status. Adèle's hands are perfectly white because she always wears dogskin gloves with gauntlets. The femininity of the laboring hands, their luxuriously aesthetic and spectacular quality, conspicuously signifies that the value of Adèle's labor does not stem from production for use: Edna "[can] not see the use" of Adèle's labor (27). Adèle's laboring hands signify her consecration to her "role" within the family, and they are marked with the gold of a thimble as Edna's are marked with the gold of a ring.

In their white, "exquisite" beauty, Adèle's hands are stably—organically—signs of her status as wealth. When Adèle jokes "with excessive naïveté" about the fear of making her husband jealous, "that made them all laugh. The right hand jealous of the left! . . . But for that matter, the Creole husband is never jealous; with him the gangrene passion is one which has become dwarfed by disuse" (29). (This ownership is not reciprocal: the question of jealousy pertains only to the husband; the wife's jealous, proprietary interest in her husband is not evoked.) Adèle's entire presence is a reminder of the property system in which woman is a form of surplus wealth whose value exists in relation to exchange. A woman of "excessive physical charm," Adèle is luxuriously draped in "pure white, with a fluffiness of ruffles that became her. The draperies and fluttering things which she wore suited her rich, luxuriant beauty" (33). Her body is as rich, white, and ornamental as her clothes; she appears "more beautiful than ever" in a negligee that leaves her arms "almost wholly bare" and "expose[s] the rich, melting curves of her white throat" (75).

In her rich and elaborate yet revealing clothing, Adèle is excessively covered while her body, already a sign of wealth, makes such coverings redundant. Adèle appears as a concretized *femme couverte.* Under the Napoleonic Code, which was still in force in Louisiana in the 1890s, wives were legally identical with their husbands; being in *couverture,* they had no separate legal or proprietary identity and could not own property in their own right. Adèle's beauty is her conspicuousness as a form of wealth: her looks are describable by "no words . . . save the old ones that have served so often to picture the bygone heroine of romance." These words—"gold," "sapphires," "cherries or some other delicious crimson fruit"—construct femininity as tangible property. The value of the woman is emphatically defined as social wealth that exists as an effect of the public circulation of the tropes, "the old [words] that have served so often," which identify her as beautiful. Her beauty is the product and representation of its own circulation. Adèle's "excessive physical charm" is a kind of currency that makes her the "embodiment of every womanly grace and charm" (26).

It is in public display that Adèle's beauty manifests itself. The sight of woman as social wealth is the starting point of Edna's self-seeking. "Mrs. Pontellier liked to sit and gaze at her fair companion as she might look upon a faultless Madonna" (29). An amateur artist, Edna finds such "joy" in looking at Adèle that she wants to "try herself on Madame Ratignolle" (30). Adèle, "seated there like some sensuous Madonna, with the gleam of the fading day enriching her splendid color" (30), appears to Edna as a particularly "tempting subject" of a sketch. This sketch becomes the second sight that Edna "survey[s] critically" (the first being her hands); finding that it "[bears] no resemblance to Madame Ratignolle" (and despite the fact that it is "a fair enough piece of work, and in many respects satisfying"), Edna enforces her proprietary rights in regard to the sketch as she smudges it and "crumple[s] the paper between her hands" (30). Edna is inspired to make another try when she visits Adèle at home in New Orleans and finds her again at her ornamental domestic labor (Adèle is unnecessarily sorting her husband's laundry). "Madame Ratignolle looked more beautiful than ever there at home. . . . 'Perhaps I shall be able to paint your picture some day,' said Edna. . . . 'I believe I ought to work again'" (75). The sight of Adèle at home inspires Edna to do the work that will help her get out of the home. Later, she will leave Léonce and support herself on the income from her art and from a legacy of her mother.

In her insistence on owning her own property and supporting herself, Edna is a model of the legal opposite of the *femme couverte*—she is the *femme seule.*

Thus Chopin connects her to the Married Women's Property Acts, property law reforms instituted in the latter part of the century that gave married women varying rights of ownership. Edna comes from "old Presbyterian Kentucky stock" (86). Kentucky belonged to the bloc of states with the most advanced separation of property in marriage. In fact, Kentucky had the most advanced Married Women's Property Act in the nation, granting married women not only the right to own separate property and make contracts, but the right to keep their earnings.

Thus Chopin connects Edna to the feminist drive for women's property rights. Elizabeth Cady Stanton, in her speech on female selfhood, makes possessive individualism the first consideration among women's rights: "In discussing the right of woman, we are to consider, first, what belongs to her as an individual." Chopin suggests that what a woman owns in owning herself is her sexual exchange value. The *femme couverte,* in being both property and the inspiration to own, allows Edna to be *femme seule.* The self she owns can be owned—is property—because it is recognizable as social wealth. Adèle, who concretizes the status of the woman and mother as domestic property, makes visible to Edna the female exchange value that constitutes a self to own. Thus Edna's possessive selfhood looks "back" to the chattel form of marriage, valorizing (in a literal sense) the woman as property. In Adèle, the "bygone heroine," Edna finds the capital that she invests to provide her market selfhood.

The way that Edna owns herself by owning her value in exchange is a form of voluntary motherhood: "Edna had once told Madame Ratignolle that she would never sacrifice herself for her children, or for any one. Then had followed a rather heated argument." In this argument Edna "explains" to Adèle, "I would give my life for my children; but I wouldn't give myself." Adèle's answer is, "a woman who would give her life for her children could do no more than that. . . . I'm sure I couldn't do more than that." Withholding nothing, Adèle cannot conceive of giving more than she already gives. Edna cannot at first identify what it is she has chosen to withhold: "I wouldn't give myself. I can't make it more clear; it's only something which . . . is revealing itself to me" (67).[2]

The self at first exists in the presumption of the right to withhold oneself as a mother. But Edna, like the feminist advocates of self-ownership, soon determines that voluntary motherhood means withholding herself sexually. After her first successful swim (during which she experiences a moment of self-support and the absolute solitariness of death), she stays on the porch, refusing Léonce's repeated orders and entreaties to come inside to bed (49–50). Later, Edna stops sleeping with her husband altogether, so that Léonce complains to the family doctor, "she's making it devilishly uncomfortable for me. . . . She's got some sort of notion in her head concerning the eternal rights of women; and—you understand—we meet in the morning at the breakfast table" (85). It is by withholding herself sexually, then, that Edna exercises the "eternal rights of women" in insisting that she has a self and that she owns that self.

The freedom to withhold oneself has its complement in the freedom to give oneself. No longer sleeping with—or even living with—her husband, Edna declares herself free to have sex with whomever she chooses. She tells Robert, "I am no longer one of Mr. Pontellier's possessions to dispose of or not. I give myself where I choose" (129). Edna supposes that her self-giving is chosen because she has presumed the choice of not giving—she has made her motherhood voluntary. Adèle, in contrast, is the mother who never withholds and thus cannot choose but to give. Will and intention seem to be with Edna, whereas Adèle exercises no will (and has no self). Yet Adèle's giving is not an involuntary and therefore selfless reflex, but a consciously and intentionally developed identity. Adèle is Grand Isle's greatest exponent of the "role" of "mother-woman," a role that is produced through deliberate public staging (26). First presented to Edna as a beautiful vision of the "Madonna," Adèle produces her maternity through public discourse. Her children are "thoughts" brought out in speech: Adèle "thinks" (out loud) of "a fourth one" and, after giving birth to it, implores Edna, in a phrase that Edna will not be able to get out of her mind, to "think of the children . . . oh think of . . . them" (132).

"Madame Ratignolle had been married seven years. About every two years she had a baby. At that time she . . . was beginning to think of a fourth one. She was always talking about her 'condition.' Her 'condition' was in no way apparent, and no one would have known a thing about it but for her persistence in making it the subject of conversation" (27). Adèle produces her role of mother-woman by thinking and provoking thought, but it is impossible to determine whether she thinks about getting pregnant—whether, that is, she practices self-ownership and voluntary motherhood by withholding herself from sex. The two-year intervals between her pregnancies might result from chance, or they might represent intentional spacing that keeps Adèle in or nearly in the "condition" that provides her identity. This ambiguity characterizes the "condition" of motherhood that Adèle is "always" producing for herself. Motherhood is a "role" and therefore consciously produced and paraded. Yet the intention and will that are used to stage the role conflict with its content, for the role of mother demands selflessness: the mother-women of Grand Isle "efface themselves as individuals" (26). Motherhood is never voluntary or involuntary. If motherhood is a social role that Adèle intentionally inhabits, it is also a condition that she can never actually choose, since intending to become pregnant cannot make her so. Thus, motherhood has a kind of built-in selflessness that is dramatically expressed in the scene when Adèle, who is usually in control of her presence, becomes pathetically hysterical and paranoiac during labor and childbirth. Here, her intentional embrace of motherhood gets its force from the unwilled nature of the "torture" that it attempts to appropriate. Hardly able to speak after her ordeal, Adèle whispers in an "exhausted" voice, "Think of the children, Edna" (132).

Adèle's histrionics insist that nothing less than the self is at stake in the speculative risk-taking that is motherhood (which includes the abstention from motherhood). The intention to become a mother is the kind of "weak" intention that Walter Benn Michaels connects with "acts that take place in the market, such as speculating in commodities." Michaels places weak intention at the center of a market selfhood whose "self-possession" and "self-interest" are grounded in "the possibility of intention and action coming apart (Michaels 1987, 237, 244, 241). Chopin's dramatization of the logic of voluntary motherhood, like Michaels' own example of Edith Wharton's self-speculating heroine Lily Bart (*The House of Mirth*), emphasizes that self-speculation is gendered.

For women, self-speculation is sexual; that is to say that sexuality is the content of the female self in the market. Contrary to Michaels' claim (240), Lily Bart is indeed "a victim of patriarchal capitalism" in a way that the male entrepreneurs in the novel are not, for the woman cannot choose whether to speculate or what to speculate in: by being a woman, she is already sexually at risk. The "voluntariness" of female self-speculation is an effect of the commodity system that constructs female value along the polarities of accessibility and rarity. Lily Bart speculates in the marriage market by withholding sexual accessibility from that market—a risky behavior that results in her death (complete with hallucinated motherhood). "Voluntary motherhood" represents the inevitable risks of female self-speculation as the risk of pregnancy—which, in the nineteenth century, was the risk of life—and points to the enforced nature of female self-speculation by identifying all women as mothers.

Adèle and Edna embody the two poles of motherhood: Adèle is the "mother-woman" and Edna is "not a mother-woman." The axis of motherhood gives Edna her original sense of identity. What makes her "not a mother-woman" is her refusal to "give" herself for her children. Unlike Adèle, Edna does not embrace the role. Her motherhood seems arbitrary, externally imposed, and unwilled, "a responsibility which she had blindly assumed." She is "fond of her children in an uneven, impulsive way. She [will] sometimes gather them passionately to her heart; she [will] sometimes forget them" (37). Her "half remembered" experience of childbirth is an "ecstasy" and a "stupor" (131). Edna's re-

fusal to give herself as a mother, rather than making her the controller and proprietor of her life, entails the passivity of thoughtlessness. In refusing to be a
mother-woman she absents herself from the motherhood that is thus all the
more arbitrarily thrust upon her.

Indeed, Edna is inescapably a mother. Motherhood is what she withholds
and thus she, too, is essentially a "mother-woman." Adèle's presence is a provo-
cation and reminder of the self-constituting function of motherhood. Her selflessness is an inducement to Edna to identify a self to give. For Edna, who "be-
com[es] herself" by "daily casting aside that fictitious self which we assumed
like a garment with which to appear before the world" (77), the friendship with
Adèle is "the most obvious . . . influence" in the loosening of Edna's "mantle of
reserve" (32). The Creole community recognizes no private sphere. Adèle's sexual and reproductive value is already located in the sphere of public exchange
(or, the public is already like the private: the Creoles are like "one large family"
[28]). In this Creole openness, Edna is inspired to resituate her sexual exchange
value in an economy of public circulation.

"The candor of [Adèle's] whole existence, which every one might read," is
part of a Creole lack of prudery that allows for the open circulation of stories
about sex and childbirth. With "profound astonishment" Edna reads "in secret
and solitude" a book that "had gone the rounds" and was openly discussed at
table. "Never would Edna Pontellier forget the shock with which she heard
Madame Ratignolle relating to old Monsieur Farival the harrowing story of
one of her *accouchements*, withholding no intimate detail. She was growing ac-
customed to like shocks, but she could not keep the mounting color back from
her cheeks." The candor of Adèle's motherhood provokes blushes that simultaneously constitute Edna's reserve and "give her away" to the public. Her body,
whether sunburned or blushing, is red from an exposure that privatizes and
valorizes that body as her domestic, private attributes—sexuality, modesty, reproduction—are manifested as social value.

Adèle has nothing to hide because her body underneath her clothes is man-
ifestly social wealth. Her bareness is as ornamentally "beautiful" as her orna-
mented, clothed self. The reserved, private, domestic self of Adèle reveals itself
to Edna as the valuable product of circulation, and this revelation prompts Edna
to explore her own possessive privacy. She becomes aware of having "thoughts
and emotions which never voiced themselves. . . . They belonged to her and
were her own" (67).[3]

Her erotic longings belong in this category. "Edna often wondered at one
propensity which sometimes had inwardly disturbed her without causing any
outward show or manifestation on her part" (36)—a propensity to become

silently infatuated with various men. These "silent" possessions of the self are owned in a way most clearly illustrated in the story of Edna's greatest infatuation, whose object was a "great tragedian."

The picture of the tragedian stood enframed upon her desk. Anyone may possess the portrait of a tragedian without exciting suspicion or comment. (This was a sinister reflection which she cherished.) In the presence of others she expressed admiration for his exalted gifts, as she handed the photograph around and dwelt upon the fidelity of the likeness. When alone she sometimes picked it up and kissed the cold glass passionately. (36)

Edna's comment on the fidelity of the likeness recapitulates the book's opening, in which Léonce's anxiety about Edna's lapse from recognizability, and his restoration of her recognizability via the wedding rings, consists of a discourse that constantly remembers and reinscribes her as a sign of him in his proprietary office. Her "fidelity" in this marital, possessive sense is her recognizability as such a sign. Edna's photograph is to Edna as Edna is to Léonce. It represents her possessive identity, her selfhood as an owner (thus there is a mirror-like quality in the "cold glass" which shows her herself kissing herself). The photograph embodies and reflects Edna's erotic desire for the tragedian. It objectifies her sexuality in an image that is handed around, praised for its "fidelity," and kissed in private.

Like Adèle, the photograph concretizes erotic value that is both publicly produced and privately owned. The erotic availability and desirability of the actor whose photograph "anyone might possess" is a product of reproduction and circulation, as Edna's own kisses are incited and followed by the circulation of the object. The mode of owning it is "handing it around" while she praises the "fidelity" of the likeness. That is, she assumes an individual possessive relationship to the photograph only in the context of its possession by any number of other owners, whose possession produces the "sinister reflection" of her own possessive, cherishing privacy. But Edna's position as an owner is not that of Adèle's husband—or of her own. Edna gives up possession in order to have this possessive relationship. In praising the "fidelity of the likeness" she does not praise its likeness to her, but emphasizes that the photograph represents and thus "belongs to" its original—a man whose inaccessibility makes her infatuation "hopeless." Edna can see her photograph as property only by seeing it as male property—just as her own hands, in their function as signs of Léonce's ownership of her, appear detachable and therefore ownable. Yet the absence of Edna in what the photograph represents allows her to imagine a possessive self that is somehow hidden and concealed—and therefore her own. Alone with her photograph, she imagines it circulating. Circulating it, she is able to imagine being secretly alone with it. In her ownership of the photograph, Edna establishes her possessive relationship to her sexuality.

"I am no longer one of Mr. Pontellier's possessions to dispose of or not. I give myself where I choose," says Edna to Robert (129). She has withheld herself from her husband in order to give herself. Instead of being property "to dispose of or not," she intends to be property that is necessarily disposed of. The forms of value in which Edna exchanges herself are the duties and functions of the woman and wife: female sexual service, motherhood, and the performance of wifely domestic/social amenities. Edna reprivatizes and reserves this value by giving up her social and domestic duties as the lady of the house, by moving out of the impressive family home into a private domestic space, the "pigeon house," and by withholding sex from her husband. This reserved self is what she gives away at her "grand dinner," when she launches her sexual exchange value into wider circulation. "Whatever came, she had resolved never again to belong to another than herself. 'I shall give a grand dinner before I leave the old house!' Edna exclaimed" (100). At the dinner, the "glittering circlet" of Edna's wedding ring (72) is now her crown.

"Something new, Edna?" exclaimed Miss Mayblunt, with lorgnette directed toward a magnificent cluster of diamonds that sparkled, that almost sputtered, in Edna's hair. . . .
   ". . . A present from my husband. . . . I may as well admit that this is my birthday. . . . In good time I expect you to drink my health. Meanwhile, I shall ask you to begin with this cocktail, composed . . . by my father in honor of Sister Janet's wedding." (108)

Her wedding rings had "sparkled," but the tiara (a conventional adornment of the "young matron") "sputters." This dinner marks the exploding of the intramarriage market, in which she repeatedly sells herself to the same man, into the public market, in which she circulates as the owner of her own sexual exchange value. In its very conception, the dinner collapses the private and public: "though Edna had spoken of the dinner as a very grand affair, it was in truth a very small affair and very select" (107). The absent beloved, Robert, is represented by Victor, his flirtatious younger brother. Flanking Edna are representatives of two modes of the market in sex value: Arobin, the gambler and playboy, represents adulterous and extramarital serial liaisons, while Monsieur Ratignolle enjoys the quasi-organic bond of Creole marriage.

The wealth of the Pontellier household is conspicuously displayed and offered to the guests. On the table "there were silver and gold . . . and crystal which glittered like the gems which the women wore" (107). The women, like the accoutrements, are presented as forms of wealth, and Edna is the queen among them. In her diamond crown, she both embodies and reigns over Léonce's riches. This dinner at which, like all women under exogamy, she leaves the "old house" is a version of the woman-giving potlatch, the marriage feast at which the father gives away the virgin daughter. The cocktail "composed" by the father for the daughter Janet's wedding is explicitly compared by Edna's lover, Arobin, to the gift of Edna herself: "it might not be amiss to start out by drinking the Colonel's health in the cocktail which he composed, on the birthday of the most charming of women—the daughter whom he invented" (108). Edna is thus the gift not just of Léonce, who makes her into a form of wealth by marking her as value, but of her father, too: that is, she is a bride. As a bride, she is an invention—man-made, brought into the world for, by, and on the occasion of the staging of ownership in the conspicuous consumption of a wedding/ potlatch.

An "invention," Edna is thoroughly representational. As a sign of value she is hailed as a sign of her father's wealth of inventiveness in making signs/wealth. The dinner dramatizes the richness of her market-determined transformations: ceremonial drink, invention, queen, luxurious gift. To say that it is her "birthday" is to say that her self is born through exchange and consists of these multiple signs that circulate in the market. What Edna wears marks her as value:

The golden shimmer of Edna's satin gown spread in rich golds on either side of her. There was a soft fall of lace encircling her shoulders. It was the color of her skin, without the glow, the myriad living tints that one may sometimes discover in vibrant flesh. There was something in her attitude, in her whole appearance . . . which suggested the regal woman, the one who rules, who looks on, who stands alone. (109)

The gold of her dress makes reference to the value in which she is robed. The lace "encircling" her shoulders refers to the skin which at the novel's opening effects Edna's transformation into "surplus." It is as if the lace is an extra skin— a conspicuously surplus skin—which in its decorative insubstantiality mirrors the meaning of Edna's skin. But the lace is not a true mirror. It points out the superior capacity of the "real" skin to change, to have "myriad tints" that allow it to be continually dissolved and re-created as a sign of value.

Edna as a sign of value is the referent of all the surrounding signs of value. She sits at the head of the table in her crown like "the regal woman, the one who rules, . . . who stands alone," as if she were the principle (and principal) of value that reigns over all its manifestations—the gold, silver, crystal, gems, and delicacies. Now Edna is like Adèle, the regal woman who has the "grace and majesty which queens are . . . supposed to possess" (31). And, like Adèle, who is tortured and "exhausted" by childbirth, Edna experiences the complement of regal power in the exhausted passivity that overcomes her after the dinner, when the celebration of private wealth moves into the realization of value through the ceremonial enactment of breakage and loss.

Edna leaves the Pontellier house with Arobin, who pauses outside the door of the "old house" to break off a spray of jessamine, enacting this defloration. He offers it to Edna: "No, I don't want anything," she answers. Emptied, she says she feels as if "something inside of [her] had snapped." This metaphorical defloration empties Edna of the erotic desire whose ownership constitutes her selfhood. Edna's shoulders are bare of the encircling lace and Arobin caresses them. Edna is passive, but Arobin feels the "response of her flesh," which, in its consecration to value, embodies the sexuality that is created in circulation. Now, after Edna's ceremonial "self-giving," this eroticism no longer constitutes a sensation that Edna can appropriate as her own desire (112–13).

The loss of the self in material bloodshedding is enacted at the end of the dinner, when the ceremony changes from a potlatch to a sacred, sacrificial rite. The desirous Mrs. Highcamp crowns Victor with a garland of yellow and red roses, effecting his magical transformation into a bacchanalian "vision of Oriental beauty." One of the transfixed guests mutters Swinburne under his breath: "There was a graven image of Desire/Painted with red blood on a ground of gold." This "graven image," like Edna's photograph, reflects her desire. Victor publicly sings the secret song that expresses the production of Edna's "private" desire as a suspicious reflection of circulation, *si tu savais ce que tes yeux me disent* ("if you knew what your eyes are saying to me") (110–11). She reacts with such consternation that she breaks her wineglass, and the contents—either red or gold, like the roses and the graven image—flow over Arobin and Mrs. Highcamp. Arobin has consecrated the evening's drinks as analogues of Edna, who has invited the guests to "drink her health"—that is, drink *her*—on her "birthday." In involuntarily shattering the glass, which, like the "cold glass" covering the photo, contains a possessive reflection of her value, Edna shatters the "mantle of reserve," symbolically releasing the maternal blood that constitutes her value.

The maternal quality of her self-giving—its involuntary and selfless aspects—overwhelms Edna again some time after the potlatch when, just as she is about to "give" herself to Robert, she is called away to witness Adèle enduring the agonies of childbirth. The sight of Adèle's "torture" overwhelms Edna (as does Adèle's exhausted plea to "think of the children"), leaving her "stunned and speechless" (132). When she returns to her little house, Robert is gone forever. Deprived of the chance to "give" herself to her desire, she spends the night thinking of her children. Later, she walks to the beach from which she will swim to her death "not thinking of these things" (136). Withholding herself from motherhood, insisting on her right to refuse to "sacrifice" herself for her children, Edna owns herself. In the logic of self-ownership and voluntary motherhood, motherhood is itself the ground on which woman claims ownership of her sexual value. Edna seizes the most extreme prerogative of this self-ownership, withholding herself from motherhood by withholding herself from life and thus giving herself in a maternal dissolution.

Edna's death in the ocean dramatizes the self-ownership rhetoric of Elizabeth Cady Stanton. Stanton argues that "self-sovereignty" is the existential birthright of both women and men, for every human being "launched on the sea of life" is unique and "alone" (248). But women's self-sovereignty specifically denotes sexual self-determination. And Stanton insists that women—that is, mothers—earn a special presumptive self-sovereignty, for "alone [woman] goes to the gates of death to give life to every man that is born into the world; no one can share her fears, no one can mitigate her pangs; and if her sorrow is greater than she can bear, alone she passes beyond the gates into the vast unknown" (251). At the moment of extreme maternal giving, the moment when motherhood takes her life, the woman owns her self by withholding herself from motherhood.

CHAPTER 2

Edith Wharton and the Problem of the Woman Author

In her memoir, *A Backward Glance,* Edith Wharton writes of "the problem" she faced in composing *The House of Mirth:* the problem of producing a work of literary value that takes as its topic a "shallow" subject. Wharton believes that the "value of a subject depends almost wholly on what the author sees in it," yet she fears that "there are certain subjects too shallow to yield anything to the most searching gaze." The subject of "fashionable New York" might fall into this category. "The problem was how to extract from such a subject the typical human significance. . . . The answer was that a frivolous society can acquire dramatic significance only through what its frivolity destroys. Its tragic implication lies in its power of debasing people and ideals. The answer, in short, was my heroine, Lily Bart" (207).

This shallow subject has value after all: the "human significance" that makes a novel great is to be found in the debasements of frivolous society it depicts. The novel's own "dramatic significance" and "tragic implication" redeem the value of "people and ideals" destroyed in this society's cheapening trade. Like its heroine, the novel itself is a product of frivolous society, which constantly collapses into and emerges as distinct from its cheapened material and cheapening context. Through this oscillation of debasement and redemption, the novel attains its stature as "tragic" art.

The stature of the novel is the stature of its author as well. As the novelist whose "searching gaze" penetrates to the tragic nature of shallowness, Wharton finds her own artistic value in the process of debasement and redemption her novel both represents and undergoes. Wharton's retrospective evaluation of the problem and achievement of *The House of Mirth* is an evaluation of herself as an author, for she recounts that in writing *The House of Mirth* on a timetable set by the publication needs of *Scribner's Magazine,* she was "turned from a drifting amateur into a professional; but that was nothing compared to the effect on my imagination of systematic daily effort" (209). When Wharton writes that she became a professional by writing *The House of Mirth,* she points to the moment at which she became celebrated as the author of a best-seller. This is both a triumph and a debasement, for her novel's popularity was due in large part to the "exasperating accusation" that she had written a high society roman à clef made up of "flesh and blood people." This reception is "dispiriting": a "born author" would never produce anything less than a creative work of the imagination, while the author of a roman à clef is hard to distinguish from a gossip columnist. Yet Wharton finally accedes to the market the power to define—and thus to debase—her work and her authorial identity. When one has "sold one's wares in the open market," she writes, "one has sold to the purchasers the right to think what they choose about one's books" (210, 212).

Wharton's professional authorship, then, is achieved through debasement in the marketplace. To trace the logic by which debasement constitutes professionalism for Wharton is to map out her divergence from the Jamesian argument with which she begins her defense of *The House of Mirth.* Wharton's beginning statement about "the value of a subject" recapitulates Henry James' "The Art of Fiction." The value of a book is in "what the writer makes of it," James insists. "We must grant the artist his subject, his idea, his *donnée.* . . . Our criticism is applied only to what he makes of it. . . . We may believe that of a certain idea even the most sincere novelist can make nothing at all . . . but the failure will have been a failure to execute" (721). Wharton's own version of "The Art of Fiction" is a 1903 magazine essay entitled "The Vice of Reading." Wharton begins by agreeing with James that a book must be "judged not by the incidents it presents but by the author's sense of their significance" (519). In this Jamesian view, a good book expresses the artist and is only as good as the artistic self expressed in it, while the product of a bad writer is shaped, not by the author, but by the market: a bad writer is concerned with what the market wants rather than with realizing his own vision.

Wharton goes on to support her repudiation of market-generated value by characterizing the reading public as unknowing and spuriously motivated. The contemporary literary audience is made up of "sense-of-duty" readers who exercise their new literacy not because they love and understand books, but because reading has become fashionable and even virtuous. This "reading deliberately undertaken . . . is no more reading than erudition is culture," Wharton complains; it is a mechanical exercise undertaken as part of the conformist striving for status. The mechanical reader, unlike the "born reader [who] reads as unconsciously as he breathes," reads on purpose—he reads with "volition." This motivated reading is "unprofitable" because "the book enters the reader's mind . . . without any of the additions and modifications inevitably produced by contact with a new body of thought" (513).

"The gravest offense of this mechanical reader," Wharton writes, is "the crime of luring creative talent into the ranks of mechanical production." The mechanical writer designs her product for the consumption of the mechanical reader. Just as the mechanical reader is motivated by external concerns and reads without engaging the inner self, so the mechanical writer puts nothing of herself into the book but writes for the market; she writes in order to have a "career" (519). Since, according to the Jamesian argument Wharton recapitulates, the value of a book is in "what the author makes of it," the career and products of a mechanical writer are without value because they result from no imaginative "making" of the author; they merely reflect the literary consumerism of the marketplace.

For Wharton as for James, then, a good book is an externalization of the author. In her discussion of this process, however, it becomes apparent that for Wharton, this author comes about only through the mediation of the market. While James assumes that the authorial self that makes literature valuable is immanent in the work, for Wharton, it is at the point of consumption that literary value—and, thus, the author's self—is manifested.

> The value of books is proportionate to what may be called their plasticity—their quality of being all things to all men, of being diversely moulded by the impact of fresh forms of thought. . . . In this sense it may be said that there is no abstract standard of values in literature: the greatest books ever written are worth to each reader only what he can get out of them. . . . There are books that are always the same—incapable of modifying or of being modified—but these do not count as factors in literature. (514)

Here, the authorial self in the work does not exist prior to the consumption of the work. For James, the author puts something into the book and thus makes it valuable; for Wharton, value—and the self that value is thought to manifest—is created at the point of "modification" by the consumer.

As the public's reception of *The House of Mirth* illustrates, this "modification" is problematic and often debasing. In her memoir, Wharton concludes from this that just as the public of purchasers must be allowed to think what they want, so the novelist must set herself up as the arbiter of value: "the novelist's best safeguard is to . . . write only for that . . . critic who dwells within the breast" (212). If writing for the market means enabling public (mis)determinations of value, it also means the dialectical creation of an interior critical self that recognizes the value unknown to the public. This critical self is constituted by the application of a value system that diverges from that of the market—that is, the critical self comes into being through awareness of the false and debasing constructions that the market imposes on the author. This authorial self has privacy, or separation from the market, as an effect of the operation of the values of the market; and this private self, Wharton argues, is the essence of the professional author. In "The Vice of Reading," Wharton argues that the essential self of the author is the source and value of good authorship and good books. She concludes that the debasement of author and book, reflected in a self that exists as the consciousness of this debasement, produces the value (or "significance," to use the terminology of her discussion of *The House of Mirth*) of both book and author.

This dialectical process in which the private self emerges out of the market's debasing misreadings is reflected in the doubleness of the term "professional," which can refer both to the expert producer of acknowledged value, a credentialed "born writer," and to the market-determined careerist. Wharton writes that composing *The House of Mirth* made her a professional, but she also points to the publication of her first collection as the moment at which she entered the literary market. This publication, she writes, gave her an authorial self, a "personality of my own." In *A Backward Glance,* Wharton writes that in 1898, after she had published *The Decoration of Houses* and some short stories in *Scribner's Magazine,* "I had as yet no real personality of my own, and was not to acquire one till my first volume of short stories was published—and that was not until 1899" (112).

The collection that produced Wharton's "own" personality was *The Greater Inclination.* This volume was made up of stories that were carefully selected by Wharton and Walter Berry. "*I* had written short stories that were thought worthy of preservation!" Wharton writes in *A Backward Glance* of her astonishment over the fact that her book was "actually thought important enough to be . . . reviewed!" (113). Like the mechanical writer, Wharton is constituted as an author by the application of external standards. Her sense of herself as an author is established only after her work has been subjected, by herself and Berry as well as by the publisher, to existing critical standards and has passed marketing trials that establish its objective marketability. As Stuart Culver points out, an anthology constructs an "author" by unifying several different texts under the principle of their origination in a single author (114–36). Out of the operation of these external systems the authorial self—an external self—emerges: "Was it the same insignificant *I* that I had always known? Any one . . . might go into any bookshop, and say: 'Please give me Edith Wharton's book'" (*Backward Glance,* 113).

Now the author is a "significant" I. "Significance" is the word Wharton uses to point to the literary value of debasement in *The House of Mirth.* The market in which her books are sold is the same "open market" in which one sells others the right to think whatever they want of one. A personality of her "own" is thus produced in a market in which her alienated identity becomes the property of—indeed, the product of—others, for in this anecdote, significance is negotiability: "anyone" in any shop can ask for the book identified by her name, "and the clerk, without bursting into incredulous laughter, would produce it, and be paid for it" (113). The interchangeability of Wharton's name and work, which are to be exchanged for money endlessly circulated, produce the private selfhood that Wharton recognizes as her "own."

Wharton's notion of authorship, insisting on the centrality to the self of value created by the interaction of public and private, is Veblen's conspicuously consuming wife (Veblen, 65–76). In Veblen's formulation, the domestic woman's status as private wealth precedes, results from, and reflects back on her status as a circulating commodity—just as the value of Wharton's private authorial self is constituted by her dedication to the market. The prostitute exemplifies this dialectic, as she commands a market price that reflects (and is thus "earned" by) the transformation of a private self into a public commodity: the body she sells is valuable because it represents value held in the domestic sphere, where it is private wealth. Like Wharton's author, the prostitute undergoes a transforming debasement (realized in market value) in which she abandons—and thus sustains the value of—her potential to be owned in private. But this analogy is not a perfect fit because authorial debasement begins not at the point of going out on the street (publication) but in the course of consumption (or its failure). The private self that is abandoned to market value exists only at and through this point of "modification."[1]

Wharton's view of authorial value is informed by the structure of woman's value in exchange. Wharton's literary self-construction—her memoir *A Backward Glance*—contains a lengthy passage about the construction of this female self that exists as the valuable object of others' possession. Beginning the story of her life with an event she identifies as productive of the first stirrings of a "self," Wharton writes, "the little girl who eventually became me, but as yet was neither me nor anybody else in particular . . . was going for a walk with her father. The episode is literally the first thing I can remember about her, and therefore I date the birth of her identity from that day" (1). On this day "she," wearing a paragraph's worth of lovingly itemized garments, "surveyed in the glass with considerable satisfaction" her "new and very pretty bonnet" before setting out for the walk with father. This walk was "particularly" eventful because the new bonnet was "so beautiful (and so becoming) that for the first time she woke to the importance of dress, and of herself as a subject for adornment—so that I may date from that hour the birth of the conscious and feminine *me* in the little girl's vague soul" (2). The tall father and the little girl meet up with tall Cousin Henry and "Cousin Henry's little boy Daniel," whom the girl feels must "somehow belong" to her. "The little boy . . . looked back with equal interest" and suddenly lifted the girl's veil and kissed her cheek. "This is my earliest definite memory . . . and it will be seen that I was wakened to conscious life by . . . love and vanity" (3).

Wharton's conscious me awakens in a nexus of objectification and possession. Her awareness of the beauty of her hat rouses her to an awareness of herself as a construct and reflection of—and thus both owner and possession of—such possessions. She becomes a conscious subject by becoming aware of herself as an object—not only an object of sight, to be enhanced by clothes, but an object of possession, a center of possessive energy around which valuable and visible things are draped. The phrase "subject for adornment" makes her a subject by making her into the object of her clothes.

This "feminine me" becomes her own only when the particularities of this possessive nexus are brought into the arena of public exchange. Walking on the street with her hand in her father's, she is publicly constituted as private property—as father's little girl. Through the intervention of publicity she belongs to her father and thus has an identity (just as the reflection of her hat in the mirror gives her an objectivity that identifies her beauty as belonging to her). In the meeting with Cousin Henry and "Cousin Henry's little boy Daniel," the girl sees another reflection: she is in the corollary position of "father's little girl." The closeness thus produced—a bond of structural homology—is perceived by the girl as a bond of possession, for all ties in this identity-producing social nexus are possessive. Daniel, she feels, "must somehow belong" to her. While he shows equal interest, it is not mutual possessiveness that awakens her to "conscious life": in lifting her veil and "boldly" kissing her, the little boy makes the appropriative gesture that simultaneously claims her as his own and exposes her to publicity.

In the birth of "a personality of my own" that attended the publication of Wharton's first collection, publicity once again secures the self-possessing self as a public self whose solidity is confirmed by the bookstore clerk's failure to burst out in "incredulous laughter." If the failure to laugh assures Wharton that the "significant I" (the marketable author) signifies the author as far as the market is concerned, it also points to the credulity of the reading public, which takes the sign for the real self. In "The Vice of Reading," she mocks the reading public for getting out of a book only what they are told is in it (its negotiability). In the modern literary market, Wharton writes, the "immense majority of book-consumers" are externally motivated, indistinguishable, "mechanical readers" who read not because they are individually drawn to reading and gifted with the organic and innate ability to read, but because the new culture of mass literacy has made reading "meritorious" as well as profitable to publishers. "The mechanical reader is incapable of discerning intuitively whether a book is worth reading or not. . . . Viewing all books from the outside, and having no point of contact with the author's mind, he makes no allowances for temperament or environment" (516). This market depersonalizes both author and reader. In his reading, the mechanical reader brings to bear on the text external social and economic forces such as the book's popularity and moral reputation and its readers' social status. In the hands of this mass readership, the author who is externalized in the book (for, if it is a good book, according to Wharton, it is an externalization of the author's self) is never "modified" by contact with the reader's self. Since no actual consumption takes place, no particular and private self uses up the author, who, never removed from the sphere of public circulation, is left to circulate.

The failure of the reader is, then, the failure of private appropriation. Private appropriation is necessary in order to have a "self"—but this self exists in the "open market." In Wharton's textualizations of this failure, the publication of letters that were originally private dramatizes the modification of the author through mass marketing that is perpetuated when private appropriation fails. Wharton's novella, *The Touchstone*, revolves around the scandalous publication of the (unsuccessful) love letters of Margaret Aubyn, a famous dead author. Aubyn is a woman whose lover fails to privatize her letters just as he fails to privatize her by marrying her. In *The Touchstone*, Wharton attacks bad readers (and bad lovers) and dramatizes the final triumph of the woman author, whose lover finally comes to value both her intellectual achievement and her femininity.

Margaret Aubyn is a literary genius—a born author such as Wharton describes in "The Vice of Reading." As such, she externalizes herself in her work, leaving herself open to a debasement in the marketplace that is, like Lily's, significant. Wharton savages the obverse of Margaret Aubyn in a satire she published in a 1901 issue of *Bookman*. This issue featured a review of a new and potentially best-selling book, *Love Letters of an Englishwoman*, which were marketed as the (anonymous) "real" letters of a young woman to her fiancé.

(For mysterious and painful reasons, the fiancé finally does not marry the letter-writer.) Wharton's parody, called "More Love Letters of an Englishwoman," was appended to a favorable review of the book; the excitement expressed in this review demonstrates that Wharton is not eccentric in basing literary and authorial value in the debasement of the female self through publication.

The reviewer of *Love Letters of an Englishwoman*, Frederic Taber Cooper, writes, "in the whole field of literature there is probably nothing more genuinely and intimately personal than the letters which just a few women possess the art of writing." "A man's letters are quite different," he goes on. "Self-consciousness," "pose," stiffness, and "company manners" mar even the most intimate letters of men.

It is only a woman, and the occasional woman at that, who has the gift of complete self-abandonment upon paper; who can open the flood-gates of her emotions and lay bare her innermost thoughts, infusing into the cold black and white of the written page a charm which is physical as well as psychic, a suggestion of a soft touch and the thrill of low-spoken words that makes such a letter quite literally and truly a human document.

Oddly, this "self-abandonment" is only achieved when the author's skill is adequate to carry out her intention of laying herself bare. Cooper writes, "that the present volume of letters was intended to be of this sort, is quite obvious; and . . . they miss their purpose by a rather narrow margin" (560).

To Wharton, the narrow "miss" creates a chasm of irony. The author's failure to abandon herself signals the absence of a self to abandon. Wharton's parody, which ridicules the Englishwoman's meretricious and vulgar pseudo-literariness as part of her calculated, sham "self-abandonment," recalls her dismissal of "mechanical" readers and writers in "The Vice of Reading." The Englishwoman writes for the market without abandoning anything to the market: she brings nothing to the market that is not demonstrably already there. Therefore, while those who buy her book think they are getting for their money the value of a private self made into a public commodity, there is nothing to be realized in the book except the reader's own external "mechanical" determinations.

What the Englishwoman supposedly puts into her letters—a conflation of her intellect and her femininity (her intellect as her femininity, since it is being sold)—is in its reflexivity to market demands merely "mechanical." Wharton's "More Love Letters of an Englishwoman" begins:

OWNEST—When I woke this morning my windows were covered with a thick, white frost. . . . I was just dangling one timorous creamy magnolia-white foot over the edge of the bed, into the icy crackling void of circumambiant cold, when the door opened and Juggins (that housemaid, Beloved, is already pensioned against senility!)—Juggins brought me Your Letter—.

My Veriest—my Mortgage on Blessedness (as George Meredith might say—you *must* try to read him, Love!)—have you ever seen . . . the virgin bosom of the Alps flush beneath the hot, passionate kiss of Phoebus? (Don't be alarmed at my learning, dear! He's only the Norse Sun-god; you'll find him in the Vedda.) Well—*I* have, Sweet—(Aunty took me up the Rhigi once). (562)

In order for the letter to "lay bare" its writer, there must be a body to expose (what Cooper calls a physical presence)—a low voice, privacy, a self that can be imagined as existing outside the market. Wharton exposes the absence of a self in a spoof of upper-class domestic femininity that has no notion of individuality. The body that is laid bare is the foot, described in mock-erotic terms that degrade its functional purpose. The affectional voice turns out to be that of "Aunty," the instructor in proper cultural and domestic deportment. The privacy or interior self of the Englishwoman is nonexistent and, in the absence of a self, there is no possessive relationship to be breached by the abandonment of possessive privacy in the literary marketplace.

In *The Decoration of Houses,* an 1897 book on interior decoration which Wharton co-wrote, the authors explain that self is the prerequisite of authentic ownership. The first two chapters of Wharton and Ogden Codman's book are devoted to arguing that the beauty of interiors should be related to usefulness, and that usefulness is relative to the individuality and needs of the occupants. Without such individuality, the possessiveness of domestic, erotic, and literary relations reflects external value systems. The parody's possessive locutions— "ownest" and "my mortgage on blessedness"—are the empty gestures of someone who, lacking self, cannot possess in her own right and can therefore merely reiterate overblown gestures of possession.

The lack of self that makes possession a sham also makes beauty and value impossible, for apparent beauty depends on inherent, functional form. The distinction between aesthetics (form) and decoration (superficial application) governs Wharton's discussions of interior decoration and literature (as it governs Selden's assessment of Lily Bart in the opening moment of *The House of Mirth*). In *The Decoration of Houses* the authors write, "rooms may be decorated in two ways: by a superficial application of ornament totally independent of structure, or by means of those architectural features which are part of the organism of every house, inside as well as out" (xix). The Englishwoman's decorative domesticity is not expressive of a real self; thus, her literary identity is similarly decorative and superficial.

An externally determined, "mechanical" writer, the Englishwoman practices literary production as an extension of her consumption practice—for, in reproducing the forms her vapid culture recommends to her, she is in essence a "mechanical reader." In "The Vice of Reading," Wharton explains that the "mechanical" consumers of culture like their literature to be measurable so that they can brag about the quantities devoured. Wharton compares people who like easily digestible literature to housewives parceling out the family's consumables: these consumers display "the cast of mind which discerns in the natural divisions of the melon an indication that it is meant to be eaten *en famille*" (514). The Englishwoman's mechanical consumption of culture is spoofed in Wharton's final parodic letter in which the Englishwoman, writing from Pisa, brags to her beloved about the sensitivity that has enabled her to "thrill" to the leaning tower of Pisa: "it is a melody in marble."

Don't laugh at me, Darling, and call me eccentric, original, romantic—but when Uncle asked me yesterday what I should like for a birthday present, I flung my arms about his neck and whispered—one of those little *Leaning Towers,* in alabaster! Beloved, I can never be thankful enough for having been born with an artistic nature. (563)

Why did Wharton go out of her way to append this parody to the review? The reviewer valorizes the amateur status of the author: this text was written for love, not money, and thus (insofar as it succeeds in giving this impression) is worth money—is valuable, in both literary and market terms. But Wharton, rather than attacking in the name of her hard-won professionalism, attacks in such a way as to cast doubt on the amateur status of the Englishwoman. This amateurishness is inseparable from femininity (these are "love letters," after all), and in her parody Wharton explodes these attributes. In exposing the letters as commodities calculated for negotiability in a particular market rather than as sincere effusions of a loving and sensitive nature, Wharton seems to be accusing the Englishwoman of being a professional—writer and woman.

Amy Kaplan argues that Wharton looked to professionalism as an escape from feminine domesticity and sentimental privacy. Kaplan writes that Wharton turned to literary professionalism in a movement toward personal independence and out of the imprisoning female role as domestic ornament and self-effacing Veblenian "sign" (65–87, 69). My reading suggests, however, that the professionalism Wharton sought—the professionalism of the "born writer" (as opposed to the mechanical professionalism of the Englishwoman)—depends precisely on the realliance of the self with a private sphere. Wharton's anxiety about professionalism is not that it will fail to remove her from a private sphere, but that it will fail to be an extension of the private sphere—that, indeed, the private sphere will itself fail. This is not an anxiety about "imprisonment" in feminine passivity; indeed, passivity is exactly what Wharton finds lacking in the self-marketing Englishwoman. It is, rather, an anxiety that centers on the public nature of privacy. Professionalism, for Wharton, is a way to reconstruct through market-generated reputation an innate private self that has been corroded.

Wharton's version of the work of authorship and the status of the author suggests that she sees literary professionalism not as a repudiation of woman's "work" of passivity and sentimental consumption, but as its extension into the market. This model of professionalism, because it depends on discontinuity between private and public spheres, raises the dangerous possibility that these spheres may collapse into each other. If the private woman is the "currency" that circulates in the market, the moment of change—the moment of debasement, of the substitution of one base of value (the private) with another (the public)—must not be dissolved. There must, then, be a "true" professional—one of inborn gifts that cannot be fully expressed as market value and will always exist in her difference from the debased market form.

In the character of Alice Waythorn, Wharton dramatizes her anxiety that the private self, marketed, may be only the marketed self. Alice Waythorn is a woman whose private self keeps reemerging as the marketed self that constructs it. The much-divorced heroine of Wharton's story "The Other Two," Alice Waythorn has the plasticity of a good book. To her brand-new third husband, Waythorn, she seems both "fresh" and "elastic," and as she pours her husband's coffee by the fire after dinner, her "flowing" and pliant femininity fills Waythorn with the "joy of possessorship." Her adaptability to his needs, like her soft appearance, makes her seem to be his property and, as such, valuable (2:381).

This pliancy, however, also works against Waythorn's sense of possessorship. As he unavoidably witnesses, Alice is equally plastic in her dealings with her two former husbands. It seems to him then that what he had taken as warmth and richness of character is actually the absence of character. He thinks, "she [is] 'as easy as an old shoe'—a shoe that too many feet [have] worn. Her elasticity [is] the result of tension in too many different directions." Now the qualities that make him feel that he owns her as his private property—her pliancy in response to his desires, her ability to create a sense of private, domestic harmony and possessorship—are what call into question the possibility of the privacy of this possessorship: these qualities and abilities that make her valuable as private property are precisely what mark her as public property. He tries to reconcile himself to his position as just another joint owner of Alice. "Was it not better," he asks himself, "to own a third of a wife who knew how to make a man happy than a whole one who had lacked the opportunity to acquire the art? For it *was* an art" (383). To own a wife who can fulfill the domestic functions of a wife is, then, to own something that cannot be private property.

Alice Waythorn's conjugal art is a version of what the author sells in the market, where she and her book are worn away, modified, stretched, and remolded by each consumer. Alice Waythorn is made into private property by each husband, just as a good reader modifies and thus privatizes a book. Yet the result of this privatizing appropriation is to relocate the commodity more firmly in the sphere of public circulation—the act of modification itself demonstrates the commodity's dedication to circulation. In Wharton's vision, the commodity remains a commodity and is not resolved into use value: that is to say, the public woman is never seen at the moment when she is (in either production or consumption) the private woman.

The commodity form of Alice Waythorn, however, can only exist via the transformation of the private, domestic self of Alice Waythorn. Waythorn finally recuperates this private self as that which is always displaced or sacrificed. As he muses, "Alice Hasket—Alice Varick—Alice Waythorn—she had been each in turn, and had left hanging to each name a little of her privacy, a little of her personality, a little of the inmost self where the unknown god abides" (383). In the sphere of circulation, there is a continually manifested discontinuity between the private self and the public commodity-self; this public self appears to be produced at the cost of the private self, which it uses up and then projects as its obverse. Circulation both effaces and produces the private self; and marriage, for a woman, as the moment at which she both enters into a private identity and loses (sells) her name and "the inmost self" it signifies, represents for Wharton the moment of publication, when the author's availability to be owned and named by others evokes a selfhood that it obliterates.

Most of Wharton's stories on this theme are about the absence and failure of marriage—as "The Other Two" shows, the failure of marriage is very much like marriage itself. In *The Touchstone*, Wharton's novella about the debasement of the woman author, the author's beloved is inadequate to the challenge of loving her back. He will not marry her, and thus her feminine passion, following her authorial identity, passes into the realm of "public property." *The Touchstone*, which was published in book form in 1900 after running as a serial in *Scribner's Magazine*, is a story about a woman author whose celebrity constitutes both the destruction and the creation of a feminine self.

The novella's protagonist, Stephen Glennard, is a struggling young lawyer who wants to marry the austerely beautiful and unpropertied Alexa Trent, but lacks the funds to keep her in decent style. *The Touchstone* opens with the text of a biographer's notice in the *Spectator,* soliciting personal letters written by the famous dead author Margaret Aubyn, "the most brilliant woman of her day" (6). Glennard is in possession of hundreds of brilliant letters from Aubyn. She and Glennard became friends as she was leaving a bad marriage and starting her writing career; then she fell in love with him (her husband died, leaving her free) and continued to love and write letters to him until her death. Glennard, however, was never able to return the passion of the unbeautiful "poor woman of genius" who "[did] not know how to do her hair." At first flattered by the "sense of mental equality" he got from their friendship, as his understanding grew he recognized her "mental ascendancy" and suffered from the "strain" of "looking up" (14). Aubyn moved to England and kept up the bond with him through her letters until she died.

Alexa Trent's family's financial problems threaten the end of her engagement to Glennard. Glennard sees a risk-free opportunity to make the money he needs to marry her by investing in a fellow clubman's patent, but he has no money with which to buy in. Using a middleman and hiding his identity as the recipient of the Aubyn letters, Glennard sells them to a publisher for $10,000 plus royalties, invests the money, and marries Alexa (who thinks he has come into an inheritance). Alexa, who has "the gift of silence," is a stunningly serene woman characterized by an unflappable, intuitive sense of justice, and the couple enjoys a peaceful, increasingly prosperous domestic life in the suburbs (44). The *Letters,* marketed as a two-volume book, is a sensational best-seller: everywhere he looks, Glennard is confronted with Margaret Aubyn's name on reviews, notices, and advertisements for the book.

Alexa asks him to pick up a copy for her: their social "set" includes women who "keep up" with the latest books and men who write for newspapers and popular literature reviews. There are discussions about the *Letters;* Alexa feels it's dastardly of the recipient to have published them and exposed Aubyn's unrequited passion. She and other women express their pity for Aubyn and their contempt for the undeserving and indiscreet recipient, while others—mostly men—take the view that the letters are literary documents, not expressions of "personal" life (47). Glennard agrees with his wife, and is tormented by guilt and self-contempt—although when the first royalty check comes, he spends it easily.

Finally, he confesses to his wife and they decide to return the money. But he then realizes that the amount has become "far-reaching" through investment (97). He learns that Alexa had guessed but kept silent about her knowledge of his complicity in the publication, caring more about his suffering than about the disgrace with which he has tainted her. Glennard begs her to dissociate herself from him in his disgrace, but she replies, "You did it for me," and tells him that he is not disgraced, but redeemed, for in his repentance he has regained himself via the "gift" of Margaret Aubyn. Glennard finally declares that Aubyn has given him, not only himself, but the Alexa he never knew.

Wharton's Margaret Aubyn is an author whose reader, Glennard, is, like the mechanical reader, "incapable." Aubyn, like a good author, writes "to the Happy Few"—not to the market; but, as Wharton points out in "The Vice of Reading," this "Happy Few" is unhappily chosen (516). Glennard's incapacity as a reader of Aubyn's letters is inseparable from his incapacity to reciprocate or respond to her womanly love: his treatment of her love, like his reception of her letters, is evasive and opportunistic. She goes away physically, but her letters importune him like an unwanted spouse whom he passively (and unsuccessfully) tries to evade: "he used to avoid looking in his letter-box when he came home to his rooms—but her writing seemed to spring out at him as he put his key in the door" (7).

Glennard's failure to reciprocate, however, is far from damaging to either Aubyn's love or her writing. He sees in her letters that the "oppressive prodigality" of her brilliance and love sustain themselves without his help. "She simply fed on her own funded passion, and the luxuries it allowed her made him . . . dimly aware that she had the secret of an inexhaustible alchemy" (8, 16). The wealth that is multiplied is a wealth of love, but its alchemical transformation occurs when it turns into brilliance. The letters, with their multiple allusions, wide range of topics, and wonderful language, are the currency of her love, the vehicle by which her private feeling is transformed into an expression of literary gifts.

As a bad reader, Glennard has no way of making contact with the real content of her letters and thus with the self who wrote them: "he was blinded to their specific meaning" (18). He evaluates them according to an external standard—"he knew, of course, that they were wonderful"—and constructs his relation to them according to an invidious system of social status: they suggest his worthiness as a friend of the genius and/or represent the unworthiness that makes him unable to reciprocate. Glennard thus brings to bear on the letters all the egregious practices of the "mechanical reader."

But this bad reading, rather than being destructive of the value of the letters, creates the condition of possibility of their value. Glennard's inability to reciprocate (or to "refund," as Wharton's metaphor has it) the passion Aubyn offers him makes her writing the vehicle of her social generosity. Giving more and more of herself, and thus having more self to give, she comes out as superior in every respect, including the moral. Her self-giving makes him feel she is his more-than wife; like the domestic woman, she pours out a personal devotion that overflows the container of his externally defined relation to her.

But it is in the literary register that the value of the letters has the most scope for multiplication. Because he cannot "read" her—cannot, that is, bring his subjectivity into relation with hers—Glennard is susceptible to what Wharton in "The Vice of Reading" identifies as the common habit of bad readers, that of "regarding reading objectively" (515). When the *Spectator* notice brings him sharply into relation with the literary market, this market's economic determinants provide Glennard with a powerful objectivity.

He had never thought of the letters objectively, as the production of a distinguished woman; had never measured the literary significance of her oppressive prodigality. He was almost frightened now at the wealth in his hands; the obligation of her love had never weighed on him like this gift of her imagination: it was as though he had accepted from her something to which even a reciprocal tenderness could not have justified his claim. (18)

In the light of this objectivity, the letters become transcendently valuable and Glennard becomes definitively unequal to their author. Aubyn, in her fame, has undergone a "gradual translation into terms of universality"; she has changed from a "person" to a "personage" (17). But Glennard, though he is a mechanical, objective reader, still retains in relation to the letters a sense of personal possessorship: the letters represent something to which he has supposedly demonstrated a particular claim. The growing inequality he feels stems from his perception that the "wealth" is social, abstract wealth, but his ownership of it is impossibly private and concrete: the wealth is something he holds "in his hands." He has always tried to shake off this sensation: where Aubyn is concerned, Glennard has always felt "the physical reluctance [that had] . . . inexplicably . . . overborne the intellectual attraction." The duality in "the strange dual impulse that drew him to her voice but drove him from her hand" is the duality of Aubyn as social wealth—as a disembodied and ubiquitous great "voice"—and Aubyn as private wealth: that is, as a woman (5, 6). Refusing, at first, to make Aubyn his own through this personal, concrete mode of possession, Glennard eventually appears incapable of making such a claim on a woman of her stature. His failure to acknowledge Aubyn the woman as his, it seems, results in her "translation" into something that conspicuously exceeds his capacity for possession.

On a literal plane, the force of Glennard's preference that she become abstract wealth so that he can get her "off his hands" is reflected in Aubyn's fate: she dedicates herself to a writing career and never remarries. The woman author turns rejection into triumph not by claiming a professional autonomy that overrides romantic rejection, as Gilbert and Gubar claim, but by showing that rejection, and her passivity in the course it sets for her, is the force that propels the externalization of self that is celebrity.[2] The "incapacity" of her love object/ reader, forcing her to sacrifice her particularity and sexuality, is an enabling condition of Aubyn's fame (and, as we have seen, of her prodigal productivity).

To Glennard, her fame means that "the public [takes] possession of Mrs. Aubyn," which eases the load on "his shoulders" to the degree that "the world . . . [has] taken her off his hands" (18). Glennard's physical metaphors are ironic, of course, since Aubyn is beyond his possession by virtue of being dead: changing from a "person" to a "personage" means dying. It is this change that makes her letters especially valuable. While love letters are accounted valuable, love letters of a tragic nature, by a dead woman writer, are the genre's most marketable form (28). Glennard's sale of the letters is the confirmation of Aubyn's disembodiment: the price they fetch confirms that their value is constructed as abstract social wealth—as money—while the transaction itself literally releases him from physical, private possession. Glennard's middleman advises him that "anything of Margaret Aubyn's is more or less public property by now" (since the author is not only famous, but dead and without heirs), suggesting that the transformation of this wealth from private and personal to social and abstract is a fait accompli which the sale will merely confirm (33). This confirmation, however, begins with the private possession of the letters; if selling them confirms that they are public property, to be public property is to be private property over which an individual has the rights of sale. Aubyn is thoroughly disembodied and translated because she was first owned (through her letters) by a single man.

If the publication of this privacy through the love letters (or "unloved letters," as one woman reader calls them) is a scandal, the "vice" of reading them ("'I believe it *is* a vice, almost, to read such a book as the *Letters*,' said Mrs. Touchett") consists in subjecting the letters to the external standards— fame, notoriety, fashion—which motivate the "mechanical" readers who are the love letters' audience (45). It is of course the book's immersion in the scandal of selling private feelings in the marketplace that constitutes its market value. In its very existence as a book (rather than as several bundles of letters in Glennard's hand), it represents debasement, embodies the operations of questionable transformations of value. While its appeal is not in one sense what Wharton would call "literary," it is as a book that the book has value for its readers. Not written *for* the market, it is written by a professional. It publishes the real privacy of Margaret Aubyn and thus achieves the realization of that author in the actual debasement of a person with serious and inborn intellectual gifts. According to Wharton's notions, then, the *Letters of Margaret Aubyn* contain the purest form of literary value.

This debasement in the market, expressed as market value, enables Glennard finally to see this debasement/transmutation and thus Aubyn's femininity. It is only when Glennard sees the letters as a book and a book as a bearer of literary value that he can see transmutation: then "he could almost fancy some alchemistic process changing [the letters] to gold as he stared" (16). Wharton's notion of "debasement" becomes more concrete in its analogical reference, as the "base" of value changes and a love-based economy becomes a gold-based economy through the mediation of a text-based economy.

A text in the literary market embodies and enacts this debasement. The text is the medium by which a particular person's mind is subjected to external construction. To be an author—someone who is published—is to be, like Margaret Aubyn, a personage whose every written word constitutes the self as published—constitutes a text. To take the logic to its limit (as does a reader when she says of the Letters, "it's the woman's soul"), to be an author is to be a text—to embody the debasing transformation of private value into public value (45).

As Glennard rediscovers, this is also what it is to be a woman. Though some time has passed since "the desiccating air of memory had turned [Aubyn] into the mere abstraction of a woman," the mills of publicity keep grinding out her celebrity. Glennard happens upon a magazine story that reproduces the photo of her that "had stood so long on his desk." When he finds in his magazine this familiar possession recirculated as one more public rehearsal of her celebrity and pathos, she seems "nearer than she had ever been in life. Was it because he understood her better? . . . Little personal traits reached out to him like caresses. . . . All that was feminine in her, the quality he had always missed, stole toward him" (75). Aubyn's femininity becomes present to him as the duality through which her debasing abstraction as a public woman offers to him, in his private possession of her likeness, the "personal traits" of the woman he has known. Finally, Glennard claims the personal Aubyn within the possessive intimacy he had always resisted. In his "better" understanding, he finds Aubyn and himself hidden in the same sphere of privacy. Like her, he has (as he puts it) "sold [him]self": his increasingly prosperous public self flourishes by transforming into money the private self that circulates as the notorious anonymous recipient of the letters.

Glennard's relation to femininity, however, is not the same as Aubyn's (or his wife's). He does not remain split. Rather than remaining a perpetual site of debasement, he moves, through the "inexhaustible alchemy" of Aubyn, from shame to redemption. His private self is brought out into the public with the help of his wife, Alexa. And Alexa is made available to him when Aubyn turns herself into Alexa, reemerging in the form of the disgraced but just and faithful wife whom Glennard has bought by selling Aubyn's letters. Seeing in Alexa the value which Aubyn, through his debasement of her love, has produced for him, Glennard again laments his inadequacy: "I despoiled her," he tells his wife, "and she's given me *you* in return!" But this very sense of self-contempt, Alexa/Aubyn counsels, constitutes a redeemed self made available, of course, through Aubyn's transmutations: "it's that she's given you to yourself. . . . That's the gift you can't escape from, the debt you're pledged to acquit" (101). Incapable of owning, Glennard, restored to himself by Aubyn, owns as himself the Aubyn who has become him.

Asserting that "the value of a book is in what the writer makes of it," Henry James insists that the author's value—the author, that is—is not what is made of him by society, with its bad reading practices informed by morality, popularity, and marketability. But for Wharton, bad reading produces "the answer . . . my heroine, Lily Bart." Lily, along with her author, must be debased in order to be herself. When Lily's vulnerable privacy is juxtaposed with her public reputation—for example, in the *tableau vivant* scene and at the novel's end, when she lies dead surrounded by her private possessions and her open account books—Selden finally loves Lily as a sign of the debasement of Lily. The private Lily, whom he might have owned and who will now be forever with him, would never have existed for him had he not seen Lily thus transformed into a "semblance" (as he calls her dead body) of the woman he knew.

   Like Margaret Aubyn's "translation into terms of universality," Lily's ascension to the "Republic of the Spirit" is always repurchased at the price of the private self that emerges through its debasing sacrifice. The debasement of Lily constitutes the "significance" and "tragic implication" that make Wharton's book valuable. A thematic container for the value created through debasement, Wharton's book circulates the author herself as a celebrity who attains her fame and infamy by marketing celebrity. Through the "significance" that debasement creates, Wharton asserts the tragic stature of her work and the seriousness of her authorial identity.

CHAPTER 3

Lily Bart at the
Point of "Modification"

At the opening of *The House of Mirth,* the "pleasure" Lawrence Selden takes in Lily Bart's "nearness" is resonant with the interest he takes in his own capacity to appreciate, and depreciate, the aesthetic appeal of Lily's body: "Selden was conscious of taking a luxurious pleasure in her nearness: in the modelling of her little ear, the crisp upward wave of her hair—was it ever so slightly brightened by art?—and the thick planting of her straight black lashes" (7). Seen through Selden's admiration, Lily's body is not a natural object but an aesthetic fabrication. Selden admires Lily's forms and colors—the "modelling of her little ear" and "the thick planting of her straight black lashes"—as if they were the creations of an artist bent on realizing aesthetic value.

In recent critical writing on consumer culture, the "aestheticization" of the body is linked to "the privilege of relative disembodiment in market culture." Mark Seltzer writes, "such a privilege of relative disembodiment . . . is one sign of the aestheticization of the natural body in market culture, and such an aestheticization of the body one sign of the achievement of personation through practices of consumption" (123, 124).

Lily's aestheticized body does indeed distinguish her from the "crowd" of women against whose "dull tints" she appears "vivid" and "conspicuous" (5–6). But Lily's exceptional status seems to depend on the backdrop of unexceptional, undifferentiated physicality. As part of his admiration of Lily's bright hair, Selden imagines duller hair while he evokes the artful diligence that might have produced Lily's brightness. Indeed, it seems that Selden cannot notice Lily's physical beauty without invoking a contrasting image in which the bright, artifactual surface that gives "luxurious pleasure" reveals a view of the body as dim and toiling.

The "modelling" and coloring of Lily's surface at once manifest and obscure this unaestheticized natural body. But far from dampening Selden's pleasure, the unstable status of Lily's beauty is essential to his aesthetic experience. The indeterminacy of what he sees and enjoys makes Selden "conscious" of his agency as the subject who creates, out of the raw material of the female body, his own "luxurious" aesthetic pleasure. If the aestheticization of Lily's body produces the "personation" of which Seltzer writes, it is Selden, not Lily herself, who attains the "person's" reflexive self-awareness and transcendence of the physical.

Throughout the novel, Lily's beauty achieves its effects precisely by lending itself to such shifting views. Though Wharton ironizes Selden's detached and self-pleasing speculations, in *A Backward Glance* she explains that she has made Lily's tragedy—and thus the literary seriousness of her novel—depend on the "debasement" such speculations entail (207). Lily's aestheticization, the narrator explains, is physically constituted: she was "fashioned to adorn and delight" (311). But the beautiful form into which her body has been molded, far from allowing Lily to transcend the body, bonds her to the physical matter in which her meaningful form inheres while it allows those among whom she circulates to experience themselves as cultural agents. In Lily, Wharton depicts the status of the female body as the substrate of value—and the object of debasement—in the discursive economies of consumer culture, sexual selection, and the literary marketplace. And in Lily's redeeming tragedy, Wharton dramatizes the cost incurred by the woman who is both destroyed and created in her role as the medium of representation.

"The Luxury of Charm"

In the passage quoted at the opening of this chapter, Selden's enjoyment of Lily's nearness embraces the experience of his own privileged freedom from necessity. Made "conscious" of himself as the possessor of "luxurious pleasure," Selden imagines himself free even from the necessity of being himself. According to Thorstein Veblen, the privilege made available by bodily aestheticization through consumption does not accrue to the fashionable woman herself. By consuming in conspicuous excess of need and displaying "physical incapacity" for work, a woman of leisure like Lily Bart "exhibit[s] the pecuniary strength of her social unit"—that is, she produces the privilege and prestige of her male owner.[1] If Lily, being unmarried, has as yet no particular owner, it is nonetheless through the structure of the marriage market, in which Lily is both a commodity and a consumer, that Selden assesses her beauty.[2] Leading Lily through, and out of, the "throng," Selden takes her from the public marketplace to his own flat. Assigning Lily the wifely job of pouring tea by his fireside, Selden allows his admiration to become a speculative appraisal of Lily as a domestic possession. "He watche[s] her hand, polished as a bit of old ivory, with its slender pink nails and the sapphire bracelet slipping over her wrist" (9). The metaphor is telling: ivory, like Lily's commodified body, is an organic substance; but, "old" and "polished," this antique ivory has been imbued with aesthetic rarity and monetary value through the long history of its status as a possession (11).

Lily's hand, decorative in itself, is accessorized by her jeweled bracelet and her "slender pink" nails. Nails are weapons of aggression and self-defense; but like the elephant killed for the ivory of its tusks, Lily, in Selden's eyes, has been defeated by the pressures that have aestheticized her. "She was so evidently the victim of the civilization which had produced her," Selden muses, "that the links of her bracelet seemed like manacles chaining her to her fate" (9).[3] Another accessory on Lily's wrist—"a little jeweled watch among her laces"—hints at the context of this servitude: as Lily (who is wont to glance at clocks and look in mirrors for facial lines) reminds Selden, "I've been about too long—people are getting tired of me; they are beginning to say I ought to marry" (11).

In Lily's aestheticization, Selden sees the sign and effect of female bondage. Marriage is the slavery to which Lily is chained—a marriage in which the beautiful Lily is to be both a valuable possession and a consumer of valuables. By her conspicuous consumption, Lily advertises her fitness for this position. Her bracelet, and the watch whose utility is obscured by jewels and laces, represent the many expensive accessories she must own and display in order to be valuable on the marriage market.

Lily's expertise in conspicuous consumption converges with her exaggerated femininity. In the novel's opening scene, these qualities emerge in contrast to the "crudity" of the women of the crowd. "[Selden] led her through the throng of returning holiday-makers, past sallow-faced girls in preposterous hats and flat-chested women struggling with paper bundles and palm-leaf fans. Was it possible that she belonged to the same race? The dinginess, the crudity of this average section of womanhood made him feel how highly specialized she was" (7). The "average" women are performing the feminine functions of holiday-making (vicarious leisure) and consumption—like Lily herself, who tells Selden she has had her maid "c[o]me up this morning to do some shopping for me" (6). Assigning the labor of shopping to her maid, Lily displaces the dingy, toiling body that underlies consumerism onto the "throng" laboriously bedecked with inappropriate accessories and encumbered with purchases. The women's "sallow" faces probably bespeak long hours at their work, and even in their consumerist leisure they remain "struggling" bodies constrained by effort and

necessity. Their possessions—the "palm-leaf fans" that accessorize their femininity—are, like their bodies, barely distinguishable from unmodified natural
objects.

Lily stands out as "highly specialized" only in reference to these unspecial-
ized women. She is distinguished, in Selden's eyes, not by having transcended the
embodied status of the average women, but as the culmination of the female
body's refashioning by culture. Selden's view of Lily falls into line with two con-
verging currents of the late-nineteenth-century scientific discourse on gender:
Darwin's theory of sexual selection and the anthropological discourse of the exchange of women. According to Darwin, the aesthetic features of women represent evolutionary adaptations to male aesthetic preference. In *The Descent of
Man, and Selection in Relation to Sex,* Darwin explains that although among
animals the female selects the male, among humans the male has preempted
"the power of [sexual] selection." As scholar Evelleen Richards explains, Darwin takes this to mean that "in human evolution, aesthetic choice was exerted
by the male, rather than the female" and therefore women's traits have adapted
to conform to "male aesthetic preference." Richards points out that Darwin
bases this reversal of animal practice on the stringent domination of females
by males in human society. The male right to choose, Darwin explains, derives
from the slavery of woman: "Man is more powerful in body and mind than
woman, and in the savage state he keeps her in a far more abject state of bondage,
than does the male of any other animal; therefore it is not surprising that he
should have gained the power of selection."[4]

In asking whether Lily "belonged to the same race" as the average women,
Selden does not so much detach Lily from the embodied masses as consider
how she arises from them. Selden's evolutionary vocabulary—"race," "average
section"—raises speculation about the physical process by which the marvelous
Lily emerges from the crude and undifferentiated femaleness of these bodies.
Lily's admirable "modelling" and vivid color, contrasted to the "flat-chested"
and "dingy" females of the crowd, represent the heightening into prominent
decorativeness of secondary sexual traits.

Color is the prototypical adaptation to sexual selection. In the animal king-
dom, where females do the selecting (Darwin explains), males develop colorful
attractants like the massive, brightly colored plumage that improves a pea-
cock's chances of mating. But the adaptations that confer an advantage in sexual selection work against survival, for conspicuous color and encumbering
appendages make the individual apparent to predators and impair his swift-
ness in pursuing food.[5] Among humans, however, it is the males who choose;
the females, therefore, develop the colors and shapes which, in Darwin's vocab-

ulary, conform them to "male aesthetic preference."[6] Although for male animals sexual adaptations mitigate against survival, the situation may be different
for human females. The "bondage" that ties women's economic survival to the
men who mate with them could mean that, for women, sexual and natural selection converge. As Gilman hypothesizes, modifications that increase a woman's
power to attract mates also favor her survival.

Selden's speculations about Lily exemplify the complicated aesthetic by
which the female body is assessed. To conform to male preference, the body
must manifest its aestheticized difference from the natural. But if the confor-
mations reflect natural selection—that is, if the femininity of the body represents adaptations that favor survival—the traits that heighten the body's decorativeness bespeak a level of existence in which both sexuality and the aesthetic
demands of the male are subordinated to brute nature. Traits that have been
produced by, and for, natural selection undermine the consumerist privilege of
the male who is attracted by them. Rather than conforming to the male's aesthetic preference, such adaptations elicit his aesthetic appreciation only to en-
cumber him with the burden of the female's survival.

The decorative Lily's material reliance on the marriage market evokes the
polarized value of her beauty. But Selden's practice—which foreshadows the
redeeming sacrifice Wharton will make of Lily's body—is to deflect onto Lily
the exigencies of physical existence that threaten him in the form of his sexual
attraction and relative poverty. Selden imagines Lily's attractiveness as her physical oppression: she is the slaughtered elephant killed to make ivory, the inert
"victim" of the marriage system whose aestheticizing "manacles" signal both
her cultural reduction to the body and her body's subjugation by the culture
that conforms it. Lily, in her beauty, is consigned to material necessity so that
Selden may imagine himself privileged to transcend materiality. (In practice,
this means that Selden's possessive relation to Lily is one of speculative admiration rather than outright "ownership/marriage," to use one of Veblen's [33]
terms.)

If the privilege of consumerism, as Seltzer reminds us, inheres in its more-
than-naturalness, its exceeding and transcending of the body and its needs,
Selden's is a consumerism so removed from need and materiality that, in its
aestheticization, it disavows even the need to own. This consumerist disavowal
(Selden imagines) has come down to him from his mother: "It was from [his
mother] that he inherited his detachment from the sumptuary side of life: the
stoic's carelessness of material things, combined with the epicurean's pleasure
in them. Life shorn of either feeling appeared to him a diminished thing, and
nowhere was the blending of the two ingredients so essential as in the character

of a pretty woman" (161). Selden's capacity to detach himself from the material (he imagines) derives from his position as the beneficiary of female corporeal endowment ("inheritance" from the female side). Through the female body, he gains access to a realm of aesthetic pleasure freed of bodily necessity. The "pretty" female body serves the perpetual bachelor as the material thing that allows him to find pleasure and disavow need. As Selden explains to Gerty, a purely "charming" woman would be out of his grasp because he could never afford to support her; but he can't see himself settling for a "nice" girl whose "utilitarian" qualities would be apt to preclude "the luxury of charm" (160). By structural definition (Selden avers), a woman he would want enough to marry would be too expensive, while any woman he could imagine himself supporting would no longer be attractive. By setting at a level beyond the realm of economic possibility the expense of an aesthetic woman, Selden ensures that he may experience his feelings of attraction while still maintaining the separation between necessity and beauty, bodily survival and embodied aesthetics.[7] Of course, by keeping his sexual desire separate from his contribution to the survival of a woman, Selden (once again) consigns to that woman the struggle for survival he refuses to own.

But if Lily's excessive aestheticization comes at the expense of her own capacity to thrive, the same could be said of the fastidious detachment that prevents Lawrence Selden from seeking riches, getting married, and reproducing. Selden's refinements recall the "derivative" adaptations described by evolutionary thinker and sociologist Lester Ward. In Ward's view, "the protection of social institutions, which had given man leisure," gave rise to "derivative faculties," which are "the chief marks by which [man] is distinguished from the animals below him." These derivative faculties are not only unconnected to survival but, like the aestheticized femininity Darwin describes, run counter to natural selection, for they often render man "unfit and almost helpless in the struggle for existence" (Stocking, 350 n. 7).

A possessor of such derivative faculties, Selden is secure enough in his institutional "protection" to afford indifference to "utilitarian" concerns. But the pleasure Selden feels in the "nearness" of Lily threateningly intimates corporeal need. Though he is sometimes brought perilously close to declaring his love for Lily, Selden manages to treat her as the paradigmatic "pretty woman" and to make his sexual attraction serve as an exemplary incursion of physical necessity into subjective agency through which he experiences his difference from (as Ward would put it) the "animals below him." Distinguishing himself from organisms that live under the compulsion of the sexual instinct, Selden converts his attraction to Lily into a heightened scrutiny of her attractiveness in which each admirable trait bespeaks *her* subjection to bodily necessity. Seeing in her bright hair an artful shift to survive, or imagining Lily's refinements as derivative traits that render her unfit to survive, Selden attains his privilege of relative disembodiment by consigning Lily to the constraints of embodiment.

"The Mingled Stuff"

Lily's aestheticization, then, does not confer on her the privilege of relative disembodiment. Her body presents itself as that which has been conformed to, and made to support, the social codes and derivative faculties that engage Selden. The continual foregrounding of Lily's body debases her; but, as Wharton's literary aspiration would have it, it also redeems her—for Wharton dramatizes the "tragic" process in which Lily's fineness is manifested by the manner of her destruction.

In her memoir, Wharton analogizes Lily's debasement to her own. The novelist complains that in *The House of Mirth* she was accused of having produced nothing more than a roman à clef whose success and popularity derived from the celebrity of "real people" whom she knew in life (210). Wharton protests that she did not merely insert real people into her fiction; yet, as she explains, *The House of Mirth* could not have existed without them. She defends the creative artistry of her rendering with an analogy in which the artist recasts, rather than appropriates, the "real" of the body. The crucial components are the market, which has initially recruited the body as the raw material of fabrication, and the "creative fires" of the artist.

The process, she writes,

is in fact inexplicable enough. . . . No "character" can be made out of nothing, still less can it be successfully pieced together out of heterogeneous scraps of the "real," like dismembered statues of which the fragments have been hopelessly mixed up by the restorer. The process is more like that by which sham Tanagra statuettes used formerly, I have been told, to be manufactured for the unsuspecting. The experts having discovered that ancient terra-cotta acquires, through long burial, a peculiar flavour, were in the habit of assuring themselves of the genuineness of the piece by tasting it. The forgers, discovering this, ground fragments of old Tanagras into powder, ran the powder into one of the old moulds, and fearlessly presented the result as an antique. Experience, observation, the looks and ways and words of "real people," all melted and fused in the white heat of the creative fires—such is the mingled stuff which the novelist pours into the firm mould of his narrative. (211, 212)[8]

The heart of Wharton's analogy is the test to which the forgery is subjected: the "assurance" of "taste," which determines whether the artifact embodies the value with which it is credited. This genuineness (or its absence) registers when the body encounters the matter of which the artifact is made; but although this is a corporeal process, the "expert" ability to distinguish genuineness, and the physical quality that registers as genuineness, derive from elaborate symbolic discernments particular to an overlapping succession of markets: the antiques market, which is propped upon the Boetian market for statuettes, which derived its value from the fashionable celebrities represented in clay.

The substance out of which the successful forgery is cast is matter that has been made into something more than matter: not merely clay, or even merely old clay, it must be clay that was made into statuettes which, "long" buried, were later (during the nineteenth-century craze for Tanagra statuettes) prized for their previous value and their historic survival. What is tested, and thereby assigned or denied value, is the manifestation of a materiality that could not exist as such without conformance to particular modes of valuing, tasting, and testing that each market passed on to succeeding markets. The matter out of which a valuable artifact is made registers on the consumer's body as "genuine" in reference to derived codes of value.

Bits of "real people" get into the artifact, then, not in their recognizably embodied identities (not as "limbs"), but after aesthetic reworking has reduced them into the pure stuff of value. Such morcelized material requires the "creative fires" of the artist to recast it into the commodity form in which its "genuineness" can be tasted by the consumer. But the successful artifact's taste of genuineness may be so convincing that the consumer thinks himself to be encountering, not art, but the "real." This is indeed ironic, for the degree of perceived genuineness indicates the thoroughness of successive recompositions comprised in the artifact.

In *The Writing of Fiction,* Wharton uses another analogy to explain how the substrate an artifact shares with that which it represents comprises the creative challenge, and the value, of aesthetic transformation.

The attempt to give back any fragment of life in painting or sculpture or music presupposes transposition, "stylization." To re-present in words is far more difficult, because the relation is so close between model and artist. The novelist works in the very material out of which the object he is trying to render is made. He must use, to express soul, the signs which soul uses to express itself. It is relatively easy to separate the artistic vision of an object from its complex and tangled actuality if one has to re-see it in paint or marble or bronze; it is infinitely difficult to render a human mind when one is employing the very word-dust with which thought is formulated. (16–17)

The artist, far from merely translating from one ontological level into another, must create a representation of the subject out of the same matter in which that subject already exists. The work this artist does is both occluded and too conspicuous. The art object made from the "very material" of its substrate may resemble the roman à clef in which the artist has merely inserted "real people," for both artifacts exhibit material continuity with their subjects. Yet the roman à clef is merely brute actuality—the given, embodied forms of reality—fashioned into the value forms of the market, while the creative work of art begins with the substance culture has produced as the medium of reembodiment.

Of course, ideally art would be an attempt not to "separate the artistic vision of an object from its . . . actuality" but to manifest through representation the essential qualities of that actuality. Wharton's analogies suggest that first among these qualities is the potential of material "actuality" to lend itself, through social fabrication, to meaningful and marketable forms. The artist, through her creative reworking, realizes the incipient meaning and value in the real. But in Wharton's Tanagra analogy, the market produces not only the process and material that are necessary to creativity, but also the artist herself. The author, producing copies ("Tanagra statuettes") of what the market already values, exercises her creativity in lending it to the "old moulds" that reproduce earlier value forms.

Part of the morcelized "real" that is consumed, tempered, distorted, and transformed in the "creative fire," then, is the talented self of the author. In writing for the market, the author fulfills her creativity by reproducing the market's arbitrary value forms (rather than by realizing the promptings of some original, artistic imagination). This means that not only are the characters ground up and recast (rather than merely "dyed" in being given fictional names), but the author herself is created through a similar process: both her imaginative vision and her own identity as an author (as a seller of "Tanagra statuettes") emerge through their relation to the market—much as genuine authorial stature emerges through the market-driven debasement of Wharton's commodified author, Margaret Aubyn.

For Wharton, the author becomes most artistic when she manifests her capacity to adopt her imaginative vision and authorial identity to the circulating forms that exist in the market—not merely to reproduce those forms, but to rework the substance of her material and her mind into conformance with them. But the analogy presses an even more radical determination by the market. As the material out of which the artist makes her "Tanagra statuette" is already the product of prior cultural fashioning, the creativity of the author is itself a social product. The work of art succeeds as such to the degree that it manifests the artist herself as a social creation whose "genuineness" registers as a taste at the point of consumption.

The crucial questions Selden poses in regard to the value of Lily's body hinge on the continuity between her marketable form and the matter of which she is made.

> [Selden] had a confused sense that she must have cost a great deal to make, that a great many dull and ugly people must, in some mysterious way, have been sacrificed to produce her. He was aware that the qualities distinguishing her from the herd of her sex were chiefly external, as though a fine glaze of beauty and fastidiousness had been applied to vulgar clay. Yet the analogy left him unsatisfied, for a coarse texture will not take a high finish; and was it not possible that the material was fine but that circumstance had fashioned it into a futile shape? (7)

Seen one way, Lily is made up of other people—"a great many dull and ugly people." This mass of undifferentiated, unindividuated human material stands in contrast to the differentiation and individuation which, as Herbert Spencer explains, is the product of evolutionary progress.[9] On this view, then, Lily's apparent aestheticization is a mere translation from base nature: she is an undifferentiated organic mass adapted to survival. An example of the unsuccessful fictional "character" "pieced together out of heterogeneous scraps of the 'real,'" like dismembered statues of which the fragments have been hopelessly mixed up by the restorer," Lily is merely real and completely unreal—that is, having no essential relation to the social form in which she appears, she manifests brute physicality and, as "Lily," has no real existence.

But Selden entertains an alternative view: the material that is "sacrificed to produce her" is "fine"; the "fine" and "strong" exterior he admires expresses its material substrate (7). But in order to imagine that the beautiful "high finish" that makes Lily appear so valuable derives from the existing value of the underlying material, Selden must conceive of this material as having been, like the Tanagra powder, subject to the market's formative (and deformative) transformations, for only through market-driven evolution could Lily's physicality (or any other substance) distinguish itself from brute matter to become recognizable to an aesthetic taste like Selden's as "fine." Seen this way, Lily's embodiment of value bespeaks the "sacrifice" of the female body through successive conformances to the markets in which it was traded. This process transforms the matter of "dull and ugly" people—the colorless female "herd" of the "throng"—into the stuff out of which culture represents itself, allowing Lily's body to be molded out of the genuinely valuable matter.

When he sees Lily as genuinely fine, Selden posits an identity between the exterior and its substrate. This identity is both a redemption (it "proves" Lily's face value) and a debasement—for in this view, Lily's very substance has been conformed to the shifting and arbitrary demands of the market, particularly the "male aesthetic preferences" described by Darwin and consumer culture's superficial and wasteful values.

In *The Decoration of Houses,* Wharton and Ogden Cogman rehearse an architectural version of the relation between substrate and exterior. The authors write that "rooms may be decorated in two ways: by a superficial application of ornament totally independent of structure, or by means of those architectural features which are part of the organism of every house, inside as well as out" (xix). The authors argue for the ontological and aesthetic superiority of the "structural," which exists for its own self-fulfilling purposes, over the "ornamental," which exists merely to induce pleasure in the spectator. Yet the value the authors attribute to structure derives from its ornamental qualities: to praise a room for being "decorated" by its own "architectural features" redeems the ornamental at the expense of the structural, whose value is seen in the aesthetic qualities it is able to express through the ornamental. Looked at as a "sacrifice" (as Selden imagines the "sacrifice" of Lily's fine material to the "high polish" of her ornamental exterior), the beauty of the decor, and thus the fineness of the structure it expresses, only comes into being by a reduction of the structural to the level of ornament.

Selden articulates a similar formulation in his polemic about the proper relation between "work" and "society." Society is all right, he announces, when used to enhance "work"; "but when it becomes the thing worked for, it distorts all the relations of life" (75). But in the antinomies that Wharton sets in play—work and society, structure and ornament, substrate and surface—the genuineness of value, beauty, and refinement is constructed only through the first term's realization through the marketable (and debasing) value that is carried in the second term. In the case of Lily, this means that her beauty is valuable only if her hair (for example), rather than having been brightened by "art," has been brightened by the body's conformance to the aesthetic codes of society. That is, Lily is valuable only if her structure and her matter have genuinely adapted to the market.

In this marketable form Lily is a commodity and, therefore, available to be consumed. And in consumption, Wharton locates the necessary test of "taste" in which (for example) the clay out of which Lily is made, like the clay of a modern Tanagra statuette, would prove its apparent market value. In "The Vice of Reading," Wharton imagines consumption as a physical process in which the consumer breaks down the commodity, encountering and remolding its matter to manifest the plasticity that enables it to embody value (514, 513). But Lawrence Selden's consumerist practice in relation to Lily rehearses his refusal to test the commodity, and his perceptions, by exercising taste in the corporeal and material plane. Though Selden has moments in which he pictures himself as the environment that would manifest Lily's value, his attraction to Lily is too compelling and her need for marriage is too material: marriage to Lily would collapse Selden's aesthetic enjoyment into the realm of necessity. Selden therefore merely imagines himself as the consumer he refuses to be (142).

Lily also imagines this relationship. Recoiling from the prospect of marrying collector/displayer Percy Gryce, Lily lovingly touches Selden's shabby armchair, his worn old books, and the other possessions whose used-up status bespeaks Selden's capacity for consumption. Despite Selden's refusal, Lily manages nonetheless to get herself consumed. Near the end of the book, Lily visits Selden and announces she is going to "leave" in his flat "the Lily Bart you knew." This immaterial Lily, she assures him, will "take up no room"—and indeed, as if she were really becoming the surface Selden values, Lily's hands appear "thin" and her body seems to have "shrunk" as the "red play of the flame" reveals, on Selden's hearth, a Lily who is wasting away (320, 321).

"A Letter in the Record of Her Past"

While Lily's body appears to be consumed by Selden's fire, the love letters Bertha has written to Selden are consigned to the flames. In burning the evidence of Bertha's love for Selden, Lily destroys the valuables she might have used to restore her reputation and even, as it turns out, to save her life (321).[10] Matching her corporeal fate to the consuming reception of these artifacts, Lily asserts continuity between the female body and the value forms in which it circulates. Wharton specifies these forms as the texts—letters and gossip columns—whose representations of Lily determine her identity, value, and destiny. Lily lives out, in the corporeal plane, the fate of a good author who (as Wharton explains in "The Vice of Reading") puts herself into the text to be recreated at the point of textual consumption.

In the previous chapter, I explored how Margaret Aubyn of *The Touchstone* undergoes "modification" by the market because of the failure of her designated consumer—the man she loves and to whom she writes her letters—to properly consume her. Lawrence Selden is as deficient as Aubyn's disappointing beloved, for he also allows the heroine to circulate in the market through the texts he ought to have privatized in consumption. Selden's epistolary negligence has put Bertha Dorset at risk; and his failure to bring Lily, the other woman who loves him, into his home leaves her to circulate in the gossip columns prompted by her near-scandalous singleness.

While Margaret Aubyn is debased by the (secretly arranged) publication of love letters, in *The House of Mirth* the withholding of letters from circulation makes the heroine the object of scandal. Like Aubyn, Lily suffers debasement through the public's relation to letters whose private context only seems to invite public circulation. In *The House of Mirth,* the cleaning woman, Mrs. Haffen, represents the ever-present, vulgar readership that commodifies the residue of incomplete consumption. Mrs. Haffen reads the trash: she has retrieved the love letters from Bertha to Selden, thinking them to be of value—for, she assumes, Lily has written them and will be motivated to keep them out of circulation.

Haffen explains,

Some of the gentlemen got the greatest sight of letters: I never saw the like of it. Their waste-paper baskets'd be fairly brimming, and papers falling over on the floor. . . . Mr. Selden . . . he was always one of the carefullest: burnt his letters in winter, and tore 'em in little bits in summer. But sometimes he'd have so many he'd just bunch 'em together, the way the others did, and tear the lot through once—like this.

Taking out one of the retrieved letters, "with a rapid gesture she laid the torn edges together" (109). Haffen shows Lily that she has many such letters, which Lily sees "had been pieced together with strips of torn paper. Some were in small fragments, the others merely torn in half" (111).

Selden's careless failure to sufficiently "modify" Bertha's letters coincides with his rejection of her love: rather than consume each letter individually, he tears through "the lot." By failing to break down Bertha's texts (as, in "The Vice of Reading," the good reader breaks down an author's work), Selden has made it possible for a bad reader like Mrs. Haffen to become a kind of anti-artist who, producing a commodity by simply piecing together heterogeneous scraps of the real, thinks herself to have reconstructed the author's creation and thus to have accessed the author herself. Putting the pieces back together between her workaday "red fists," Haffen subjects the text to the literal or surface level she inhabits—that is, she is a forger, for she understands the letters to be Lily's and thus gives them a market form which, ignorant of the presence (or absence) of the author in the work, has no relation to the authorial essence from which the text is fashioned.[11]

Yet the marketing of the letters involves Lily with and in this essence. "[Lily] had no idea of reading the letters; even to unfold Mrs. Haffen's dirty newspaper [wrapper] would have seemed degrading," the narrator explains. But while Lily leaves the letters unread and untouched, Bertha's words "leap" into her mind and shriek at her with Bertha's voice, while Bertha's "hand" immediately communicates both her identity and the meaning of her letters (112). Conflated, at the level of marketing, with the loving woman in the letters, Lily is forced into bodily contact—even into bodily identification—with the person Mrs. Haffen supposes her to be, "the writer of the letters." Thus Lily does, in a sense, become the author—and as such she is debased, for the monetary value placed on the love Bertha has for Selden debases Lily's love for him as well. In order to save herself as a loving woman, Lily has to save the man she loves by "purchasing" his reputation with her love expressed in the debasing form of money. If Haffen's false attribution of authorship is, then, made true at the point of the letters' marketing, her false sense of their value to Lily is, likewise, a truth in the context of the market: the letters do indeed represent both Lily's love for Selden and her marriageability—for Lily can use the letters to blackmail Bertha. And to remain both loving and valuable, Lily herself has to take a hand in the debasing marketing of herself through and in the letters.[12]

The two textual forms Wharton emphasizes—correspondence and gossip columns—derive their value from the persons whose identity or essence these texts embody and signify. The meaning and value of letters derive from their writer and recipient, while gossip columns reflect the social status of their subject. Both forms advertise privileged access to a "private" self they publicly construct: as we saw in the previous chapter, letters attain value as commodities by debasing—creating a debased version of—the personal identities of writer and recipient. Gossip columns, in like manner, construct the private persons they "reveal."

The identity and value of Lily Bart depend on her relation to these textual forms, particularly the letters. Will Lily sell the letters to Bertha? If so, Lily would both be an agent who creates her own identity in the market and a passive construct of the market—she would, that is, be like a published author, for to sell the letters is to realize the self through the textual market, while to exchange them is to subject that self to the market's debasing constructions (which, in Lily's case, equate her marriageability to Bertha's sham reputability). If, alternatively, Lily should choose to hide or destroy the letters, she would incur inevitable debasement as a perpetually and scandalously unmarried beauty who provides grist for the gossip columns.

Both courses of action (and she has to take one) are forms of publication—of subjecting the self, through the medium of a text, to the debasing construction of the market. But if publication is both inevitable and inevitably debasing, Lily finds a way to manifest this capacity to be debased as creative artistry. Before her death, Lily rereads, so to speak, the "letters" in which she has circulated and been "enveloped"—that is, she reviews her dresses, saving for last the dress in which she appeared in the Reynolds *tableau vivant*.

An association lurked in every fold: each fall of lace and gleam of embroidery was like a letter in the record of her past. . . . She was startled to find how the atmosphere of her old life enveloped her. . . . Last of all, she drew forth . . . a heap of white drapery. . . . It was the Reynolds dress she had worn in the Bry tableaux. . . . She had just closed her trunk on the white folds of the Reynolds dress when she heard a tap at her door, and the red fist of the Irish maidservant thrust in a belated letter. (329–30)

Lily ends her review with the Reynolds dress, whose "white folds" suggest in their blankness not any particular "letter" but the capacity to be inscribed with, and to circulate, meaning and value.[13] The Reynolds tableau for which Lily wears the white dress reproduces the portrait of Joanna Leigh who, pictured before her marriage, is gracefully carving the name of Lloyd, her future first husband, into a tree. The activity depicted in Reynolds' portrait—along with Ned Van Alstyne's comment, "deuced bold thing to show herself in that get-up; but gad, there isn't a break in the lines anywhere, and I suppose she wanted us to know it!"—has been cited as evidence that Lily's tableau is a scene of writing.[14] But it is more precise to call it a scene of publication—one in which Lily (like "Joanna Leigh" in the process of becoming "Mrs. Lloyd") manifests her status as a medium of textualization that circulates the identity and value inscribed in and on it.

I call this a scene of publication because if Van Alstyne's comment about "lines" suggests writing, then writing is "showing oneself." And if the black-and-white Reynolds tableau suggests text, it images even more directly the black-and-white magazine depictions of "typical" American women with which the market was flooded (Banta, 212). What is stunningly "shown" in Lily's tableau is her capacity to represent an aggregate or public identity—the woman as "type": Lily "had shown her artistic intelligence in selecting a type so like her own that she could embody the person represented without ceasing to be herself" (141). The genre of the *tableau vivant* reprises the representational practices of the Tanagra analogy. Like the reconstituted "Tanagra statuette," the *tableau vivant* succeeds through simultaneous conformance to and difference from the "original" it represents—an original that is already (like the Boetian statuette of "people of fashion") a representation of a value form (the marriageable woman), much as Lily's self-presentation succeeds, not in reference to the self-originating production of writing, but as the recirculation of cultural material. The value of the tableau derives from the preexisting market value of the painting, whose recognizability and marketability as an image are lent to the tableau that successfully reproduces it. In choosing to reproduce a form of which she is already a recognizable version, Lily draws attention to her likeness to that form. But since the stunning artistry of the tableau is available only through the realization that it is a representation (that Lily is *not* the portrait), Lily's con-spicuous artistry is in the difference between Lily and what she manifests—is in, that is, her unexhausted capacity to represent.[15]

This representational virtuosity inheres in Lily's body. Both the difference and the continuity between Lily and "type she embodies" is Lily's body itself, which seems to have "stepped, not out of, but into, Reynolds' canvas" (141). If the tableau is the textual form through which Lily shows her "artistic intelli-gence," the medium of this form (and of the self of/as the artist) is the female body, whose "plastic possibilities" the tableaux put on display. In the tableaux, the female body manifests its involvement in the many levels of representation: all the tableaux feature women dressed up—or semi-undressed—to reenact famous paintings which themselves rehearse the status of the female body as the subject of representation. The stunning feat of a tableau is its use of the three-dimensional real of the female body to create an impression of the two-dimensional representation of the body. But since what the arranged bodies represent are representations of women's bodies, the tableau in general stages what Lily's tableau particularly emphasizes: the capacity of the female body to represent an actuality—in Lily's case, a "self"—that is already a representation. Thus Lily Bart is strikingly present in her tableau by enacting "the portrait of Miss Bart" (141). Like the reconstituted statuette made, as Wharton writes, in the "white heat of the creative fires," this copy of the form of an already valu-able artifact is not a base forgery but a recirculation and renovation of the mat-ter of which value is made—the female body, which is already made through representative practices.

Another popular representational practice, trompe l'oeil, features "a mate-rial equivalence between the representation and the objects represented" (Michaels 1987, 162, discussing the "flatness" of what is depicted in trompe l'oeil paintings). The level at which *tableau vivant* features "material equiva-lence" is both essential and forever deferred. Using three-dimensional female bodies to portray flat paintings of female bodies, the material equivalence is mediated by a layer of representation—the paintings—which are indispens-able to the success of the "equivalence," for between the "illusion" (the posed bodies) and the "reality" that illusion evokes (the posed bodies) intercedes cul-tural creation both in the representational capacity of the female body and in the spectatorial agency of the onlooker who experiences himself as giving rise to that capacity—for the tableau, Wharton emphasizes, produces in the spec-tator a pleasurable awareness of his own capacity to adjust his "mental vision" (140). As the perpetual spectator of Lily's body, Selden experiences pleasure and privilege in shifting his view from the aesthetic effect of Lily's body to speculation, provoked by that effect, about the "real" matter that supports this effect. But in the pure success of the tableau, Selden's speculations allow him to feel that the "real" of the body already is constituted to support his aesthetic practices.

Lily succeeds in representing the portrait to the degree that her body dispenses with its "material equivalence" to its own three-dimensionality. It is, therefore, precisely because Lily *is* embodied that she affords her audience an experience of their own spectatorial agency. Ned Van Alstyne, as impressed as anyone with the success of Lily's presentation, aggressively secures the best possible view of Lily's "female outline." "Bold," says Van Alstyne; "there isn't a break in the lines anywhere, and I suppose she wanted us to know it!" (142). As Van Alstyne insists on the sexy conspicuousness of Lily's body, we should remember that Lily's is the most conspicuous body because her performance puts into most conspicuous relief the representative capacity—the femininity—of the female body. If the female outline of Lily's body, which shows through the white dress, invites Van Alstyne to shift his vision between looking at and seeing through the aestheticization the culture has imposed on the body, the bold self-awareness Van Alstyne attributes to Lily reflects her apparent understanding of her body as already representational: making her audience "know" that she "knows," Lily shows her audience that the female body exists by representing (first) itself. The body's very materiality comprises the continuity—the unbroken "lines"—between Lily's bodily presence and preceding products of cultural fashioning: the embodied femaleness which, under the pressure of consumer culture and natural selection, has been molded, circulated, broken down, and reformed.[16]

Color and ornament represent adaptations to particular environments: the specific aesthetic demands of a particular market in women produce adaptations that bespeak the values that have formed them. The white dress that shows off Lily's body, in contrast, can be "seen through," as it were, because in the pictorial language of color, white is universal: it represents the capacity to represent.[17] Seeing Lily in white, Selden exercises the purest kind of spectatorial awareness, in which the form becomes indifferent, allowing him pure access to representative capacity in itself and thus to an unmediated experience of his "vision-building faculty" (141). Seen thus, Lily transcends the accident of material form and accedes to a realm like "the Republic of the Spirit" as, for a moment, Selden sees "the real Lily Bart, divested of the trivialities of her little world and catching for a moment a note of that eternal harmony of which her beauty was a part." Lily becomes herself in showing a self that is the representation of a self: and "here there could be no mistaking the predominance of personality" (141). That the body Lily publicizes immediately circulates as the subject of sexual gossip only confirms her representationally derived identity by enforcing the "modifications" of the market. The female body so stunningly revealed by the white dress "shows itself" as already the expression of culture: not a counterfeit, it is an aesthetic creation which, in expressing its own representational constitution, confirms the subjective agency of all members of the culture.

At the novel's end Lily makes another publishing gesture. Before lying down to die she lays out as if for display two letters. One contains the incoming legacy check, which she addresses to her bank to deposit; the other contains her outgoing check to Gus Trenor. Now, as her perfectly balanced, open account book shows, her outgo is perfectly equal to her income. This momentary equivalence between published versions, like Lily's fitness to represent the Reynolds painting, suspends the contingencies of local forms and freezes for a moment the structure of Lily's representationality in itself, effecting a self that rises above its representations in the local economy (of sex, money, texts) and transcends even the vehicle of the female body—which Selden sees, in its static deadness, as the medium that has let her represent herself, "the semblance of Lily Bart."

Thus the "real Lily" (that which is not the "semblance") emerges through the derivative value forms of the market supported by the female body. Constrained (indeed, constituted) to circulate the abstractions that make up value and aesthetics, Lily's body is always, as a body, "disembodied"—more than natural and never merely itself. In the female body this exceeding of the natural is not a privileging move away from the body, but a sign of the female body's irreducibility as the chief construct of "civilization." Lily's aestheticized female body manifests its self-sacrifice as the substrate of marketable forms of value, beauty, and personal fineness. By performing the embodiment of circulating representations, Lily renovates them through the infusion of her material fineness and displays the indispensability of woman, whose body is the material prop and whose plastic possibilities are the means by which the organic world is transmuted into the forms of value and meaning. Finally giving up her body in death, Lily transmits to Selden through the medium of her body this redeemed sense of value in the form of a "word."

PART Two

The Great White Slavery Scare

HAVE YOU A GIRL TO SPARE?

Sixty Thousand White Slaves die every year. The Vice Resorts cannot run without this number is replaced annually. Are you willing to give your daughter to keep up this terrible business?

From Clifford Roe, *The Great War on White Slavery*, 1911.

CHAPTER 4

"No Girl Is Safe!"

The Girl That Disappears

The year is 1912; the scene is the dissection room at Chicago's Cook County Hospital. "A second year medical student" and his classmate were about to share a body for dissection practice. "This being a female body," the narrator explains, "a few remarks passed among the students, of a smutty and indiscreet nature." The classmate "began cutting the body, especially the left hip and thigh," while the student himself, feeling unaccountably "nervous and creepy," began "cutting open at the right side of the face."

"Just for curiousity's sake," the student examined a piece of paper tangled in the hair of the corpse. It was a note which read,

My Dear Mother,
that same day father left me [in the city] that traveling man took me to the theater and bought some candy while we looked at the play. . . . We finished it . . . in a taxicab. I became suddenly ill and lost consciousness.

I do not know how long it was before I came to full consciousness, but I was in a strange house, undressed in bed. . . . I tried all kinds of ways to get away, but simply in vain. . . . I had simply to do what they said in the house.

After I got out of that house . . . I could not bear to go home in the condition I was [in]. . . . It got worse and worse, until I got shot.

I have not got an envelope . . . so I will put this in my hair. Maybe the undertaker will send it to you, dear mother. I cannot tell you what horrible things I have gone through. . . . I am innocent! The virtue of a girl ruined takes all her power away from her.

The student read to the signature—"your daughter, 'A'"—then "staggered to the window and fell."

This white slavery narrative, "Brother Cutting Up His Own Sister," is the centerpiece of Dr. C. C. Quale's 1912 white slavery pamphlet entitled "Thrilling Stories of Eye-Opener on White Slavery" (20–22). The years from 1909 to 1914 saw a huge outpouring of white slavery materials in the United States. Pamphlets, magazine articles, plays, novels, and even movies—including the first feature-length movie, *The Traffic in Souls*—were eagerly consumed by the public. Twenty-two book-length white slavery collections appeared during these years; a prominent example is Clifford Roe's *The Great War on White Slavery, or Fighting for the Protection of Our Girls,* whose title page promises a "truthful and chaste account of the hideous trade of buying and selling young girls" and which features "startling disclosures," "astounding confessions," and "graphic accounts" of the methods used to capture women and hold them as unwilling prostitutes. Roe's book also promises "a full account of the great fight for the suppression of white slavery," which, having been State's Attorney for Cook County (the Chicago area) before becoming a full-time antivice reformer, Roe was able to provide at first hand.[1] Typically, white slavery compendiums also offered earnest essays by religious activists and social workers attesting to the innocence of the victims and urging the reader to join with "the great public" in the "crusade" against white slavery (Roe title page).

The set piece of all white slavery writing is the white slavery narrative, which tells of a naive and virtuous young woman unwillingly caught up in the wickedness of commercialized vice. She may be rescued and restored to her family, or she may be found dead, a tragic victim. A genre of melodrama that brings together absolute innocence and unspeakable evil in the mysterious setting of the big city, white slavery literature has ties to the detective story and descends from the genre known as "mysteries and miseries of the city" as well as from the captivity narrative.[2]

In Europe, white slavery was a sensational issue as early as the 1880s; but to the American public, it became a major concern only after a series of muckraking magazine articles exposed commercial vice operations. In 1907, *McClure's* magazine writer George Kibbe Turner, with the help of Clifford Roe, wrote a sensational series on vice in Chicago, describing the "loosely organized association" that furnished Chicago with its tens of thousands of prostitutes. Turner inspired journalists in Chicago and other cities to look into the conditions that allowed the vice industry to flourish; a series on official corruption in Chicago's vice district was particularly scandalous.[3] Exposés of big-city vice in other cities followed, and growing public outcry provoked the Senate to pass legislation extending the government's power to bar and deport aliens suspected of trafficking in "white slaves," while the Mann Act (also known as the White Slave Traffic

Act), passed by Congress in 1910, made it a felony to aid, entice, or force a woman to cross state lines "for the purpose of prostitution or debauchery, or for any other immoral purpose" (Connelly, 128; Cordasco, 33).[4] Most major cities set up Vice Commissions to uncover local branches of the white slavery conspiracy; but while these investigative bodies found flourishing businesses in prostitution and related enterprises, they consistently failed to produce evidence of the organized, conspiratorial trafficking and enforced prostitution described by white slavery literature.[5] Skeptics became more vocal after the commission results were known; yet despite the lack of evidence and the public testimony of vice workers who admitted they had never come across a "white slave," white slavery, as one skeptical commentator noted, was an idea "in which the public veritably revels."[6]

In its success in getting public attention, white slavery was "probably the most notable crusade of the Progressive Period" (Cordasco, 18). Widely circulated in the expanding journalistic market, white slavery literature offered titillating and scandalous content—sex, drugs, crime, tragedy, and heroism— made acceptable by its moralistic and alarmed reformist stance. But in addition to providing entertaining narratives and the sensational appeal of scandal, white slavery addressed concerns that were central to the Progressive Era. What distinguished white slavery from ordinary prostitution, according to writers like Clifford Roe, was its advanced level of commercialization: "The traffic in women slaves . . . is hundreds of years old, but it has remained for the present age to see it crystallized into a well defined commercial business" (96–97). With the formation of corporations, trusts, and monopolies, along with the growth of marketing, economic interests had consolidated a vast amount of power; and white slavery's vision of a commercial network that corrupts civic justice and overrides individual freedom expresses the fear of economic coercion—and the impulse to fight it—which scholars consider characteristic of Progressive reformism. The 1910 New York Vice Commission reports that its white slavery investigation, though it may not have unearthed a conspiracy, uncovered an alarming threat: the erosion of democracy by commercialization.

It is not the "demand and supply" which makes the public tolerate this abnormal, artificially stimulated vice situation, but the business interests and political expediency— things which we are learning are undermining political freedom and economic independence as well as menacing the moral integrity of men, women and children. (The Research Committee of the Committee of Fourteen for the Suppression of the "Raines Law Hotels" in New York City, *Social Evil*, xxxiii)[7]

In its depiction of an all-powerful, criminal commercial conspiracy engaged in "commercialized vice," white slavery literature focused Progressive Era anxiety about the effects of big business on a democratic society. In white slavery's mysterious bosses conducting their inexorable, backroom deals with the connivance of corrupt officials, the public was given a concrete image of the enemy being conjured up in exposés of crime and big business.

In the earliest American white slavery literature, the traffickers are immigrants (most often Mediterranean or Jewish) who conspire to import their corruption to the United States (Cordasco, 8). Because white slavery literature foregrounds a Progressive Era concern about non-nationals, historians see it as a nativist reaction to immigration (see, e.g., Connelly, 118). Certainly, white slavery writing responds with fear to the presence of the "alien." But as it developed into a domestic American discourse that called on the citizenry to unite around the cause of "free, glad, safe womanhood," white slavery writing, hailing the "great public" to take part in reform, became part of the process by which aliens were assimilated (Bell, 11; Reverend J. G. Shearer in Bell, 19). White slavery writing envisions a national unity made up of diverse groups that come together to protect women from illegitimate traders. White slavery reform's "great public" is a social network in which diversity contributes to unity: in the economy of exchange in which groups transact across their borders, the separations between groups are the points at which groups cooperate. In its reformist outrage at the practices of prostitutors, white slavery literature links these mutually exchanging groups into a community that shares a common commitment to the legitimate exchange of the women whom Roe and Bell refer to as "our girls."

In its response to immigration, as in its response to big business, white slavery literature was more than reaction—it was reform. Its revelations of the evil practiced by white slavers require the reader to revise his view of society and his place in it. And in these revisions, purely discursive though they are, the reader is invited to empower himself in relation to the changing public sphere of the Progressive Era. White slavery's central premise hardly seems empowering at first glance: the public sphere, according to its depictions, is most accurately seen as a vast market in which women are exchanged as sexual chattel. "Most large cities are in fact market places where girls are sold and bought," explains Clifford Roe (169). But if the revelation of the white slave trade calls for strenuous action, the reform to be enacted is not the restoration of the women's freedom, but their reclamation by the ordinary man. In white slavery's view, if the United States is to be the "land of the free, home of the brave," its women must be freed by "men brave enough to protect our girls" who will keep them "glad and safe" (Bell, 11). Women will enjoy this protection when men reclaim their proprietary rights: "it is our daughters they are selling body and soul," Roe exhorts, reiterating white slavery's premise that the women sold in the market are the property of the family man (169).

This is precisely what the brother in C. C. Quale's narrative learns. Reading the note tangled in the hair of the "female body," he discovers "his own sister." Though the body is a commodity in the medical education market, prostitution is the obvious subtext; and in another section of his pamphlet "Thrilling Stories of Eye-Opener on White Slavery," Quale describes the hierarchy of sexual markets through which a white slave like the sister passes. When first "brought into the traffic," he explains, a young woman will be "sold and ruined at the highest places" until, becoming less valuable, she is "transferred to lower" and still lower places, "winding up at Cook County Hospital." Trafficking does not cease when "finally [she] passes on to the other world": under this rubric Quale refers to the bodies' further stops at "the morgue of the Cook County Hospital," "the potter's field," or "the different medical colleges" (24–25). This young woman shared among the males is a prostitute who has been passed from hand to hand in the market in women's bodies—a market in which the brother is a customer whose medical school fees purchase educational items such as this body. It is "customary" in the medical school, explains Quale, that "two or more students are given one body to dissect"; and along with the body, the young men share some sexual comments ("this being a female body, a few remarks passed among the students, of a smutty and indiscreet nature"). When the brother "[goes] to the body and begins cutting," then, he joins his fellows in violating the sexually degraded "female body" (though, as the author pruriently stipulates, it is the classmate who cuts into the groin, while the brother dissects the face).

Using the body in the manner for which the medical school has purchased it, the brother quite strikingly perceives the body only through its status as an item of trade: even as he investigates the structure of the woman's face, he has no perception of "his own sister." Quale's narrative literalizes the white slavery precept that women, once fallen into the clutches of traffickers, simply vanish. "The girl that disappears" was a "familiar phrase" in the literature, explains Laura Hapke (1989, 117). And though it is supposedly into death that the women vanish—"60,000 girls a year" are needed, Roe explains, "to replace that number that will die" at the hands of white slavery—it is an axiom of white slavery writing that the woman who becomes a white slave is never again to be seen, not even in the form of a dead body. The 1911 white slavery book by ex–New York City Police Chief Theodore Bingham, *The Girl That Disappears*, begins by telling of a frequent event: when an anonymous female body has been found in the public domain, relatives "flock to the morgue" in the always futile search for their girl's remains (7–9).[8]

If white slavers make women disappear, white slavery literature presents itself as the intervention that will bring them back. The sister reappears to her brother through the note in her hair, an account of her capture and ruin that is a white slavery narrative within the "brother" narrative. While Theodore Bingham inquires about the "thousands of young girls" who yearly "disappear," "where do they go? . . . Into whose hands?" Quale, in the pamphlet containing the "brother" narrative, challenges the reader to provide the answer: "Some of you who are sure that you are very honest, clean, respectable people," he writes, "think back and see how many girls, perhaps, you have robbed of . . . purity, home and honor" (10). Prostitutes end up in the hands of the vice business's public clientele, just as the sister ends up under her brother's knife. While the chances are not great that the prostitute you patronize will turn out to be your own sister, she almost certainly, as Quale suggests, is someone's sister.

This is the great "eye-opener" of Quale's narrative: "our girls," who have vanished in such vast numbers, are to be found in the women offered for sale in the market—just as the brother discovers "his own sister" in the "female body" into which he cuts. Incest, of course, is the subtextual shocker of Quale's narrative; and the brother's dramatic reaction to his discovery reflects the gravity of incestuous transgressions: he "staggered to the window and fell." But in the specifics of the brother's expression, Quale points to the underlying structural imperative that makes incest so horrifying. As Claude Lévi-Strauss famously argues in *The Elementary Structures of Kinship* (his structural analysis of the anthropological discourse of the exchange of woman), the prohibition against incest is secondary to the imperative to forge bonds with outside groups through the practice of reciprocity. Incest is merely a (variable) designation of some women as prohibited in order that the males of the group be required to give these women to another group and receive that group's women in exchange. That is, the prohibition of incest is the requirement to practice some form of exogamy, which ensures that each family group (however defined) must position itself in relation to other groups, relying on these outside groups for a basic necessity and thus avoiding what might otherwise occur: a sort of social implosion, a hermeticism figured here in the brother's claustrophobic rush toward the world outside the room where he has possessed "his own sister" (chaps. 5 and 29, esp. 480).

Depicting an economy in which women are traded as sexual chattel and women's owners enjoy a total power in their possessorship, white slavery literature takes the exchange of women to the limit of literalness. In Quale's drama-tization, the "female body" is so totally defined through its status in exchange that, it seems, the only impact death makes on this status is to affect the body's current sale price. A certain pity attaches to this reduction of a woman to an object; but the narrative's horror and shock are reserved for the fate of the brother—in fact, it is the brother who seems to be the imprisoned one, as he staggers to the window in a manner reminiscent of the characteristic (and equally futile) escape attempt of the white slave. (For example, Roe depicts one Mildred Clark desperately calling for help out the brothel window [119].)

"It is our daughters they are selling, body and soul," as Roe puts it (169). The peculiar claim of white slavery literature is not, of course, that there are fe-male bodies for sale, but that the sexual marketing of women is inseparable from the abduction and enslavement of women—"our" women. The brother's experience fleshes out this claim: to understand that his sister is being sold for the profit of traffickers is to understand, simultaneously, his own loss of her—or, more precisely, his loss of the value she brings in exchange. (Of course, one of the parties who profits from her sale might be the sister herself, and in a later section of this chapter I discuss the literature's response to this possibility.) In the hyperbolic and melodramatic mode of the genre, Quale's narrative makes this loss as devastating as possible. Not only is the marketed woman the brother's "own" and thus a woman whose exchange value he should have had a stake in, but the brother, rather than enjoying his rights in her value, has actually paid out money for his "own" woman. In buying his own woman, he at once dis-covers his loss and reaches the absolute end of any prospect of recuperation. That is, it is not possible for him to imagine that in losing his woman he will be recompensed with a woman in exchange, for he has already received the woman in exchange—and that woman, being "his own sister," is marked by the code of incest as having no value to him except insofar as he can realize her value by alienating it in exchange. The traffickers, however, have already done this in his stead. In fact, so thoroughly have they emptied out the sister's ex-change value that she has come to the lowest point of the market, the medical school dissection table, from which she will go to a public grave in the pot-ter's field.

What the slavers have stolen from the brother is not, then, his sister per se; he gets her back, in the end. Rather, what has been stolen are his rights in the exchange value of his sister. In order to realize this value, the brother must have a market for her—a market that observes his rights in her value (his rights, that is, to receive the equivalent of her value in exchange). But the slavers have saturated the marketplace with their own agents, taking up all of the market's advantageous transactional positions and relegating the brother to a position outside the benefits of exchange, where he provides the original wealth without recompense and then pays the traffickers to get it back when its value has been emptied out.

In the ubiquity of the white slave organization it imagines, white slavery writing reacts to the consolidation of big businesses through "vertical integration." A contemporary observer remarked of Andrew Carnegie's vertically integrated operation that "there was never a price, profit or royalty paid to an outsider" (American Social History Project, *Who Built America?*, 2:31). The white slavers have aggrandized all the profits and benefits yielded by trading in the sister so that the brother is deprived not only of her exchange value, but of her use value as well: accordingly (the reader must assume), he is forced to stop the dissection. Without a market for his sister—without, that is, the prospect of realizing her value—the recognition of the sister as "his own" positions the brother at a claustrophobic dead end.

The white slavery narrative presents its shocking revelation in order, as Quale puts it, that by knowing this truth you will "know how to fight this great evil." The same central truth—that the female body sold in the market is one's "own"—constitutes both the evil the reader must acknowledge and the knowledge with which to fight that evil. Mrs. Ophelia Amhigh, Superintendent of the Illinois Training School for Girls, testifies in Reverend Ernest Bell's white slavery compendium that white slavery narratives "have done great good . . . [for] they have stirred to a sense of alarm . . . parents who were asleep in a false . . . security." Amhigh urges the families of women to understand, from reading these revelations of white slavery, that women have a value in exchange that must be observed and protected. Warning that "in this day and age of the world no young girl is safe," Amhigh addresses parents as follows:

If you had something of great value which needed to be protected day and night, would you select for such a task a blind watchman? or one who was firmly possessed of the idea that there was really no danger, no occasion for watchfulness? Certainly not! There is nothing in the world of such priceless value to a father or mother as the honor, the purity, the good character of a daughter. (Bell, 118, 119)

It is because they are valuable property appropriated by traffickers that women in the home are understood as valuable property to be possessed—but never to be "firmly possessed," for only in its imminent alienation by those who covet it is the "priceless value" that constitutes the true nature of "a daughter" recognized and owned by the parents.

Revelations of white slavery, then, reveal the sister in the prostitute along with the prostitute in the sister. If white slavery's public of readers must learn to possess their women more rigorously, they will be rewarded with enrichment, for the woman treasured in the home will not be relinquished without due recompense for her value (and respectful tribute to the possessive rights of family members in their own women). In the case of the brother who cuts up his own sister, the white slavers have successfully monopolized all the value of his own woman; but if the brother is undone, the reader of the white slavery narrative, "stirred to a sense of alarm" (as Amhigh puts it) and duly enlightened by the brother's fate, knows to take possession of his own woman within the market white slavery literature has revealed.

White slavery literature opens the reader's eyes to the value of a woman by pointing out the structure of exchange, in which one's "own" woman is destined to be appropriated by a group outside one's own. Indeed, Quale's narrative demonstrates that this exchangeable status is what makes the woman recognizable (from the brother's point of view, for example) as one's "own." This understanding, tragically, comes too late to the family of the sister who gets cut up. The parents whose desire to "send their daughter to the university" lands her on a dissection table, Quale explains, are "a very fine and well-educated family" who, in sending their daughter off to become "well-educated" herself, seem to imagine that their daughter cannot be alienated—they assume, that is, that in going out among strangers the daughter will live out her similarity and affiliation to the parents themselves.

White slavery intervenes to make it clear that, on the contrary, daughters belong to their families through their status as items of exchange: it is not through her likeness to her family, but through her potential for alienation from it— her destined affiliation with alien groups—that the daughter constitutes familial property. These parents who are blind to the exchange system fail to see the otherness of strangers; accordingly, they invest an ingratiating young "traveling man" who appears at their door to peddle pianolas with the powers of a surrogate parent. This salesman makes his sale by playing on the parents' delusion that they can at once keep their daughter and send her away: he demonstrates that the pianola "could play two of the pieces that the girl played," and "the parents thought it would be nice to have it while their daughter was away."[9] The parents seem to think that they can "have" their daughter while she is "away" by substituting something similar—a pianola that plays the same tunes. This commodity that affords the parents a false sense of possession is, of course, not a version of the daughter but an equivalent received in exchange for her, and the parents relinquish the daughter herself when they hand over to the salesman the cost of the pianola along with "the whole story" of the daughter's imminent departure for the city. Once in possession of this information, the sinister sales-

man need only promise to "make the necessary arrangements" in the city—
and, as the poor sister's note attests, these arrangements are most efficiently
carried out.

Amhigh would place these parents among those who deludedly act as if they
were "firmly possessed" of their daughter; those who, that is, lack the understanding that they possess their daughter through a system that destines her to
be possessed by outsiders. In the brother's tragic discovery of "his own sister,"
the family finally confronts the true nature of familial possession and the consequence of failing to lay claim to familial property. The white slavers, of
course, are well aware of the value of daughters. They are able to take a valuable
daughter and give back a daughter who is emptied of value only because the
family is blind to what it owns in owning its own woman. In fact, in returning
the sister to the brother to be cut up, the slavers give back to the family a literal
version of what the family owned from its own (deluded) point of view: a
woman with no exchange value.

Taking something of value and returning something worthless, the white
slavers have violated the rule of reciprocity; but the revelations of white slavery
can, in and of themselves, enforce this rule. To understand white slavery is to
understand the "priceless value" (to use Amhigh's term) that is one's daughter,
endowed with exchange value that is one's own property. Such an understanding will, of course, enable an owner to insist on a fair equivalent in exchange for
the daughter. But more immediately, the family of such a daughter is also enriched simply by acquiring this understanding. To know that one's own daughter is valuable in exchange (a knowledge that comes through knowledge of her
value to the traffickers) is to come into possession of the value in exchange of
that daughter; that is, a woman who is one's own, and whose exchange value one
knows, is already the equivalent of the exchange value endowed in her by the
market in women. Thus the awareness of women's market value—an awareness which, white slavery literature explains, comes only through revelations of
the practices of white slavers—in itself corrects the slavers' capacity to violate
reciprocity and forces from them the return of the value of one's own woman.

The Big Chief

Although white slavery literature seems to emphasize the implacable power
of the white slavery organization, it actually invites the reader to position himself, by means of its revelations, as one who determines, owns, and enforces
reciprocation of the value of his "own" women. "It is your bounded duty . . .
that you know how to combat this great evil and you can only know how by
Reading this Great Work," Quale tells the reader; he might well have said that

to read works such as his own pamphlet is in itself to undo the evil. The wide-spread appeal of white slavery literature is not hard to grasp: in the population at large, almost every male (and even many women serving as heads of families) could identify themselves as possessors of their "own" woman. In this book's final chapter I consider what white slavery offered to women in particular; to all members of the Progressive public, white slavery literature was a timely response to the growing power and consolidation of big business. In its horror over the breach of reciprocity, and in its invitation to imagine oneself enriched and empowered in the exchange system, the literature responded to the multilevel integration that big business undertook in the first years of the century.

The standard model of the big business was the Standard Oil Trust, made familiar to the public by Ida Tarbell's *History of the Standard Oil Company,* which ran in *McClure's* in 1902, 1903, and 1904. Standard Oil's horizontal and vertical integration brought many plants and facilities under centralized management, while every component of the business, from mining and production to shipping, distribution, packaging, sales, and marketing, was controlled by Rockefeller. Tarbell's series made Rockefeller a familiar public figure.[10] Though Tarbell tended to praise the rationality and efficiency of Rockefeller's operation, she also depicted its ruthlessness and disregard of social consequences. By the Progressive Era, the term "trust" evoked a self-enriching operation which, working only for its own profit, amassed a disproportionate share of social influence and economic leverage. In some white slavery writing, the trust serves as the paradigm of the lawless business syndicate; for example, in Turner's New York City exposé, ex–police chief Theodore Bingham asserts that the city's white slavery organization is "a regular trust" (Cordasco, 28).

It is perhaps not surprising that John D. Rockefeller Jr., son of the most successful of trust builders, put his faith and money behind the proposition that white slavery was indeed a trust.[11] The elaborate and thorough investigation that Rockefeller funded and headed, the New York Commission, very famously could not find any evidence that such a centralized organization existed (see n. 5). Nonetheless the public continued to believe in the white slavery conspiracy. White slavery's rendering of an economy in which organized operatives monopolize all the raw wealth, manage all the transactions, saturate and control the market, and put all the profits into their own pockets, provided the public with a version of the trust as an unequivocal evil—a version they could symbolically defeat and reform.

Roe's "wanted poster" reading, "Wanted. Sixty Thousand GIRLS to take the place of 60,000 white slaves who will die this year," suggests that the white slavery "syndicate" (as Reverend Bell calls it) keeps taking and taking, providing itself with more and more stolen girls to replace those whose exchange value it has emptied out—just as, in the "brother" narrative, the slavers deplete the sister's market value through successive exchanges (Roe, 49; Bell, 57). The slavers violate the rule of reciprocity by failing to yield an equivalent for the sister. Returning an unrecognizable body to the family, the slavers have caused the sister, as a valuable possession, to vanish from the point of view of her familial possessors.

Quale's story of the sister who disappears into prostitution extrapolates the white slavery trope of the "girl that disappears." This trope was strikingly counterfactual, for the "commercialization" of vice lamented in white slavery literature actually meant that prostitutes and prostitution were far more visible than ever; in fact, it was hard *not* to see a prostitute in the Progressive Era city (or at least in parts of it).[12] Jane Addams reports the dismay caused by the display of prostitutes, commenting that "the suggestive presence of such women on the streets is perhaps one of the most demoralizing influences in a large city" (1912, 47). The "girl that disappears," then, appears alongside the emphatic visibility of large numbers of prostitutes. But when Bingham considers the disappearance of women, he poses the question, "Where have they gone?" by asking "into whose hands" they have fallen. By focusing on the women's new owners, whose resistance to reciprocity makes them secretive and unaccountable, Bingham's rhetoric explains how such conspicuous women nonetheless become "girls that disappear."

The Rockefeller Commission failed to find any organized white slavery conspiracy. Bingham explains, however, that this finding indicates not that the white slavery organization does not exist but that its criminal enterprise is highly successful. The undetectability of the white slavery organization is a necessary component of its refusal to practice reciprocity in exchange. By providing no visible point of contact that would make it accessible to those outside the organization, by offering no boundary or point of interface, the organization ensures that no outside group can negotiate deals with it. In this sense, then—the structural sense informing the symbolic economy of white slavery—white slavers constitute an "undetectable" group. This is not to say (as was said after the Rockefeller finding) that they do not exist as a criminal conspiracy; on the contrary, to assert their undetectability is to assert the absolute criminality and seamless organization of their practices.

White slavers carry on their business so quietly and shrewdly that "detection and conviction is almost impossible" (Bingham, 21). And to the degree that these expropriators of women cannot be made visible, the women they own, as defined by their status in exchange, are equally undetectable. Like the sister whose body lies before the brother but who is herself completely invisible, the women taken by the slavers have disappeared from the point of view of Bingham's reader, for the exchange value they comprise has fallen into the hands of the criminals who sequester that value within their secret organization.

Not to be seen, the white slavers are also not to be located in place or time: they are nowhere and everywhere. Roe charges that "most large cities are in fact market places where girls are bought and sold," but he stipulates that "by market it is not meant that there are public places . . . where girls are sold. . . . Neither is there an open meeting together of people, at a stated time and place." Instead, this market is "an opportunity for selling anything; demand; traffic; and exchange or purchase and sale" (169). C. C. Quale, more imaginatively, envisions this market as a network of ubiquitous, immaterial "wires." Quale asks the reader to imagine that "wires were strung" between all the points of trafficking in girls; were these wires material (rather than place-holders for the immaterial links of what Roe calls "opportunity for selling"), "you could not pass as much as half a block in any section of the entire city where you would not run up against a wire" (24). In fact, you might be unable even to get out of your door: "any wire from potter's field to your house?" Quale asks. The wires of selling and buying, demand and supply, make a network so tight that, while it causes women to vanish from their homes, it virtually imprisons the women's rightful, familial possessors within, where they can take no profitable part in the market that surrounds them.[13]

Undetectable and ubiquitous, the white slavery network is subtended by countless agents: but who are they? The ingratiating, all-American pianola salesman who lures the sister to her doom is a typical example of the white slave scout who pursues his prey in the disguise of a wholesome "boy next door." In *The Traffic in Souls,* the head of the white slavery syndicate turns out to be the city's most admired business leader. In a similar vein, Quale addresses himself to "you, who are living a double life," and admonishes in particular "you men higher up, polished and refined" who are often "the wolves." Indeed, Quale goes so far as to suggest that any of his readers may be this "you": in order to find an agent of white slavery, one might need to look no farther than himself ("any wire from the potter's field to your house?"). In white slavery literature's nightmarish vision of the corporation, the corporation has incorporated "you." Seamlessly fused with its self-serving economic agenda, the citizen has no vantage point; and unless the situation can be changed, he has no leverage point from which to extract his economic due.

As a "trust," then, white slavery not only has consolidated into its centralized network all the various phases of its operations but has integrated the entire society into its operations. This saturation allows the white slavery organization to escape all boundaries and become both omnipresent and undetectable. This depiction of the white slavery "trust" would seem to posit, indirectly but forcefully, the benefits of social demarcations. Boundaries setting off groups from each other, divisions of difference or even of manageable opposition, are structurally indispensable to the practice of reciprocity in exchange. If white slavery literature confronts the reader with its vision of the saturating presence of the criminal "trust," it offers along with this revelation—or, more precisely, in the form of this revelation—the corrective to that evil when, by revealing the criminal practices of slavers, it offers a shocking vision of the "otherness" within society.

White slavery literature forces white slavers into visibility by delineating their radical "difference"—their criminality, their secrecy, their chilling unanimity in opposition to the legitimate practices of the respectable public. The literature's promises of "thrilling . . . eye-opener" are made good in the moments in which it defamiliarizes the familiar. The young salesman and the business leader are revealed as denizens of another order of society; your own home ("any wire from the potter's field to your house?") is revealed as a starting point on the well-worn route to the most sordid of public venues. And even more shocking than the strange in the familiar is the familiar in the strange: the female body quite logically (as it turns out) makes the brother feel "creepy," for it is, in fact, the body of "his own sister."

These uncoverings of the exotic in the mundane, as supports to the general claim that American society harbors a ubiquitous domestic enemy, distinguish the fully developed U.S. discourse from its European predecessor. European white slavery was xenophobic: the enemy, essentially, was made up of foreign nationals in league with hostile colonial subjects. As first adopted from the European discourse, American white slavery expressed a similar concern about non-nationals. The focus of early American white slavery writing was the alleged trafficking by immigrants in immigrant women, as reflected, for example, in the 1910 U.S. Immigration Commission Report, *Importation and Harboring of Women for Immoral Purposes,* which explains that "the ease and apparent certainty of profit have led thousands of our younger men, usually those of foreign birth or the immediate sons of foreigners, to abandon the useful arts of life to undertake the most accursed business ever devised by man"— the business, that is, of trafficking in white slaves (quoted in Connelly, 48).

But as concern over "commercialized" prostitution took hold in the United States, the trafficker's alien status became less and less a matter of literal foreignness. Clifford Roe explains that as the business grew, aspiring native-born men, seeing how white slave trading enriched "these men of foreign birth," were "prompted . . . to adopt the same methods" (101). Quale's fine "gentleman high up," the ingratiating pianola salesman—even "you," the collaborating reader himself—comprise the criminal white slavery syndicate. The panderer Paul Sinclair, "one of the most clever procurers that operated in the United States," whose lengthy reformation narrative is discussed in the following chapter, is described as a mirror image of Roe himself: white, mild-faced, and clean-shaven (to judge by the photograph inside Roe's book cover) (Roe, 68).

No longer necessarily "other" by birth or ethnicity, the white slave trafficker becomes "other" by virtue of his structural opposition to those who would enforce legitimacy in exchange. This structural otherness is often portrayed, in white slavery literature, as an archaic lawlessness associated with the barbarian stage that preceded the civil order of modern society. The brothel madam enforcing her "Turkish misrule" is one such exotic figure (Roe, 104). In his depiction of the white slavery tycoon, Reverend Ernest A. Bell invokes the archaic barbarian described in anthropological accounts of the origins of woman-exchange. Bell writes,

the white slave traffic is a system operated by a syndicate which has its ramifications from the Atlantic seaboard to the Pacific ocean, with "clearing houses" or distributing centers in nearly all of the larger cities. . . . It is a definite organization sending its hunters regularly to scour [Europe and Canada]. . . . The man at the head of this unthinkable enterprise is known among his hunters as "The Big Chief." (57)

In this anthropologized figure, the rational, ruthless modern businessman becomes a predaceous tribal chieftain with his band of "hunters." Where Tarbell might portray Rockefeller pulling the strings of his vast industrial empire, Bell imagines this barbarian overseeing the seizure and accumulation of the women and the wealth that women produce.

Bell derives his tribal chief from the anthropological accounts of barbarism and its stages. The Big Chief pursues what anthropologists identified as the predatory barbarian's main form of "exploit": the "seizure of women" from the opposing group. In its primitive form, this practice of raiding the enemy for one's women, as long as the enemy engaged in the same practice with about the same level of success, constituted an exchange system. But the Big Chief takes power only after economic development has reached the point that supports accumulation and capitalization. This transition, so the anthropological account explains, comes about when economic practices begin to generate surplus wealth consisting of slaves (i.e., women), cattle, and the products they provide. Such surplus, Veblen writes, allows for a new standard of "reputability" in which honor and power accrue to those who, systematically putting their riches to use to acquire ever-vaster holdings, come to control great quantities of the available wealth. In this protocapitalist phase of barbarism the desultory raids and hunting parties characteristic of earlier "predatory exploit" evolved into what Veblen calls "industrial aggression" (35, 37).

The social unit expanded along with the economy as tribes—consolidations of kin groups under a strong leader—began to take over from families. Organizing the little bands of hunters into an army of economic aggression, the kin leader evolved into the tribal chieftain, bringing to bear the ancient authority of the patriarch over this newly expanded province of linked kin groups and far-reaching economic power—much as Bell's patriarchal yet businesslike Big Chief reigns over his great syndicated enterprise for exploiting the wealth that is woman (Veblen, 37, 52).

White slavery's "Big Chief" takes form through the anthropological account of barbarism. Surviving into the succeeding stages of social evolution, he is exotic and alien in relation to the generic urban citizen of the rationalized modern order. As an archaic figure, the Big Chief would probably have resonated with the stereotype of the "new immigrants" arriving from the peasant cultures of Eastern Europe, bringing with them unfamiliar traditions and practices rooted deep in the past. The Big Chief and his hunters might also have invoked the stereotype of that other resident alien, the Indian chief and his braves. In fact, according to one influential paradigm of racial difference, the Big Chief's archaism itself marked him as racially "other." Within the evolutionary model in which different races represent successive stages in an evolutionary telos, the Chief's archaism associates him not only with a different developmental stage but with an alien race.[14]

Because white slavery literature foregrounds a Progressive Era concern about "aliens," scholars have classed it among the reactions to immigration. Mark Connelly explains that race and nationalism were one important context for white slavery, which served as a container for nativist reactions to immigration and urbanization. According to this view, it appears that the American discourse, in taking up the European discourse and its concern over the non-national who preys on European women, puts an immigrant in the place of the colonial subject, while the ungovernable, envious "foreign" world of the colony becomes the booming city (Connelly, 118ff.). Fear of immigrants—or, more precisely, fear of the immigrants' difference—accounts, in this view, for the popularity of white slavery literature's strident and counterfactual alarms.

Nativist fear and hostility certainly characterized the attitudes and actions of Progressivism—white slavery not excepted. But while white slavery writing makes use of this fearful concern over the presence of immigrant "others" by invoking the alien in association with the white slaver, it actually expresses a wish for the structural persistence of otherness as it goes about uncovering and delineating, with its "eye-opening" revelations, the "other" among us. This other, like the Big Chief (and unlike the immigrant per se), manifests a difference that inheres not in his literal ethnic or racial derivation, but in his woman-exchanging practice. White slavers are "other" in that they are criminals who violate the rules of exchange. This in itself makes them "different"—shocking, exotic, and "unthinkable" in reference to the mundane social sphere of the average reader.

The white slave trafficker is a criminal "other" because of his refusal to engage in the reciprocal relations through which the social network is formed. In white slavery literature, alienness becomes structural: the Big Chief is other, not because he is an immigrant, but because of his illegitimate trading practices. In the revelations of the white slave trade, otherness comes about by distinguishing illegitimate expropriators from those who observe the rule of reciprocity.

White slavery literature uncovers the presence of this other in order to reform the social order. This reform, rather than doing away with otherness, enlists it. In seeing the other who desires one's own woman, the reader, as a member of the "great public," learns how to possess what Amhigh calls the "priceless value" of his own woman. Seeing these criminals and their practices means seeing the value of the illegitimately expropriated woman in the trafficker's possession and forcing the white slavers to return that value.

White slavery writing thus integrates the presence of otherness into the common social aim of realizing women's value and implementing the productive social relations made possible by owning and exchanging women. The structurally alien status of the white slaver is no less useful for being nonessential—in fact, because it is performative rather than inherent, it is usefully inexhaustible. White slavery literature sets out with a vision of the social network as an exchange system that requires reciprocity—and, therefore, difference—between groups. Difference enables harmonious mutual enrichment within society; and structural (rather than inherent) differences may be generated endlessly. In making the exchange of woman the governing mode of social life, the literature animates a model of social collectivity that requires boundaries over which women can be exchanged. Insofar, then, as American white slavery responds to immigration and the uneasy proximity of different classes in the crowded cities, in its vision of the exchange of woman the literature responds to this diversity not through a wish for assimilation (elision of difference) but through the accommodation of difference into the harmonious functioning of a larger whole.

In the anthropological discourse used by white slavery writers, this mode of interconnection is affinity—that is, relation through marriage. Affinity is socially foundational but (strictly speaking) consensual. It is a socially created and ever-expandable bond of mutual obligation that authenticates itself by simulating the flesh-and-blood bond of biological kinship. Affinity is a very apt paradigm of the quasi-familial, quasi-racial collectivity that is the public sphere under construction in the Progressive Era—in fact, affinity is a perfect model for the public sphere of the democratic nation in general, as it invokes the paradigm of blood relation (one's affines are both like one's own family and the means for increasing that family) while, being instituted through contract, it mobilizes the mutual obligations and mutual observance of rights and privileges that belong to the civil sphere.

Generally, scholars see race as the paradigm of Progressive nationalism.[15] Like race, affinity proceeds from the presumed bedrock of the family and its bond of blood, enlarges the scope of that system through the metaphorical "family" of kin, and organizes the collectivity into a mutually identifying, coherent whole. An advantage of affinity as a national paradigm in the Progressive Era is that, within limits, it uses the demarcations between differing groups to forge the populace into a collectivity. While the nation at large made no serious commitment to the assimilation of blacks, it did set out fitfully to include other groups, especially Jews, Italians, and other Eastern Europeans, which were designated in the dominant racial discourse as racially other.[16] Affinity created through the exchange of woman provides a way of including the "other" without rendering him "same"; thus otherness is domesticated, so to speak, while the daunting challenge of overcoming difference is deflected by a unifying vision.

The Traffic in White Women

White slavery literature, in uncovering the radical otherness stalking the public sphere, delineates boundaries that serve, in its symbolic economy, as points at which relations between groups are mediated through the exchange of women. As we saw in the analysis of "Brother Cutting Up His Own Sister," white slavery's revelation of the evil done by this "other" constitutes its reformation: to see the white slavers' practices is already to force them into the position of reciprocal partners in exchange. But in order to integrate the other as such into the unified whole of the exchange network, white slavery must segregate women into the separate category of exchangeable property. And if the groups that exchange women must somehow be different from each other, the women, in contrast, must be inherently indistinguishable insofar as they represent property that a member of any group might own. Any inherent qualities that would indelibly signify a woman's alliance to a particular group would disqualify her as an item of exchange among groups. If white slavery imagines demarcations among the population of exchangers, then, it puts women in the place of the universal.

As American white slavery literature increasingly addresses itself to the enlightenment and reform of the national "great public," it asks its readers to regard the woman at stake as the "daughter" of every citizen. In the domestic American version of white slavery, the white slave, previously designated an immigrant woman trafficked by immigrants, becomes more and more frequently a native-born American woman. Legal historian Frederick Grittner recounts that in the debate preceding passage of the Mann Act, "concerns about immigrant women gave way to fear of immigrant men corrupting native-born women" (96). A contributor to Bell's 1910 compendium writes, "I hope soon to see the time when the laws of the land will as carefully protect the daughters of the United States from the destroying hand of the white slave trader as the international treaty agreements now protect the girl who is brought in from foreign shores" (Bell, 17). And, in 1910, Clifford Roe would write that "in the United States, at least three-fourths of the girl slave victims have been inveigled from our own farms, homes, towns and cities, but it was the foreigner who taught the American this dastardly business." [17]

In the nationalistic rhetoric of American white slavery literature, fair access to the exchange value of the white slave becomes the common interest of all nationals. White slaves (or potential white slaves), each one a "daughter of the United States," are interchangeable in their status as women whom any U.S. citizen could recognize as his "own." It would be wrong, however, to say that as items of exchange these "daughters" bear no distinguishing markings, for they are marked by their current status in the exchange network. The sister who comes to the brother in the form of an anonymous "female body" bears no sign of his proprietary relation to her: the identity of this body is determined by those who have exercised the rights of possession and exchange over the body as it passes through the market. The sister's invisibility in the body may seem a nightmarish proposition, but the narrative shows that the body's capacity to bespeak the proprietary identities of those who claim ownership of it—the capacity that hides the sister behind the prostitute—also enables the sister to reappear through the agency of the reader. Cued by the white slavery narrative, the reader (in this case, the brother) reinscribes on the female body the marks of his own proprietary rights and thus brings into being the woman that is "his own."

The white slave is inscribed and reinscribed by her current owner in the exchange network, and has no specific qualities of her own that would mitigate against her possession by any group. But the term "white slave" seems to contradict this nonspecificity, at least insofar as "whiteness" designates a particular racial identity. However, Clifford Roe explains that the term has no racial referent: "The phrase, white slave traffic, is a misnomer, for there is a traffic in yellow and black women and girls, as well as in white girls" (97). The "misnomer" stuck, however; and recent scholarship on the development of America's racial discourse helps explain how whiteness can at once designate race and float free of racial categories. As Ruth Frankenberg explains in her book on white women, whiteness has often been considered the absence of racial marking, a "nonracial or racially neutral" identity.[18] Just as the associations connected with the national, ethnic, and racial "alien" were metaphorically employed, in the American discourse, to characterize the trafficker within his structural alienness, attributes connected to racial whiteness were attached to the white slave, whose whiteness is a lack of specific group identity that makes her available to be owned and exchanged by any number of different groups.

The absence of particularizing identity signified by whiteness has a positive value within the economy of the exchange of woman. Applied to the woman of exchange, whiteness denotes the value that makes her desirable as property. This association derives from the European colonial discourse. The European anti–white slavery crusade was a colonial discourse in which female European nationals, it was feared, were coming into the possession of colonial subjects who stole them as a way of usurping the privilege of the colonizer. The anti–white slavery movement, which had begun as a domestic British reform movement, came to focus on international trafficking during the mid- and late nineteenth century, when British and continental anxiety over the weakening of colonial domination was growing. In this context, racial demarcations between colonizer and colonized were mobilized to shore up power, making "whiteness" denote European national identity. Increasingly, the term "white slavery" came to refer to an international traffic in European and North American women, in which women were moved out of their homelands into lives of sexual exploitation abroad.[19]

Colonial white slavery literature reflects this racialized nationalist anxiety. In *The White Slave Market,* published in London in 1909 by Mrs. Archibald MacKirdy (a British colonist of India) and W. N. Willis (an ex-MP of Australia), the white slave is a European or North American immigrant woman prostituted in a colonial locale. To these authors, who allied themselves with the national interests of the European colonial powers, the white woman, as the prized property of this dominant group, was imagined as inherently desirable to men of the subject populations. In chapters such as "Christian Slaves in the East" and "The Pimps' Club at Singapore," the authors describe the brutal lust of the "black" and "Asiatic" patrons of white slave dens. "An Asiatic will sometimes pay ten times the usual price to associate with an American woman, and such association will serve him as a thing to sneer and gibe over at the expense of the Western whites for a full year," explain the authors. The undermining of national prestige by free access to white women is described in a chapter anxiously devoted to "American Women in the East," where the authors warn that "any Western nation that coolly stands by and views with complacency their women prostitute their bodies to Asiatics—who, of course, include Indians, Malays, Chinese, Cingalese, Siamese, Filipinos, etc.—quickly loses the last fragment of respect the Asiatic may have for it" (186).

In the European discourse, whiteness, as a racialized designation of national status, marks women as at once our "own" and (for that reason) valuable to (and thus likely to be appropriated by) the "other." Though the American white slave was misnamed (according to Roe), her structural position correlates exactly to that of her predecessor: the "whiteness" she shares with the European is her value to all and her capacity to be owned by all. This economic sense of whiteness conflates the metaphorized racial meanings with a reference to female chastity as a moral "whiteness" in which women's relative inaccessibility adds to their value.[20] White racial purity may signify sexual inaccessibility (and thus value) in American writing as well. In his chapter on "Procuring Country Girls for City Resorts," for example, Clifford Roe describes the hunting and capture of white slave victims whose rural isolation has preserved both the sexual innocence and the Nordic purity reflected in their "blond hair and large blue eyes" and "pure red blood" (154, 164–65, 157).

But white slave victims in general, as Roe points out, are neither particularly white-skinned nor sheltered within a homogeneous rural enclave. The American white slavery discourse, as it developed, borrowed the racialized desirability attached to "white" women within the colonial context of European white slavery and applied it to the generic class of young women. An undoubted advantage of the term for American usage is that it helped distinguish sexual slavery per se from black chattel slavery and the absolute sexual accessibility of the black slave woman (in contrast to the relative inaccessibility of the "white" woman). While Roe writes that the traffic includes "black girls," the narratives in fact do not recount the capture of black women: white racism would have designated black women, in their status as ex-slaves, as a specific kind of sexual chattel already the property of slave-owners and not imaginable as the (generic, white) reader's "own" women.

Whiteness, then, in the metaphorical sense used in American white slavery, is an inherent neutrality that allows the white slave a potentially endless series of affiliations. In the term "white slave," white is a gender designation: it designates the capacity to be exchanged that is attributed to women in the discourse of exchange. In the preceding chapter, we saw that this use of whiteness is not limited to white slavery literature. In Edith Wharton's novel *The House of Mirth*, whiteness, as I argued, images the female body's status as the medium through which possessors (or speculative buyers) access their own capacity to recognize the value in the woman. The white dress Lily Bart wears in the Wellington Brys' *tableau vivant* entertainment images the essential blankness that allows Lily to "publish" herself (as I put it) as the medium upon which are inscribed, and through which are circulated, the values and codes of the various social and aesthetic economies that make up her shifting contexts—contexts such as Lawrence Selden's privatizing home, "Town Talk"'s promiscuous sexual gossip-market, and the Brys' artful representation of half-dressed married and marriageable women. Though it is Lily's dress that is white, it is Lily's body, which the dress does not so much cover as manifest, which presents its "lines" so that the audience might delight in the representational capacity associated with the female body.

Standing in front of her audience, her female body showing through her white dress, Lily is like the white slave whose body has the capacity to manifest various identities in the eyes of its beholders and owners (or potential owners). And the plot of Wharton's novel shades into the white slavery narrative: like the victim of white slavery, Lily is an unprotected heroine circulating in a market where, if her rightful protector fails to claim her, she falls into the hands of "alien" marketeers from *arriviste* classes. (Sim Rosedale, in fact, like the paradigmatic white slave trafficker of the earlier white slavery discourse, is both a Jew and a financial schemer.) Like the white slave, Lily dramatizes the plight of the woman debased in a sexual economy; and Wharton's novel shifts toward the melodrama that is characteristic of white slavery as Lily dies debased yet innocent.[21]

The whiteness of the dress Lily wears in her tableau performance, as I argued, has specific associations with social universality. In reference to Reynolds, the artist whose portrait Lily's tableau reproduces, whiteness is part of the pictorial privileging of civic universality over local particularity; in Reynolds' practice, whiteness was used to consolidate British nationalism. The whiteness that manifests Lily's inexhaustible representational capacity has, then, an immediate resonance with the whiteness of the white slave, who is the universal commodity in a diverse populace. The white slave's whiteness, we have seen, is not literally racial, but is associated with the exchanged female body that is both one's "own" and, as such, the property (or potential property) of an other. In this context, whiteness signals the absence of any particularizing designation; it denotes a sort of blankness at the site where group or kinship affinity is inscribed— a blankness that makes women available to be appropriated and reappropriated, symbolically reconstituted as they are inscribed with the value and identity assigned by the possessors.

Wharton's fiction of the woman of exchange uses the tropes of reading and writing to figure the inscription of value and identity on the white woman. Wharton dramatizes the publication (or suppression) of textualized female value and identity in the paper-like "white folds" of Lily's dress, the many envelopes and letters, the ledgers, the gossip sheets, and the Reynolds tableau. These texts determine the "readings" which, by indicating Lily's value, finally determine her destiny. In "Brother Cutting Up His Own Sister," as we have seen, the written note on the woman's body transforms her status and her value; similarly, the white slavery genre as a whole appeals to the public to reform the treatment of women by reading (its own literature). In her use of the technologies of writing, reading, and the circulation of texts, Wharton develops a trope that is central to white slavery.

As a textualized body in the frame of her tableau performance, Lily experiences a triumph: as she stands before the audience framed within the preexisting "portrait," she appears for a moment not as a stunningly feminine body inscribed by the Reynolds portrait and the meanings it has for her audience but as herself inserted into the text of the tableau and, by her presence, giving that text its rich and multifarious meaning and value. But the triumph is fleeting: the femaleness of Lily's body, which allows her so powerfully to arrange her "lines" so as to reproduce the portrait, is successful precisely because it invites the tableau audience to impose their own readings on her. And in the context of an economy in which women are exchanged in the service of sexual titillation and commercial self-aggrandizement, the meanings Lily makes herself available to represent are inevitably debasing.[22]

Wharton, like the writers of white slavery literature, dramatizes the debasement of women in a sexual market in which a woman's body is inscribed with the values of those who possess, exchange, and speculate about her. Also, like white slavery writers, Wharton offers to the readers of her narrative the experience of their own capacity to see (or to imagine seeing) the debased woman differently, to endow her with the value that counters those debasing inscriptions. In Wharton's novel, Lawrence Selden acts the part of this reader. Wharton sets up Selden not only as the character who possesses the capacity to impose his own, redeeming reading on Lily, but also as the one whose vision of a valuable Lily depends on his reading, in Lily, the debasing inscriptions of others.

Selden (echoing the reader, who expects him to act heroically) accusingly asks himself, "How could he lift Lily to a freer vision of life if his own view of her was to be coloured by any mind in which he saw her reflected?" (167). But in fact Selden's reading task is not a simple matter of imposing his own "colour" on Lily's whiteness in order to see her only through the lens of his "freer vision." What Selden loves in Lily is her capacity to be colored by various readings—that is, her whiteness. Seeing Lily in white is seeing Lily seen by everyone else: it is only as a spectator among spectators—as a spectator of the Lily who is seen by many—that Selden sees and loves the "real Lily Bart." The views of these other spectators, being debasing, make apparent to him the value he sees in the "real Lily": "It was as though her beauty, thus detached from all that cheapened and vulgarized it, had held out suppliant hands to him," the narrator explains: the Lily Selden recognizes as (potentially) his own manifests herself to him only in relation to the debased Lily circulated among the undiscriminating mass of the tableau audience (142). Seeing her thus "divested of the trivialities of her little world" he is able to imagine owning her: "He would lift her out of [her element] and take her beyond!" (167).

In the two scenes where Selden's reading of Lily is crucial—the *tableau vivant* and the death scene—Selden, like the reader of white slavery literature, looks at the exposed female body represented through its debasing value in exchange and experiences his own capacity to read her differently. Wharton even hints at Selden's similarity to the white slavery readership when she makes Lily a figurative slave whom Selden wants to release from bondage: "He knew that Perseus' task is not done when he has loosed Andromeda's chains, for her limbs are numb with bondage and she cannot rise and walk, but clings to him with dragging arms as he beats back to land with his burden" (167). And, like the white slavery reader who is enjoined to claim his "own" woman through the structures of kinship, Selden shares his fleeting view of a redeemed and rescued Lily with Gertrude Farish, another audience member who, not insignificantly, is his cousin. Together, Selden and Gerty, a kin group, see in the publicly circulated female body a woman they can claim. "The real Lily . . . the Lily we know" appears to them only through the Lily known by others (142).

Like the brother who cuts up his own sister, Selden comes to know his own woman by seeing her, in her status as exchangeable sexual property, debased. In the novel's final scene, Selden sits alongside Lily's dead body, a representational medium he understands as "the semblance of Lily Bart" which forever defers his access to "the real Lily" he might have claimed. Appropriately, Selden (like the brother who cuts up his own sister) has been set a forensic task: dispatched to Lily's little room to sift through her things before the authorities arrive to make their definitive account, Selden attempts to read Lily's story (and, thus, her identity) in the body and what surrounds it—the open books, the sealed envelopes, the desultory notes and papers, the bottle of sleeping potion on the nightstand. Two pieces of paper strike him as significant: a note he himself wrote asking Lily "when may I come to you?" and an envelope bearing the name of Gus Trenor (who, the reader will recall, had connived to make Lily a sexual commodity).

The note, like the narrative in the sister's hair, designates Lily as Selden's own; but Selden's recognition of Lily as his own comes to him only through the power of Gus Trenor's inscription. Admitting to the determining power of Trenor's view of Lily, Selden "was too honest to disown his cowardice now, for had not all his old doubts started to life again at the mere sight of Trenor's name on an envelope?" In light of Trenor's inscription, Selden's reading of his own note "overwhelmed him with a realization of [his] cowardice" in not claiming Lily for his own (341). That is, only in reference to Trenor's claim on Lily does Selden understand her as his own, much as the brother recognizes "his own sister" only in the convergence of the trafficked woman and the note that connects her to him as his sister. The death scene, then, like the dissection room where the degraded sister lies, by presenting Lily to be read as the debased property of others, manifests her as Selden's own.

Of course, the envelope addressed to Gus Trenor (in conjunction with the open account books) proves Lily's absolute noncompliance in her trafficking: like the female body of the white slave, the debased "semblance" into which Lily has been transformed is the result, not of her own venality, but of the practices of those who assess and exploit her. This is the tragedy of Lily and the white slave alike; but without this tragic innocence, the woman could not truly be debased and therefore be valuable as one's "own" lost woman. In Selden's reliance on the debasement of Lily for his vision of a valuable Lily and, particularly, in the tragic consequence attendant on his pleasurable practice of speculation in regard to Lily, Wharton seems to express her disapproval of this genre in which both she and white slavery writers work—the genre that depends, for its pathos, its shock, or its "tragic significance" (to use Wharton's term) on an account of woman's debasement and the experience thus afforded to the reader of his own capacity to see (and, in imagination, to claim) the "real" undebased woman.[23]

Selden and the brother in Quale's narrative both attest to the power of the reader to determine the identity and fate of the white woman. The disappearance of the sister into the female body that gets cut up demonstrates the white slavers' power to determine how the trafficked woman is perceived—to determine, indeed, who she is perceived to be. But this disappearance testifies, as well, to the potential power of the brother, and of the reader who identifies with him, to restore the sister by their own rereading of her—a reading produced by the white slavery narrative that tells her story.

In his "brother" narrative, Quale illustrates with uncanny literalness a passage in which Lévi-Strauss elaborates the "objective" structural designations by which women are perceived in exchange. Of the formal nature of incest prohibitions, the anthropologist writes:

> If there is a prohibition [against receiving a certain woman], it is not because there is some feature of the object which excludes it from the number of possibilities. . . . Speaking objectively, a woman, like the moiety from which she derives her civil status, has no specific or individual characteristics . . . which make her unfit for commerce with men bearing the same name. The sole reason is that she is same whereas she must (and therefore can) become other. Once she becomes other (by her allocation to men of the opposite moiety), she therefore becomes liable to play the same role, vis à vis the men of her own moiety, as she originally played to the men of the opposite moiety. . . . The same women that were originally offered can be exchanged in return. All that is necessary on either side is the sign of otherness, which is the outcome of a certain position in a structure and not of any innate characteristics. (Lévi-Strauss, 114)

So literal is the sister's reduction to her status within exchange that when she returns to the brother with the "sign of otherness," she is no longer "his own sister." But having established this capacity of the female body for inscription, white slavery literature positions itself as the intervention by which women are reinscribed—this time by their rightful protectors and owners. Inaccessible in the form of the "female body" provided by the traffickers, the sister is restored by the narrative in her hair. The narrative dramatizes that it is the reader who must finally assume the power to bring back the vanished women. "It is your bounded duty . . . that you know how to combat this great evil and you can only know how by Reading this Great Work," Quale declares.

It is ironic that whiteness makes the woman's very identity subject to her owners. In the original coinage of "white slave," the term "white" signaled an inherent entitlement that made subjection to economic powers illegitimate rather than (as in antivice white slavery) structurally inevitable. Catherine Gallagher explains that the term "white slave" was coined by eighteenth-century anti-abolitionist industrial reformers who unfavorably compared the condition of England's "free" poor—those "whites" entitled, as such, to citizenship—to that of her colonial black slaves.[24] As first used in early industrial Britain, then, "white slavery" indicted the coercive power industrial interests illicitly wielded over putatively free wage workers: the "white" of white slave referred to a citizen (male) entitled to a race privilege illicitly nullified by economic oppression. As a polemical term, then, "white slavery" is an antinomy that does more than point to the "similarities" between hard-pressed workers and slaves; "wage slavery" would do that just as well (Gallagher 1985, 11). *White* slavery denounced the scandalous and hypocritical denial of citizenship rights and protections to *entitled* citizens—to, that is, generic (male) whites.

Over the middle and late decades of the nineteenth century, the term gradually became associated with prostitutes; this new meaning was first put in circulation by British social purity reformers, who referred to prostitutes in Britain as "white slaves." [25] Eventually, "white" slavery came to mean sexual slavery: thus the term, which assumes that such prostitutes were always women, depends on the notion that embodiment as a female specifically renders the subject vulnerable to absolute exploitation. (The fact that this usage only began after black slavery was abolished in the British Empire in the 1830s suggests that in antivice white slavery, anxiety over the coercive determinations of embodiment previously contained by black slaves was projected onto women.) By the second half of the century, common usage had made "white slave" a synonym for prostitute, though the term also retained its original industrial context well into the 1880s (Gallagher 1985, 53–54).

The original, industrial use of "white slavery" depends for its meaning on the presumption that the nonwhite subject is likely to be a slave (a noncitizen), while the generic (male) "white" subject is entitled, as an abstracted individual endowed with the rights of citizenship, to inclusion in the universalizing sphere of civil freedom, where he is protected from absolutist powers, including those of the economic sphere.[26] As the term came to be used for prostitutes, the colonial context of European white slavery retained this association of whiteness with political rights in that the prostitution of European women abroad was protested as an infringement of the right to protection from degrading economic exploitation due to the women as European nationals. As Donna Guy explains, sometimes the recuperation of national prestige meant protecting these women nationals by extending their citizenship entitlements; most often, however, it meant abridging women's freedoms and shipping them back home.[27] But the rights at issue in the prostitution usage of "white slave" are predominantly those, not of the women, but of their rightful owners, who by the traffickers' illegitimate expropriations are stripped of the possession and exchange value of their "own" women.

Wharton's rich evocation of whiteness in *The House of Mirth* offers a helpful perspective on the shift in usage that occurs as the discourse of exchange joins the nationalist context from which "white" derives its meanings. In Reynolds' pictorial language, whiteness recalls the entitlements referred to by the industrial term "white slave": it points to a sphere of civic universality which, transcending particular and local affiliations, includes the subject as an abstract individual in the collective national citizenry. In a society structured through the exchange of women, however, this is a universality to which a woman—Lily, for example—gives access but from which she herself is barred. It is not the white woman herself, but her speculative owner—in this case, Selden—who accedes by means of her whiteness to "citizenship" in his imagined "republic of the spirit," a realm of freedom "from all the material accidents" (72, 73, 74).

Selden's speculative practices, which engage him in constant shifts of vision, remove him to an imagined realm in which he is the potential exchanger of, and with, everything and everyone and the actual, committed buyer of nothing. As such he remains free from any fixed relation to the material world of embodied value. Though Selden uses a civic term, his "republic" more closely resembles an abstracted market in which, as an exchanger/"citizen," Selden fancies himself able to occupy all positions (as owner, seller, buyer, abstainer) in the exchange system. The whiteness of the woman of exchange is a space that invites the exchanger to inscribe and reinscribe his mark. Never indelibly inscribed, and therefore always available to be inscribed, this blankness allows the exchanger to reposition himself endlessly. Through his relation to this whiteness, which he experiences in his self-congratulatory exercise of shifting his view of Lily, Selden finds his way to a version of civic humanism.[28]

While Selden's "republic" is only metaphorically national, some American white slavery rhetoric specifically makes the whiteness of the woman of exchange into a field of national commonality, sometimes by resurrecting the abolitionist rhetoric of the mid-nineteenth century. "Can democracy find no other way of controlling its strong and protecting its weak members? If not, whose fair, tenderly loved daughters are to be taken?" asks Reverend Shearer in his contribution to Roe's volume. Addressing the "great public," which he enjoins to arise and fight for the national ideal of "democracy," this white slavery writer imagines the fight against vice as an abolitionist struggle to save the Union and its unifying values. The "great public" Shearer addresses is a nationalist public, aroused to its essential national purpose and collective identity: "at last, the great public is coming to recognize that there is a White Slave Traffic, infinitely more inhuman than the black slave traffic" (Roe, 23, 19).

In projecting a national entity that comes together against the practice of slavery, this author clearly relies on the historical nearness of the Unionist abolitionism of Civil War times. Civil War abolitionism was framed as the struggle to form a democratic "Union" against the barbaric and feudal practice of slavery; white slavery takes up the antislavery rhetoric of that earlier struggle to buttress its own Progressivist nationalism. However, as the period's increasingly vociferous antiblack racism emphasized, the abolition of black slavery had not resulted in the freeing of blacks into democratic inclusion. White slavery writers, by calling on the public to give themselves to this new abolitionist fight, collude with the continuing exclusion of blacks by turning the public's attention to their urgent call for a new and even more dire abolitionist struggle that deflects awareness of that older struggle's ultimate failure. Indeed, a contributor to the compendium entitled *The White Slave Hell* suggests that by taking a stand against white slavery, each member of the public could renovate not only his own abolitionist credentials, but those of the great democratic Union and its "dear old flag" (all without relinquishing antiblack racism). "The slave-coffle of the trader," writes this contributor, "is brought back from the years of memory. . . . Under the shadows of the dear old flag has sprung into existence a slavery that to-day outrivals in cunning and cruelty that of the Black Slave Master; viz., the White Slave trade. It reaches from shore to shore and counts its victims by multiplied thousands" (Lehman 1910, 71).

In white slavery abolitionism, gender, understood through the discourse of the exchange of woman, provides the structure through which the nation will unify itself. A collective dedicated to democracy, the nation comes together to "free" the white slaves in resistance against coercive economic powers. And in the face of the population's growing diversity, the Union re-forms around its commitment to the legitimate exchange ("emancipation") of its women. Diversity need not be elided—indeed, in the minds of Progressives its elision must have seemed unlikely; but in the symbolic economy of exchange, the differences among groups brings them together around their common interest in the fair exchange among them of the "white" woman who is their common property.

CHAPTER *5*

Papa's Girl

An Elaborate System

Summing up its 1910 white slavery investigation, the New York Vice Commission concludes:

The analysis of the laws . . . shows that prostitution is no longer the simple process of a man seeking a woman in a place kept for such a purpose, or that only men who are looking for such places or women who wish to live in them, are to be found there. . . . This form of prostitution exists merely as the center of an elaborate system which has been fostered by business interests rather than as a consequence of emotional demand. . . . The procurer and the combined interests are aware that if the safeguards of childhood can be broken down, the work of procuring women and patrons is easier. (The Research Committee of the Committee of Fourteen for the Suppression of the "Raines Law Hotels" in New York City, *Social Evil*, xxxii, xxxiii)

The Commissioners imagine that before prostitution became commercialized, the brothel was part of a "simple process" put in motion by the unmediated wishes of the inmate and the desires of the patron. This precommercial brothel bears a close resemblance to the traditional home: a special place where a woman lives in order to serve a man's spontaneously arising "emotional demand," it provides a version of the marital relation and ratifies the male's "right" of conjugal access to a woman. And, the Commissioners suggest, parental rights are also conserved in the brothel of old, for only with commercialization has prostitution breached the sanctity of the domestic boundary to violate the "safeguards of childhood." [1]

In contrast, the brothel of the modern vice market serves the purposes of a far-flung network of marketeers. No longer spontaneously generated by men's and women's needs, the brothel has been integrated into the "elaborate system" of modern "business." The brothel, and prostitution in general, the Commissioners warn, "is not a problem in a class by itself. . . . This may be seen from those who share the profits." The many contractees who profit from the prostitution business include the landlord, the janitor, the "middleman," the "brewer," the "druggist," and the "midwife." The profits of the vice business also go into "police protection," payments to the "telephone company and messenger service," and money due the "keeper, 'cadet,' or protector." These "combined interests," incorporating the brothel into their interlocking commercial system, have appropriated the women who in simpler times served the purpose of the seeking man. Indeed, they have also "procured" the man himself: the desire that brings a man to the brothel, the Commissioners explain, is no longer his own, for the linked businesses "vastly increase the stimulation because of the multiplied interests which must have their share of the proceeds" (xxxiii). The men now found in the brothel are not there because they wish to be. The male desire that once provided the central "purpose" of the brothel now serves as the raw material which, amplified and exploited, generates profits for the business interests.

Commandeering both the male desire to go to the brothel and the female wish to live there, luring children away from the authority of their parental homes, the commercializers of prostitution, the Commissioners charge, have usurped the rights, relations, and services proper to the family. But what is most horrible in commercialized vice—its replication of familial relations, which enables it to supplant the family—is also what is most promising. Seen as an appropriation of the family, the commercial system is subject to being reclaimed by and for the family. This reform would not merely restore the family of old, but would bring the family into the market, installing the prerogatives of the husband and parent at the center of the commercialized system. In this vision—the vision of white slavery literature—the commercial capitalization of women and children, the proliferation of sites where women serve men, and the intensification of the male desire whose "demand" gives rise to that service provide the infrastructure of an empowering expansion of the family into the public realm.

White slavery literature projects this vision in its reforming heroes who act on behalf of traditional family values, particularly to protect women who are seen as helpless against the powers of commerce. To "control the evil," the New York Commissioners recommend, an army of lawmen, educators, and investigators must infuse the public sphere to enforce the "moral integrity" of the people and the "collective will of the community" (xiv, xv). The most active of these reformers are the brothel-raiding lawmen written up in white slavery

"MY GOD! IF ONLY I COULD GET OUT OF HERE"
The midnight shriek of a young girl in the vice district of a large
city, heard by two worthy men, started a crusade which resulted in
closing up the dens of shame in that city.

From Ernest Bell, *Fighting the Traffic in Young Girls,* 1910.

crime-fighting narratives. Such men reclaim the potency and purpose of the male subject whose agency and desire have been diverted by the business network. In narrative accounts of brothel raids, the literature tells of men who go to the brothel with a purpose: they go to seek out and reclaim the women whom commercialization has appropriated.

The same commercial system that "stimulates" male desire works on women to elicit, magnify, and profit from the dependency and servitude of woman's social position. In the market, white slavery writers imagine, women retain their functional position as dependents; but the material dependency met, within the family, by one provider becomes the unlimited need of the consumerist woman. The manifold agents of marketing, constantly eliciting the woman's need for goods she can never provide for herself, force her to rely on any number of providers. The state of need is the starting point of a woman's fall into white slavery: the servitude that comes with dependency, exploited for commercial purposes, is the "enslavement" that befalls women in the public sphere. Rescuers of white slaves find them languishing in this abject dependency and "free" them into their rightful status as consumers who depend on familial support.

The quintessentially feminine "love of fine clothing" and weakness for "finery," the narratives explain, make it easy for procurers to ensnare thousands of women simply by holding out "promises of an easy time, plenty of money," and, above all, "fine clothes" (Bell 1910, 57, 58). And because of their consumerism, women are as readily enslaved as they are trapped. The persistent feminine craving for fine clothes makes women the indebted thralls of their keepers, who elicit women's need and control their access to clothing through a practice known as the "clothing switch." Roe (240) describes this as a common ploy, while Bell, in an account of a typical brothel raid, explains how it works:

When once a white slave is sold and landed in a house or dive she becomes a prisoner. The raids disclosed the fact that in each of these places is a room having but one door, to which the keeper holds the key. In here are locked all the street clothes . . . of a woman. . . . The finery which is provided for the girl for house wear is of a nature to make her appearance on the street impossible. Then added to this handicap, is the fact that at once the girl is placed in debt to the keeper for a wardrobe of "fancy" clothes which are charged to her at preposterous prices. She cannot escape while she is in debt to the keeper—and she is never allowed to get out of debt—at least until all desire to leave the life is dead within her. (Bell, 58, 59)

The woman is held in bondage, but the street clothes are locked up in a dungeon. The woman's possession of a set of street clothes might seem to signify her status as a possessive individual; but in the white slave house, the possession of commodities signifies instead the woman's need for (more) commodities—a need that the keeper, as an operator in the commercial domain, can elicit and exploit.

Bell gestures toward a logical reason for the efficacy of the clothing switch: the slave needs clothing because the keeper has locked up her street clothes. But the slave does not purchase a replacement for her street clothes; instead, she accepts a set of "finery" that is continually renewed in a perpetual cycle of buying, indebtedness, and servitude. But if the efficacy of the clothing switch is logically vague, it is rhetorically clear: the woman's consumerism allows the keeper to enslave her, and the street clothes he incarcerates signify and enable the woman's consumerism. The street is the realm of shopping where women pursue the enticing commodities displayed in stores and windows, and the possession of street clothes shows that the woman not only has been shopping, but has equipped herself for more shopping. When the keeper locks up the woman's street clothes, he symbolically contains and appropriates her consumerism. Possessing her clothes, he extorts and controls her consumerist need, becoming her only source of goods and the economic benefactee of all her transactions. As the woman's creditor, the keeper lays claim to the economic value she can render—namely, her value in exchange. Not by separating the woman from her street clothes, then, but by enforcing her perpetual connection with them—a connection that is figured in the mirrored imprisonment of the woman and her clothes—the keeper makes the woman his slave.

Though the woman makes purchases, and pays for them with her exchange value as a prostitute, her buying never leads to owning. It is as if, with every exchange into which she enters, the keeper's rights of ownership over the slave increase, while the state of need that prompts the woman to enter into the purchasing contract is not alleviated but deepened. For her purchases, the woman pays with her value in exchange; but this payment, rendered as service in the brothel, puts her in need of more boudoir clothing, which she must purchase at the price of her continued sexual bondage. Every time the woman takes part in an exchange, she magnifies and perpetuates her neediness and therefore deepens the subjugating dependency of her feminine status. The keeper, in contrast, like a capitalist who makes his profits through others' efforts and transactions, grows in wealth and power with every purchase and payment.

Contract making, far from ratifying the woman's status as an equal, enforces and perpetuates her subjugation. Within the walls of the white slave house, the woman lives out her feminized position in the market where, as in the home, her contractual relations are subject to, and produce profit for, the male proprietor. The clothing switch reveals that the market is a sphere of compulsion for the woman; but for the keeper who gains from the woman's contract making, the market offers, along with profit through contractual exchange, freedom from the obligations of contract. The keeper not only forces the woman to engage in contractual relations, but he controls the terms of these agreements: the slave has no power to set the terms or prices of her purchases. But even more unequal is the keeper's freedom to exempt himself from obligation. The slave, through the contractual exchanges that generate profit for the keeper, frees the keeper from the contractee's obligation to reciprocate, for he uses the profits earned by the slave to purchase the "finery" for which he forces her to pay. Like the husband Veblen describes, who accumulates reputability through the vicarious consumption he assigns to his wife, the keeper of the consuming woman seizes the value and acquires the social stature generated through the woman's contractual relations. Within the domain of his possessive authority over the woman, the keeper, like the husband, is a sovereign and not a contractee.

According to antivice writer Charles Crittendon, the street prostitute is similarly exploited through her contract making. Though not confined within a prison-like brothel, the everyday prostitute Crittendon describes is made a "slave" by the men with whom she must reach agreements in the market. While the brothel inmate is subjugated as a consumer who needs a "provider," the street prostitute is exploited through her need for that related feminine requirement, "protection." Writing in Bell's white slavery compendium, Crittendon, who founded the Crittendon Mission for wayward women, reports of his work among prostitutes:

What impressed me most in coming close in touch with the subject, was that almost every girl that I met in a house of sin was supporting some man from her ill-gotten earnings. . . . In addition to this form of slavery I also found that the majority had to pay a certain percentage of their earnings to some individual or organization who had promised them immunity from arrest and to whom they looked for protection. (127)

Crittendon focuses on the prostitute's protection contract, and on her support of "some man," to suggest that in giving up a portion of her proceeds the prostitute shows that the value she exchanges is actually owned by the men who profit from it. The prostitute exchanges her sexual value for money; but (Crittendon emphasizes) she uses the money to purchase the protection she requires to go on exchanging herself for money with which she will pay for protection, and so on. Because she participates in the market and its contractual agreements, the prostitute is forced to generate, for the profit of exploiting men, more market value in the form of protection from the market.

This situation, Crittendon argues, shows that the market, far from being a place that entitles the woman to own and profit by herself through contract, is a place where she is forced to realize her value through exchange in order that it be taken from her. Although the ostensible purpose of the prostitute's protection contract is to keep her value for herself, the fact that she must make payments to prevent the market's commercial operators from seizing and exploiting her value, Crittendon intimates, shows that she is already the object of exploitation—for the market extorts money in return for the protection which it necessitates and which, being protection from extortion in the market, it cannot provide.

Far from manifesting her self-ownership, the prostitute's participation in contract-making signifies and regenerates her status as a sexual object who, upon entering the market, is required there to render up her value in exchange to male "owners." These men exercise their freedom by creating the conditions that force the prostitute to enter into all sorts of agreements and thus to generate more profit. Crittendon imagines, then, that each contract the prostitute makes is not only compelled but compelling, and deepens her subjection. Crittendon's account of the prostitute's contractual relations resembles Carole Pateman's description of the wife's domestic subjection. Pateman writes that women are subordinated in their familial role through a nominal "agreement," which Pateman calls the marriage contract. The terms of this agreement, which is compulsory for women as a class, require a woman to exchange "obedience for protection." Predicated on the inequality it perpetuates (the woman needs "protection" because of her weakness and inequality), the marriage contract renders the woman, like a slave, a life-long servant in her gender-specific status as "wife."[2]

In the clothing switch and the enslaving "protection" contract, white slavery writers depict the woman in the market as a version of the domestic woman: needing protection and material goods she can never provide for herself, the woman in the market gives obedience and sexual services to her providers and protectors. But unlike the household head who provides for the domestic woman, the business interests elicit, magnify, and perpetuate the woman's state of need, making capital of the sexual exchange value she renders through the perpetual contract making of the consumer.

The All-Absorbing Street

White slavery literature, in imagining that women are brought into the market as they are brought into the family—as dependents and sexual property—invites the family and its agents to reassert familial authority over women. But in order to reclaim the women whom the market has commercialized, the traditional family must conform itself to the realities of the new economic order.

The old-fashioned family, Jane Addams writes, retains attitudes and traditions that are not in accord with modern-day "actual fact," and will not reclaim its women until such fact is understood. Women's present-day involvement with the market, Addams suggests, entails both a need for commodities and a capacity to earn wages. Both these circumstances enthrall women to the commercial powers, for in the view of white slavery literature, the possession of money—like the possession of street clothes—merely sets the stage for the disastrous compulsions of consumerism.

Of the traditional family in general, Addams writes, "it has always been difficult for the family to regard the daughter otherwise than as a family possession."[3] Traditional parents—particularly, in Addams' examples, unassimilated immigrant parents—ignore both the consumerism and the economic self-sufficiency of the modern working woman. Despite the fact that daughters now earn wages, traditional families treat even their working daughters "as if the tradition of woman's dependence upon her family for support held long after the actual fact had changed, or as if the tyranny established through generations when daughters could be starved into submission to a father's will, continued" (Addams 1912, 82). But because of white slavery, Addams warns, some of the old-fashioned parental practices are now dangerous: for example, routine confiscation of a working daughter's earnings creates a perilous situation for the young woman, who is thus deprived of the means to satisfy her compelling desire for clothes. Such a daughter, in obedience to her consumerist desire, deceives her family by withholding extra earnings. All the money such daughters can keep for themselves, Addams writes, is "invariably spent upon . . . clothing" that their parents, through obliviousness or misguided strictness, will not allow them (82).

Many young women turn to prostitution to support their buying. Addams tells of one Polish mother who, following the moral code of traditional culture, thought she was doing her parental duty when she "so conscientiously punished a daughter who was 'too crazy for clothes.'" This unassimilated immigrant is oblivious both to the compelling consumer culture that has recruited her daughter and to the threat posed by traffickers and white slavers who gain access to women through their consumerism. Such an unassimilated mother, Addams warns, "could never of course comprehend how dangerous a combination is the girl with an unsatisfied love for finery and the opportunities for illicit earning afforded on the street. Yet many sad cases may be traced to such lack of comprehension" (82, 83, 84).

Clearly, Addams' appeal to the "danger" posed by sexual traffickers is meant to reinforce her argument that parents should liberalize their treatment of daughters, allowing them to assimilate, by their participation in consumer culture, into the American middle class. But in Addams' depiction of the young daughter's relation to the street, it seems as if the daughter is already held in erotic captivity, seduced and abducted by the appeals of marketing which elicit, along with her desire for goods, her escapist dreams of "romance" and adventure. The street "absorbs" the young woman of the tenement, whose crowded family dwelling provides her

no room in which to receive her friends or to read the books through which she shares the lives of assorted heroines, or, better still, dreams of them as of herself. . . . And she finds upon the street her entire social field; the shop windows with their desirable garments hastily clothe her heroines as they travel the old roads of romance, the street cars rumbling noisily by suggest a delectable somewhere far away, and the young men who pass offer possibilities of the most delightful acquaintance. It is not astonishing that she insists upon clothing which conforms to the ideals of this all-absorbing street and that she will unhesitatingly deceive an uncomprehending family which does not recognize its importance. (82, 83)

To keep the girl from disappearing into the "all-absorbing street," the parents must provide "room" in which the daughter can entertain and satisfy her consumerist desires. Ceasing to be "an uncomprehending family," the family must expand to comprehend the rambling dreams, propped up by clothing, through which the daughter responds to the elicitations of marketing. Given "room" and permission by the reformed parents, the daughter's consumerist life will remain within the domain of the family home.

Though Addams proposes that in comprehending the daughter's consumerist life the family adjusts to "actual fact," this familial stance of containment and permission giving runs counter to the fact at issue: that the daughter pursues her desires with her own earnings. Addams' model of the reformed family actually revives the very ideology she sets out to revise—the traditional familial view in which daughters, because they are seen as dependent on their fathers for provisions, are treated as possessions subject to absolute rule. Like the traditional family, which thinks itself entitled to "starve a daughter into submission," the reformed family Addams imagines acts as the source of a daughter's provisions. But, enlightened and liberalized, the comprehending family, rather than starving its daughter, chooses instead to "allow" her the goods she craves. Women's consumerism calls, not for the dismantling of parental possessiveness, but for its renovation.

By making room for the daughter's consumerist life, the family retains possession of the daughter—for the alternatives to familial comprehension, as Addams evokes them, hint at the clandestine confinement of the white slave. The traditionally treated daughter who is left with no spending money will contrive to get money to buy "her own clothing, which she, of course, cannot wear at

The Cab Route.

A pander from the Madam's low retreat
Makes ruin of our Innocence complete.

From Rev. F. M. Lehman and Rev. N. K. Clarkson, *The White Slave Hell,* 1910.

home, but which gives her great satisfaction upon the streets" (82). Imagining a site, located somewhere in the uncharted territory of "the street," where the daughter stores the secret wardrobe for which she has become a prostitute, Addams reflects the white slave house in reverse. In the white slave house, the incarceration of the woman's street clothes makes "her appearance on the street impossible"; in the "all-absorbing street" into which the daughter has disappeared, a wardrobe is secreted along with the daughter whose appearance at home, dressed in her new clothing, would be equally impossible. The commercial operators have usurped the role abdicated by the "uncomprehending" familial providers. Like the keeper who uses his inmate's earnings to provide the finery required for the sexual marketing of the white slave, the commercial operators, by accommodating the daughter's consumerist life, are able to exploit her market value.

At stake in the family's ability to "comprehend" female consumerism, then, is nothing less than possession of the woman herself, who through her recruitment into consumer culture becomes a repository of market value the family may retain or lose. Addams bolsters the persuasiveness of her reform proposals by holding out a class incentive to the "working people" and inhabitants of "crowded tenements" whom she hopes to liberalize (81, 82). The daughter of a family that provides "room" for her consumerism, Addams writes, will consume not only clothes but "books"—that is, she will join the middle class as a consumer of leisure and leisure goods. As such, like the conspicuously consuming woman Veblen describes, who consumes surplus wealth and performs vicarious leisure to enhance the reputability of her "owner," the consuming daughter enjoying her finery and reading her books in the family "room" will enhance the family's social status. Addams advises, then, that a traditional family that relinquishes its claim to the daughter's earnings will find itself possessed of something much more valuable: the books and finery, and the daughter who possesses them, will distinguish the family as the possessor of surplus wealth. Working-class families, Addams imagines, assimilate and move upward in social class through their daughters' involvement in consumer culture. And because it is the daughter's own earnings that pay for the goods reputably consumed in the family home, such a family can attain status through the possession of surplus wealth without itself providing the surplus income required. The limit of such a family's potential reputability is marked only by the limit of the daughter's capacity and desire to consume.

Addams presents her reforms as a means of promoting the tradition and sanctity of the family. When familial possessiveness is enlarged to encompass the daughter's consumerism along with the daughter, the family not only remains a family, retaining its traditional identity as the possessor of a daughter, but it rises in class status to become more solid and prestigious. A white slavery narrative included in Bell's compendium describes a family that in many ways exemplifies Addams' vision of this renovated patriarchal possessiveness. "The True Story of Estelle Ramon of Kentucky" by Principal D. F. Sutherland of Red Water, Texas, describes a family headed by the old-fashioned John Ramon. A traditional patriarchal husband and father who works the land and provides for his women, John Ramon, like the liberalized parent Addams imagines, consolidates his patriarchal authority by accommodating a consuming woman. But Sutherland, by making the daughter Estelle a victim of white slavery, portrays with dramatic starkness the encounter between familial and commercial possessors of women. In this extended narrative, the author imagines how the father's traditional possessive rights, challenged by the recruitment of women into commercial exploitation, may be extended over the woman in her status as a commodity in the modern marketplace.

As the story opens, the reader is introduced to John Ramon, a husband and father whose sterling attributes and "roman" name denote his fineness in the classical masculinist tradition. "One of these great, big, good-looking, honest and hard-working men from the mountains," John Ramon derives his identity from his laboring body and the land on which he labors. In his powerful size, good looks, integrity, and industriousness, John epitomizes an economy situated far from the urban centers of exchange—an economy in which, the author seems to imagine, wealth and identity are not the results of exchanges, but derive from the inalienable property, character, and work of the man himself, just as John himself is "honest" and true to type.

In contrast to John, Amanda Ramon, the social-climbing wife and mother, constantly strives to become someone else. Amanda derives her identity from the class codes of consumer society. "A refined and well educated Kentucky woman and a woman who loved to be with the 'society' folks," Amanda engages in untrammeled conspicuous consumption: she "loved to wear fine dresses and spent more in this way than her husband could really afford." It turns out, however, that Amanda's overspending, far from depleting the security and success of the Ramon estate, brings about its rapid enrichment. Amanda's love for "fine dresses," which makes her spend "more . . . than her husband could really afford . . . caused him to have to work very hard early and late," Sutherland explains; and all this hard work means that John clears more land and improves his farm, quickly becoming a rich man (Bell 1910, 80).

Sutherland mentions the material gains that are part of John's success; but John's transformation into a man of notable stature seems to take place when he acquires reputability in the eyes of his admiring neighbors. Seen meeting the burden of Amanda's debts through his strenuous labor, John has "everybody . . . talking about what a noble fellow young John Ramon was" (80). Like Ben Franklin's conspicuous industriousness, John's work is efficacious as a performance: the strikingly long hours and the apparent strenuousness of his "very hard" labor performed "early and late" make John "noble" in his neighbors' eyes. What distinguishes John's work—and, thus, the "noble" John himself—is not productivity in itself, but a reputation for excessiveness that is created and reproduced through the circulation of his neighbors' "talk." The excessiveness of John's performance as a provider derives from the excessive consumption of his wife. Showing himself prepared to work without stint, John meets and exceeds Amanda's spending of "more than he can afford." Forever extending the limit of his capacity to provide, John becomes a rich man, his material position rising commensurately with the ever-expanding limit of Amanda's capacity to spend.

Amanda's practice of appearing in "fine clothes" gives rise to John's striking manifestation as a fine man. The neighbors' admiration of John's "nobility" recalls Veblen's account of the honorific status earned through conspicuous consumption. Veblen explains that the supporter of a conspicuously consuming wife accedes to a position of honor that derives from the barbarian admiration of predatory prowess (Veblen, 27, 65–67). John, in similar fashion, is endowed with an anachronistic kind of honor: the "nobility" of a feudal lord. Fittingly, in his dealings with his family John claims the authority that goes with this status. Although John has promised Amanda that when their daughter Estelle reached school age he would "sell out" and make the move into town Amanda so eagerly anticipates, when the time comes, John peremptorily breaks his promise and forbids the move. In explanation, he gestures to his rich estate and remarks that in town he "had nothing . . . and no work." John grounds his right to rule the family by his gesture to what he—and therefore his dependents—have at their disposal: in the role of provider, John claims absolute patriarchal authority. The assumption of this role harks back to a time before the "actual fact" (to use Addams' term) of large-scale female employment. In aligning himself with the providing patriarch of old, John also alludes to an archaic rural economy in which males, who owned and managed the land, produced the family's wealth. Saying that in town he "had nothing . . . and no work," John collapses his wealth into his work. His refusal to "sell out" and move to town is a refusal to perform the transformation of his labor into exchangeables—a refusal to admit that what he "has" comes to him through the mediation of the market in which he sells his labor (81). By not "selling out," John maintains the symbolic economy in which his labor is both the source and the repository of the family's wealth and, as such, is the basis of his old-fashioned patriarchal absolutism.

Asserting his power by evoking an archaic, premarket economy, John Ramon seems to be the "ideological" patriarch Stuart Ewen describes. Ewen writes that patriarchal power, based in the father's role as provider, lost its economic underpinning as industrialization moved production out of the home and into the capitalists' domain. But the disappearance of its economic base, Ewen explains, did not make the patriarchal family vanish. Instead, "the [patriarchal] internal authority of the family, as more and more of the workers' world became bought rather than produced, became symbolic—real for those who experienced it, yet unsupported by the priorities of an industrializing world" (Ewen, 117).

Ewen suggests that patriarchy maintained itself, albeit only ideologically, in the face of its displacement by industrialization and the market. But the example of John Ramon suggests that, in white slavery's discourse, the market—and particularly women's engagement therein—generates this ideological patriarchy. Like the possessive immigrant parents of whom Addams writes, John Ramon acquires and enforces his traditional patriarchal prerogatives through his relation to the family's consumerist women. John lives his patriarchal role by at once providing for Amanda's perpetual consumerism and by claiming (on the ground of his success in this role) the right to distance himself from exchange. Like the white slave housekeeper, John rules over a female subject whose engagement in contracts makes him free to exempt himself from contractual relations: when John refuses to "sell out," and when he ignores his promise to Amanda, he manifests his privileged exemption from the obligations of contract. And like the keeper who profits by the "debt" his slave incurs, John grows rich and reputable to the degree that Amanda overspends. The debt Amanda incurs allows John to perform the labor by which he outstrips debt (stays ahead of Amanda's spending) and thus transcends the obligations of contract—at least in his social identity as a "noble" and self-sufficient producer.

Amanda's subjection to the market, then, makes possible John's ideological freedom from the market; and when John forbids the move off his farm and into the city, it is not that he keeps Amanda out of the realm of consumerism, but rather that he possesses her, in her consumerism, within the domain of his patriarchal authority. Like the white slave house, the Ramon household is a sphere of compulsion for the woman, who remains a dependent through her perpetual purchases of fine clothing. The "finery" purchased by the white slave, Bell recounts, "makes her appearance on the street impossible." Like Amanda, the white slave is enthralled through the consumerism in which she is a perpetual participant. If these women are deprived of the freedom to make their appearance in consumerism's domain of the street, that is because they are already there.

Papa's Girl

John Ramon, of course, is an object of admiration, while the white slave-keeper who exploits his victim by assuming the role of the provider represents the epitome of evil. Usurping familial rule, displacing good husbands and fathers like John Ramon, white slavers turn provisioning into exploitation and protection into imprisonment. However, it is not the differences, but the correspondences between the father and the slaver that point the way to the restitution and reform of paternal authority. The slaver is able to assume absolute power by displacing and mimicking the father, whose traditional role he expands into the market, setting the stage for the legitimate familial male to reclaim, in its newly commercialized and expanded version, his time-honored role as the custodian of women.

In the imagined contest over the white slave, the family and the commercial powers seek to displace each other. The common procurement ruse of the fake marriage figures both the evil and the thrilling promise of this conflation of the family with white slavery. Charles Crittendon, writing of this procurement technique, suggests how easily a woman's dependence on the family for domestic, erotic, and material fulfillment can make her subject to commercial exploitation.

Crittendon writes of the young woman who, thinking she is going to her marital home, finds she has been sold into a white slave house by her new "husband."

Can you imagine any greater horror than that of this trusting child wife, when she realizes she is a prisoner and a slave in that den of shame? And such slavery! the blackest that has ever stained human history. Shut up beyond the reach of friends. . . . Surely no hell in the other world can be more dreadful than a house of shame in this world. (Bell, 131, 132)

The "horror," Crittendon suggests, is in the shock of discontinuity as the dependent, domestic innocent, the "child wife," finds herself a sexual commodity and an exploited "slave." Yet Crittendon's depiction, like the false marriage ploy itself, insists on the easy conflation, more than on the disjunction, of wifehood and prostitution. A brothel inmate yet still both a "child" and a "wife," Crittendon's white slave dramatizes the functional similarities between a domestic woman and a sexual commodity. Finding, to her distress, that her route to the house quite readily leads instead to a "house of shame," the white slave's story intimates that the wife not only arrives in her domicile through exchange, but that (like Amanda Ramon) she performs her familial duties through involvement in the market.

The success of the false marriage ploy emphasizes these convergences; and if they elicit the "horror" Crittendon invites the reader to feel, they also provide the thrilling promise offered by white slavery literature. By proclaiming that the traffickers enforce continuity between the domestic woman and the prostitute, white slavery writers remind the family that it possesses commodified women. With his rubric "child wife," Crittendon rhetorically collapses the domestic and the commodified woman to suggest that familial protection produces commodified women. "Child wife" conflates the woman protected by the family and the woman exchanged by the family; the term reminds the reader that the "child," the object of familial protection, inevitably becomes the wife, the sexualized object of familial exchange. If the figure of the falsely married white slave shows how slavers make prostitutes of wives, Crittendon, with his "child wife," invites the family into the arena of woman-exchange by evoking the corresponding process by which the family makes wives of its children.

Crittendon produces white slavery's characteristic thrill of mingled horror and promise by collapsing the domestic woman into the woman who circulates in the market. Sutherland, in contrast, portentously keeps these two female roles apart: in the Ramon family, Amanda does all the shopping while the daughter, Estelle, who is indifferent to the market, is a dedicated "papa's girl." Sutherland's drama moves toward the climactic moment when the papa's girl and the woman in the market are collapsed in the white slave—for Estelle, perfectly epitomizing the "trusting child wife," falls victim to the false marriage ploy and finds herself a prisoner of the white slave house. Estelle is eventually rescued and once again married—this time by her childhood sweetheart, William Scott, who has been appointed Estelle's protector by John Ramon. Sutherland's unusually long and complex narrative works out the reformist proposal implicit in white slavery's conflation of the child, the wife, and the prostitute, detailing how, by the intercession of white slavery, the father's possessive stake in his child is translated into the ownership of a commodified woman that a reformed (version of the) patriarch can exercise. As a rescued and married white slave, Estelle is at once the child of John, the wife of William, and a fully capitalized sexual commodity through which the traditionally possessive family renovates itself in the arena of the market.

The story begins on the Ramon lands. A "papa's girl," Estelle appears to derive wholly from John. Sutherland recounts, "from the time she could toddle around she had been constantly with her father"; "in the fields making the hay, gathering the crops, seeing after the stock, you would find Estelle and her father always together" (81). Like the hay, the crops, and the healthy livestock, Estelle, it seems, is an effect of John's labor. Even her capacity for mobility firmly links her to her father's work and possessorship, as she moves about only within the realm of his possessions and in tandem with his labor. And the author suggests that John has given figurative birth to Estelle: the family doctor, Sutherland explains, attributes Estelle's survival of a childhood bout with typhoid to John's refusal to leave her bedside over eight sleepless days and nights, until finally she awakens to ask, "Is this you, Papa?" (83).

It is as if John has brought Estelle into being as an effect of his paternal labors; and, like the other wealth he claims through his performance of labor and refuses ever to "sell out," Estelle is not regarded as exchangeable. John imagines that Estelle's eventual movement into marriage will be like her movement around the fields as she follows him in his work—that is, her marriage will express his identity as a laboring man. Accordingly, John's preference for her future husband is, as he says, the man Estelle herself prefers. Of course the father and the papa's girl are of one mind: both prefer Estelle's childhood sweetheart, William Scott. William is the son of David Scott, owner of the adjoining farm. David Scott, whose yeoman-like name evokes Sir Walter Scott's medieval tales, is strikingly similar to John Ramon: like the honest and noble John an indigene of the "mountains" of Kentucky, David is "as true a man as ever lived among the hills." David's son William Scott, "as noble a lad as ever lived," could be a son of John (84, 85). Fittingly, William's relation to the slightly younger Estelle is distinctly brotherly. Playmates from "early childhood," William and Estelle "had told each other from childhood that when they got old enough they were going to get married." William is what the French call the *petit mari*—the childhood mate who seems kin from the earliest years (86).

In choosing William as his son-in-law, John imagines Estelle's married state as a continuation of her childhood. John's possessiveness toward Estelle may seem protective; but the narrative suggests that John's refusal to give her in marriage actually means that Estelle is abandoned to confront the market as a helpless child, for after John's sudden death the tractable papa's girl is pressured by Amanda into a false marriage with a flashy white slave scout. John's death, which is so disastrous for Estelle, dramatizes his unbending stance of resistance to the market. This catastrophe comes, logically, as Estelle nears the age of marriageability. At this point—as at the precursor crisis when Estelle reached school age—John's relation to "selling out" once again takes the foreground. Suddenly, Sutherland reveals that the Ramon economy in which, as John likes to see it, all that John "has" is his work, actually involves a significant amount of selling. But, adhering to the ideology that privileges labor, the author makes this selling conspicuously laborious and physically heroic. "John Ramon was working hard," Sutherland recounts, to make log rafts of the Ramon timber to be floated down the Cumberland River to market in Nashville. John and his men ready themselves to take advantage of a "head rise" that is coming down the river. One dark night finds them out on the rafts, which they ride and wrestle while waiting for the current. As the river grows wilder, John mounts a log to cut loose a raft of his timber. Straddling his market-bound log in the middle of the night on the raging river, John's act of selling is a hypermasculine, heroic bodily feat—and one at which the productive John turns out to be all too effective, for the goods rush to market with uncontrollable speed, the rapids pulling the rafts apart and propelling the timber so abruptly that John is unseated and falls among the logs to be pulled under and drowned (87).

By having John himself become "entangled among some of the logs" that are market-bound, Sutherland both connects and opposes John's death to the market. Killing off John in the act of selling out, the author suggests that John is subsumed in the selling of his products and disappears into the commodities that comprise his laboring self. But the author also suggests that John's antipathy to selling is so total as to make it a kind of death: a working man pulled under by the fatal current of commodity capitalism, John is reified in his resistance to the market. The liquidation of John's estate completes the impression that he cannot be transformed into his equivalent in exchangeables: for Amanda comes into possession of, and quickly loses, the $5,000 life insurance payment, which she gives, along with Estelle and the other proceeds of the estate, into the keeping of the white slaver/"husband" she sends to the city to found a new family home.

With his last breath John has shouted out to William Scott, "Promise me that you will take care of Estelle." "I swear to you that I will do it," William replies (87). But it is Amanda who takes possession of Estelle, rushing her off to market and thus symbolically destroying the "papa's girl" along with the noble John. William, though he advises against this "marriage," takes no action to prevent it. It seems as if, in his role as John's surrogate, William shares John's resistance to recognizing the value in exchange of the "child" he possesses. William knows Estelle as the girl who has always been his; but in relation to the Estelle who is subject to exchange, William (like the dead John) vacates. Thus unimpeded, the phony "husband" completely sells out the Ramon estate, turning the Ramon cash and John Ramon's daughter into traffickers' profits. The cash will never be reclaimed; but in the woman sold in the marketplace, William

Scott, activated by white slavery, will find and reclaim the papa's girl, who is now his own woman and the wife he will "take . . . home" (95).

She Was Estelle

Once Estelle and the Ramon cash have vanished into the city, William is suddenly transformed: he becomes a man of action endowed with relentless purposefulness. William undertakes a tireless search through the vice districts of the northern cities, "for he intended to find her, if alive." As Sutherland narrates William's adventures, he adopts a choppy, matter-of-fact narrative style familiar from the law enforcement narrative and the detective story:

No sooner had suspicions of foul play been aroused . . . than young Scott took the train for Cincinnati. There he employed a detective to aid him in his search for Estelle. After one week of close search . . . the place was found where the "artist" and Estelle boarded. . . . He advertised for her in the newspapers and secured the services of detectives in several cities. (93)

Not only an employer of detectives, the once-rustic William becomes a sort of detective himself: he packs two revolvers, keeps his own counsel, and is supported, in his investigative mission, with funds sent by his neighbors back home.[4] Stealthily and with absolute firmness of purpose, William makes a brothel-to-brothel tour through the red light districts of at least three major cities. Though he fails for several months to find a "clew" to Estelle's whereabouts, through extensive surveillance he becomes adept in the ways of the criminal underworld, learning its codes and adopting its secretiveness so that he is able to seize upon a useful hint and follow up on it. One night in a hotel lobby William overhears one "gambler" tell another about a "beautiful girl" "at a certain place" in Cleveland, who had "fought [him] like a tiger." The savvy William knows enough not to "seek further information from the gambler"; but his knowledge also enables him to extrapolate from what he has heard.

He was fully convinced that Estelle was in a house of ill-fame in that city. By this time he had learned that it would not do him any good to tell his troubles to the police, for some of them would be more likely to help the madam secrete the girl than to help him get her away. On reaching Cleveland, he determined to tell no one of his mission or why he was there. He determined to form his own plans and carry them out. . . . He determined to visit every house of prostitution in the city or find her. (94)

William's knowingness and determination, as he makes his tour through the vice districts to reclaim the stolen woman, recall the stern purpose of the lawmen whose dangerous exploits are recounted in other white slavery literature.

Crime-fighting narratives introduce agents such as "Hon. Edwin W. Sims, the man most feared by all white slave traders" (Bell, frontispiece) and "three . . . [detective sergeants] attached to the author's office whose work at catching White Slave traders has struck terror into their hearts" (Roe, frontispiece). William, with his secret agenda, his special knowledge, and his two revolvers, attains a potency that rivals that of these lawmen; and he resembles them also in the moral code he imports into the domain of commercialized prostitution. Bringing the possessive rights and the protective mandate of John Ramon into the vice network, William becomes one of the crime fighters whom the New York Vice Commissioners charge with the job of enforcing "moral integrity" and the "collective will of the community."

The prominent anti–white-slavery crusader Clifford Roe, in one of his chapters on crime-fighting, produces a reformed criminal to bear witness to the potency of Roe's moral authority. Roe embeds the lengthy testimony of reformed trafficker Paul Sinclair in a chapter on his own adventures as Assistant State's Attorney. Jailed and "shamed" by Roe, Sinclair recounts how he was converted by the lawman from a panderer into a crusader against white slavery. Sinclair testifies that Roe, though blander and younger than the conventional patriarch, nonetheless has all the moral force of that traditional figure. The converted criminal repeats the command with which Roe began his reformation: "You must tell me the absolute truth." Expecting to find himself brought to judgment by a "fierce individual with a bristling beard and mustache and horns and raucous voice, etc.," Sinclair is surprised to find that Roe is a "quiet, mild mannered young man very nearly my own age." This modernized disciplinarian, for all his mildness, very easily induces "uneasiness" and shame in the hardened criminal, getting a full confession and a revealing conversion narrative (Roe, 68).

Not only does Sinclair directly attest to Roe's moral efficacy, but by lending his narrative to the chapter that frames and appropriates it, Sinclair adopts a textual position as an object of Roe's reforming power. Most of Roe's chapter 4 is narrated in Sinclair's voice, with Roe introducing Sinclair as the man who, at the lawman's command, gave up a career as "one of the most clever procurers that operated in the United States" (67). By embedding Sinclair's narrative within his own, Roe incorporates, as his own expert knowledge, the special competency of the panderer, and he appropriates the masculine power of this successful trafficker in women.

Roe's textual appropriation of Sinclair mimics white slavery reform's fantasized appropriation of commercialized vice by the family man. And the content of Sinclair's narrative reiterates this fantasy, for Sinclair's criminal career begins, as he recounts, when he marries a white slave and tests her conjugal devotion by requiring her to prostitute herself for his benefit. Sinclair tells how rescuing the young white slave named Grace, to whom he became both husband and pimp, transformed him from a wanderer of the vice districts to a purposeful and powerful possessor of women.

The panderer's story begins when, at age twelve, he is "seized with an uncontrollable desire to travel around." For a time the boy repeatedly runs away from home, sometimes finding a niche as a worker in a brothel and, in his teenage years, becoming the virtual sexual "commodity" of Cora, a prostitute "nearly forty years old." At one point stricken with typhoid, abandoned on the streets, hospitalized, and returned to his mother, Sinclair goes through the kinds of adventures that usually make up the story of the white slave herself (Roe, 69, 70). Sinclair's years as a wanderer also evoke the New York Vice Commission's portrayal of the male brothel patron. Roaming through the city streets, enticed and commodified by the marketeers who exploit him, Sinclair, like the patron of commercialized vice, is "procured" into the brothel.

But Sinclair's story is exemplary of male reempowerment: the period of passive mobility gives way to a more substantial life as a husband and pimp, which begins when, finding himself at a brothel, Sinclair responds to the plight of a sobbing young inmate by rescuing her. He marries the white slave he has freed and, before long, he turns her out on the street to earn money for him (75). Sinclair's wife Grace proves her marital fidelity through her exemplary diligence as a prostitute. "I have never known a woman so faithful, so noble as she. Over this one woman I had the power to make of her good or evil, and I chose the latter" (81).

By imagining that Grace's work as a prostitute reflects her wifely devotion, Sinclair reclaims prostitution for the purpose of the family man. Subject to other men because she is Sinclair's marital slave, Grace shows that commercialization, properly understood (seen, that is, from the dual perspective of the trafficker and the moral reformer), extends womanly dependence and provides wives by making women accessible as prostitutes. In Sinclair's narrative, the commercial explosion of brothels which, the New York Commissioners fear, fragments and appropriates a man's desire, no longer undermines the conjugal prerogative that constitutes the "purpose" of a man in the commercial sphere. Just as Grace's movements through the vice markets reflect Sinclair's power, the proliferating sites of the vice business merely multiply the authority of the husband. The presence of a woman in each place of prostitution, like the presence of a woman in each home, attests to the feminine subordination to men that makes wives and daughters subject to patriarchal authority.

Sinclair achieves white slavery reform's central aim of turning white slaves into family women—and he does so by showing that white slaves are already perfect wives. From Sinclair's point of view, the expanded network of vice is a source of women who are, in effect, already possessions of the family man, for the prostitute proves woman's fitness for wifehood, just as Grace proves her marital devotion by working the streets. All that is needed to realize the wife in the prostitute is the reclamation of the prostitute (as the prostitute) by the family man. With his white slave/wife, Sinclair models the two sides of this reclamation: a trafficker who turns wives into white slaves, he also becomes the reformer who turns white slaves into wives. His dual experience as a trafficker and a husband leads directly to the moral insight—the patriarchal view of women—which grounds his reforming career. Pimping has shown him that women are to be claimed and protected, for every woman is completely subject to the power of a man: "show me a bad woman and I'll show you a man who made her bad. . . . Yes and I'll show you a man who might have saved her" (68).

Clifford Roe, appropriating Sinclair's achievement and agency as he subsumes Sinclair's narrative, models the renovated patriarch who brings into the market the fiercely moral father reincarnated in the bland, middle-class family man. In the story of William Scott, Sutherland depicts how such a family man invades the brothel to find and claim his wife. Taking up the mandate of John Ramon, but translating that traditional patriarchal agency into the Roe-like efficiency of a reformer, William moves through the vice districts to find and marry the woman who is his own.

Making commercialized prostitution serve the male's conjugal prerogative, William exemplifies the crusading reformer of commercialized vice. But, as Estelle's intended husband, William has also played a part in turning wifehood into prostitution. Though it is the phony "husband" who actually sells Estelle to the brothel, William makes no effort to save her. In Sutherland's story, as in the story of Paul Sinclair and his wife Grace, marriage and prostitution are mutually constituted. Before becoming a woman that William can claim as his own, Estelle first passes through the hands of the manifold "commercial interests" who, sharing her value among them, ratify her status as a marketable possession.

The path that finally leads to Estelle takes William through the tortuous realms of the market. Reaching Cleveland with his determination intact, William follows up on the gambler's hint and finds his way to the brothel. Knowing by now just how to ask—and to pay—for a likely woman, "he told [the madam] he would not object if she had one real pretty." Informed of the "fighting girl from the country" being kept upstairs, William cooly pays the madam and heads for the room housing the unnamed woman. "He felt sure that she was Estelle, and that he was going to meet her now. The door was unlocked, and he entered. . . . He turned on the light" and looked into the face of the sleeping woman. "She was Estelle!"

When Estelle was a child, her father brought her out of a deathly coma; when she is awakened again from the sleep that claims her, this time it is William who reconstitutes her in her familial role. Laying his two revolvers on the side table, "for he had resolved to take her out of this place," William awakens Estelle with an announcement of his name and purpose—which comprise her own destiny and identity: "It is William Scott . . . come to take you home." Estelle faints, but he revives her, letting her know that "he determined to steal her out of the house quietly and get away" (95, 96).

Taking Estelle from the white slave house, William obtains his wife through the two methods by which brides are acquired in the system of woman-exchange. Paying the madam for access to the girl upstairs, William buys her; tying bedsheets into a rope on which to carry Estelle out of the brothel window, William captures her. The five dollars William pays the madam is merely a means for securing the exclusive possession that is his right by decree of the patriarch John Ramon. Like the early patriarch described by anthropologists, who institutes the individual right of the husband and father in the new, monog-amous regime, through bride-capture William defeats group marriage and its matrilineal descent to assert the male's individual possession of his woman.[5]

Seeking Estelle, William adheres to the purpose that makes him an agent in the commercial sphere and a sovereign in the domain of his family. As the be-quest of John Ramon, Estelle has not evoked William's possessive agency. Only after she has vanished into the market from which, in obedience to John, William can restore her, does Estelle become recognizable to William as his own wife. It is white slavery—or, more precisely, William's thorough knowl-edge of white slavery—that enables him to locate, recognize, and possess the woman who is his own. Knowing the ways of white slavery means knowing "it was Estelle" even before he sees her. Opening his eyes to the marketing of his own woman, William knows what the brother of Quale's narrative disastrously ignores: the female body which is his to purchase is his to claim, as he expands the domain of patriarchal rights through white slavery's commercialized own-ership of women.

"Our daughters are . . . sold for fabulous sums (a flattering unction this)," scoffs "Madeleine," an ex-prostitute and ex-madam whose 1919 memoir de-flates the myth of white slavery ("Madeleine," 322). But, as we have seen, the imagined value of daughters' bodies, far from "flattering" or enriching the women themselves, destines them to be the familial and commodified property of men. The exchange value of women's bodies accrues, not to the women themselves, but to their individual and collective male possessors. White slavery literature insists on the market value of women in order to propose that ordinary men like William Scott, acting out their traditional, familial relations to women, are comparable in wealth and power to the commercial operators in the booming market.

Nevertheless, the myth does harbor an implicit flattery of women themselves. White slavery may not always ascribe "fabulous" value to women's bodies (Estelle, for example, is sold to the madam for fifty dollars), but it depicts the female body as the fundamental item of trade: the modern city, Roe asserts, can be summed up as a "market in women." As the chief form of wealth held, displayed, circulated, and protected by parents and husbands, woman is also the linchpin of the family's enrichment and empowerment in market society.

In white slavery, woman is both the repository of economic value and the medium of economic and social relations. As Madeleine suggests, this vision seems to argue for a new empowerment and exaltation of woman. In her white slavery book, *A New Conscience and an Ancient Evil,* Jane Addams attempts to flesh out such a view. Woman, Addams argues, embodies value in which all members of society hold a stake; therefore, she must be recognized and honored as a fully entitled member of the public. Though as an individual, a woman cannot claim title to the value that inheres in her exchangeable status, collective womanhood can accede to social power: indeed, Addams urges, this reform must be made in order to protect woman's value. In Addams' vision, the flattery implicit in the market price of the white slave, and the tragic subjection of her commodification, propel the feminist demand for female citizenship.

Conclusion

Victims of Commercialism

In Jane Addams' *A New Conscience and an Ancient Evil,* white slavery reform epitomizes the Progressive Era struggle against economic coercion. Addams writes,

A generation which has gone through so many successive revolts against commercial aggression and lawlessness, will at last lead one more revolt on behalf of the young girls who are the victims of the basest and vilest commercialism (218).

A New Conscience, like all white slavery writing, portrays women as absolutely passive in relation to commercial powers. Whether working, looking for work, shopping, or enjoying recreation, the women Addams writes of require careful and extensive "protection" if they are to be kept from the predations of the traffickers (11).

It seems odd that a feminist—the most prominent feminist of the Progressive Era—would stress woman's passivity and helplessness. But Addams appeals to the myth of woman's inevitable vulnerability to traffickers, not in order to return her to the private realm of the traditional family, but to argue that she must have an equal voice in government. In part, Addams argues from need: woman's vulnerability makes her a deserving object of the protections offered by the "state," which Addams describes, in a classic account of Progressivist reform, as increasingly involved in protective and custodial interventions (93). But Addams also suggests that woman—or, more precisely, woman's body—as the market's primary commodity already endows her with a fully public social and economic role; and this role makes her indispensable to the public sphere. The object of both commercial exploitation and social protection, woman's body, as seen in the pages of *A New Conscience,* is occupied, coerced, defended, and fought over. Not a merely private domain, the female body is the site of contests over power, regulation, and democratic inclusion. In Addams' white slavery writing, the commercialized female body stands for the Progressive Era's public sphere, where the defenders of democracy do battle with the enslaving powers of commercial enterprise.

The previous chapter explored Addams' proposals for reforming the family into a modern protective agency that could oversee the expanded economic lives of its women. In this reformed family, Addams imagines, woman is still understood as a dependent: but now her consumerism brings her, inevitably, in contact with the commercial interests who activate the market value that makes her the treasure of her family. Addams' own life work, however—the settlement "house," which is a socialized version of the family—attests to the inadequacy of the traditional family. The settlement house collectivizes the job of providing for daughters and protecting their value. The reformed state Addams envisages in *A New Conscience* would, similarly, take on the functions no longer performed by the traditional family. White slavery writing, by dramatizing woman's consumerist need and her resulting vulnerability to commercial powers, gives emphasis to Addams' demand that the state bring woman fully into its democratic order as a protected and entitled citizen.

Addams follows other white slavery writers in imagining that woman, when separated from familial providers by her entry into the public sphere, lives out a disastrously intensified consumerist dependency. In an account that is typical of white slavery writing, Reverend Bell describes how procurers ensnare their victims by eliciting the characteristic female desire for expensive pleasures. Once a girl has been separated from her "associates," Bell explains, "then the only thing is to accomplish her ruin by the shortest route." Most often, "promises" of luxurious leisure and provisions—"an easy time . . . money, fine clothes" or a "fake marriage" to a wealthy man—will do the trick. If these "allurements" fail, "harsher methods," including rape, beatings, and drugging, may be brought to bear (57, 58). But in most cases, the activation of women's compelling and irresistible consumerist desire renders them abject slaves.

Addams, who attributes many women's "downfall" to their "love of pleasure [and] desire for finery," joins other white slavery writers in tracing a direct route from female consumerism to forced prostitution (Addams 1912, 59). Like Charlotte Perkins Gilman, who theorizes that woman had evolved to adapt to her status as a consuming dependent, Addams embraces the evolutionary discourse to imagine the consumerist drive as a constituent of female embodiment. In *Women and Economics,* Gilman argues that woman's consumerism is a perversion of true femaleness: adapting to her dependent status, woman leaves behind her "human" love of work and her caretaking instincts, becoming a selfish parasite who cannot mother (see the introduction for a discussion of Gilman's argument).

Addams asserts, however, that the consumerism attributed to women is not unfeminine and selfish; rather, it expresses a maternal orientation toward acquiring, conserving, and nurturing. Addams was the American popularizer of the evolutionary theorist Patrick Geddes. As historian Jill Conway explains, Geddes claims that "sex differences should be viewed as arising from a basic difference in cell metabolism." "At the level of the cell," Geddes teaches, "maleness was characterized by the tendency to dissipate energy, femaleness by the capacity to store or build up energy." Extrapolating from his cellular theory, in which "male aggression aris[es] from the male tendency to dissipate energy and female passivity flow[s] from the complementary tendency to conserve energy sources," Geddes maps out the sexes' "entire evolutionary progression" and role differentiation (Conway, 143, 144).

Geddes explains that every cell in a woman's body tends to store, conserve, and build energy because woman is a nurturer and provider. Addams, in her depictions of consumerist women, adds acquisitiveness to conservation: if woman is subject to an insatiable consumerist desire, it is the maternal drive that propels this economic behavior. In Addams' portrayals of consumerist women, even the eroticized "love of pleasure" and "desire for finery" imputed to the woman who falls into prostitution bespeak the domestic orientation whose endpoint is successful propagation. The need expressed in female consumerism, Addams urges, is not a selfish but a social need: felt on behalf of the offspring who are so essential to the social order, women's consumerist desire seeks to contribute to the perpetuation of society.

This view underlies Addams' account of the working woman who is so vulnerable to white slavers. In *A New Conscience and an Ancient Evil,* white slavery enters the picture to indict the social conditions that have thrust women into self-support without ensuring adequate resources or providing a sheltered sphere for mothering. In her account of the salesgirl who becomes a white slave, Addams imagines the prostitute as a woman who, in being driven to extremes by unfulfilled consumerist need, epitomizes the maternal woman.

Standing Alone in the Midst of Trade

In *A New Conscience and an Ancient Evil,* Addams represents the needy working woman as a department store salesgirl who stands at her post, surrounded by commodities she cannot have.

The department store has brought together, as has never been done before in history, a bewildering mass of delicate and beautiful fabrics, jewelry and household decorations such as women covet. . . . And in the midst of this bulk of desirable possessions is placed an untrained girl, [a member of] . . . the first generation of girls which has stood alone in the midst of trade (65, 66).

Work, asserts Charlotte Perkins Gilman, is the antidote to woman's extreme consumerism and the sexual commodification that accompanies her dependency. Gilman argues that by working, the individual woman escapes her privatized parasitism; and as more women go to work, through evolutionary modification woman will finally shed her specialized adaptation to consumerism, taking her place as a "human" in the great collective endeavor that is production and exchange (Gilman, 21).

In the years following 1899, when Gilman published her attack on the sexuo-economic market, women entered the workplace in impressive numbers (Gilman, 44). "Self-supporting girls are increasing steadily in number each decade," Addams remarks (56).[1] But the "self-supporting" woman depicted in *A New Conscience* has not left her dependency behind. Passively "placed" yet dutifully upright among the "bewildering mass" of commodities that threatens engulfment, the "untrained" feminine body of the "first-generation" girl so abruptly detached from traditional female dependency is not adapted to the demands of her economic situation.

Addams suggests that the historical dislocation encountered by the working woman is not the transition to female self-support but the overwhelming immediacy and profusion of commodities—commodities "never before . . . in history" brought together—to which she is exposed. Standing among these goods, whose abundance mocks her relative poverty, the salesgirl suffers chronic desire and deprivation. The requirements of the job, Addams imagines, intensify the salesgirl's bodily and emotional need. Though she may be "faint for want of food," the salesgirl "may not sit down" or eat. As uncared for as she is unprovisioned, she suffers "lonely" longings on the job that requires her to "smile affably" at throngs of strangers, reflecting their prospective fulfillment in a contemplated purchase that is always beyond her reach (65, 66).

Work intensifies need; and for Addams, as for other white slavery writers, what women need most is clothing and the enticing "fabrics" from which it is made. The circumstance which, above all others, typifies the saleswoman's suffering is her deprived relationship to the abundant yet inaccessible clothing that surrounds her. The saleswoman, Addams imagines, may herself be "without adequate clothing" while she "stands in an emporium where it is piled about her, literally as high as her head." Though it seems unlikely that an inadequately clothed saleswoman could remain at her post, her imagined shortage of sartorial possessions reflects the exploitative nature of her employment: required to sell clothes, she is prohibited from buying them. The scarcity she endures is a relative, perpetual lack imaged by the body that stands, dwarfed and depleted, maintaining its post by the towering piles of clothing that must be sold.

Like the saleswoman's need for food, sympathy, and rest, her need for clothing is elicited by her work. If, as Addams often reminds her reader, women go to work to be able to buy clothes—clothes their meager wages barely provide—women need clothes to be able to go to work (76). Simply by working, the woman experiences the inadequacy of her wardrobe and is put in perpetual need of more clothing. Like the white slave subjected to the "clothing switch" ploy, the salesgirl needs clothing because her body is publicly accessible—she stands all day in a public place—while she makes her body accessible because only in this way can she earn money to fulfill the demand of her job: the demand that she have more clothing.

The impossible burdens and grinding deprivations of this posture of self-support, Addams suggests, finally bring the salesgirl to the edge of an ultrafeminizing swoon. Standing precariously "in the midst of trade," the salesgirl, when she loses her footing, will "faint" into a passive, sexualized body as she slips into the virtual flood of commodities to be conflated with the other "desirable possessions." "Easy of access" in the department store, the working woman is herself a commodity. Her body, projected in the "filmy fabrics" that elicit her sensuality and in the piles of clothing as high as her head, and surrounded by the household goods that emphasize female functions, is offered to the public in the simulated home that is the department store.

While the girl yearns for a "future lover" who will provide a real home, it is the white slave procurer who approaches her with promises. "It is perhaps in the department store more than anywhere else that every possible weakness in a girl is detected and traded upon," Addams warns. "The . . . man who approaches her there acting upon the knowledge of this inner life of hers in order to despoil her" knows that her consumerism is fueled by the maternal drive. "Because she is young and feminine, her mind secretly dwells upon a future lover, upon a home, adorned with the most enticing of the household goods about her, upon a child dressed in the filmy fabrics she tenderly touches" (66).

Through her fantasized possession of commodities, the working woman imagines herself a domestic woman. In the fulfilled consumerism of her fantasy life, the deprivation and exhaustion associated with work is compensated by an eroticized plenitude associated with motherhood, wifehood, and domesticity. The saleswoman's job may leave her fainting at her post, but in her "secret" corporeal dream-life she is a swooning mother experiencing, perhaps, the luxurious languidness of pregnancy as she anticipates the baby by going over the nursery items.

In the eyes of the knowing slave procurer, the woman relates to consumer goods with all the involuntary tropism of a maternal body bonding with its offspring. Instinctual in its affinity for the "filmy fabrics" that appeal to the erotic drive and to the exquisite protectiveness of a doting maternalism, the woman's body "tenderly touches" the luxurious commodities that bespeak the fulfillments of wifehood and maternity (and may also express, through identification with the dependent infant, the mother's own need for support and nurture).

If the duties of the workplace impose impossible demands on the salesgirl's body, her "inner life" (and its fantasized context, the home) expresses the determinations of female embodiment that render the working woman a "victim of commercialism." The young working woman is exposed to a public sphere that at once promises and denies the fulfillment of her instinctual needs: for the department store, with its profusion of "household goods," forcibly elicits her dream of domesticity, and the procurer enters the salesgirl's dream merely by approaching her in this site where the objects of her instinctual desires are at once offered and withheld.

The man who knows the salesgirl's "inner life" takes possession of her by promising the goods that represent wifehood and maternity—"enticing" goods such as the "filmy fabrics" she desires. In the presence of the white slave trader, the woman's secret dreams are made to effect a clothing switch: the fantasized exchange of her working clothes for "filmy fabrics" becomes a real exchange in which she dons the "flimsy finery" of the boudoir costume and thereby gives purer expression to the bodily accessibility which, Addams stresses, is the basic requirement of her job. In a sense, the white slave procurer is redundant; the salesgirl standing erect in the department store is already like the white slave who, forced to remain in the domestic version of the market that is the white slave "house," must make herself available to the public. The salesgirl's bosses, like the white slave keepers, ensure her accessibility by inducing a perpetual state of active desire—desire for the goods and, even more deeply (as the white slaver understands), desire for herself as the possessor of the goods. The insatiable and exploitable desire of the consuming woman, Addams shows, expresses the feminine drive toward wifehood and maternity; and, as white slavery proves, the working woman is the consuming woman brought to the extremity of need.

Social Housekeeping

The white slave procurer enters the department store to dramatize Addams' thesis that work ("self-support"), by exposing the woman to the public sphere of commodity capitalism, enforces her status as a commodity. Thus Addams refutes Gilman's argument that, in getting out of the home and into the work-place, woman will be freed from the determinations of her sexual embodiment. Addams uses white slavery and its discourse of female consumerism to portray the workplace as another site at which woman lives out her status as a depen-dent and a sexual chattel.

But if the conditions of the market mean that woman's innate nurturing in-stincts are publicly exposed and exploited, this public exposure in itself grounds the reforms Addams calls for. As historian Aileen S. Kraditor explains, Progres-sivism's main feminist reform ideology, social housekeeping, points out that women's traditional roles and functions are no longer confined to the private home, but instead must be seen within an expanded social and political con-text; and in her use of white slavery, Addams places woman, in her embodied femaleness, within the economic sphere.

Kraditor explains that Addams, as the Progressive Era's best exponent of so-cial housekeeping, argues that under modern conditions a woman can no longer fulfill her domestic and motherly duties without having a hand in "pub-lic affairs lying quite outside of her immediate household." Addams gives "ideal expression," writes Kraditor, to the argument that the newly socialized context of woman's traditional, domestic labor means that women must be em-powered legislatively, politically, and economically so that they can effectively carry out their womanly duties. This may involve helping build up a "code of legislation" to regulate public sanitation, commodity safety, conditions of pro-duction, and so on (Kraditor, 67ff.). For example, in the 1909 essay, "Why Women Should Vote," Addams argues that "a woman cannot care properly for her family if she has no voice in making the laws and electing the officials that determine whether her home has pure water, fresh food, proper sanitation, and adequate police protection; municipal government is housekeeping on a large scale."[2]

Social housekeeping assumes a gendered division of labor that aligns domes-tic tasks with the assumed functional attributes of the female body: provision-ing, conserving, protecting. In a 1906 *Chicago Sunday Record-Herald* newspaper essay, Addams appeals to the embodied status of this domesticity, translated to the public sphere through female consumerism, as the ground for universal womanhood suffrage. The franchise, writes Addams, must be extended to all women regardless of education or class because "those matters in which woman's judgement is most needed are far too primitive and basic to be largely influenced by what we call education" (quoted in Kraditor, 143). The adjectives "primi-tive" and "basic" modify not only the "matters" having to do with basic bodily needs, but also the "woman's judgement" with which any and all women are endowed. Such woman's judgment, Addams insists, is innate and inborn in every woman: it is a condition of female embodiment.

The matters on which female embodiment qualifies every woman to judge are consumerist matters: pure food and water for one's family, good public sanitation to protect the family against disease. In social housekeeping, the embodied consumerism of women, already put in a social context by its elicitation and exploitation in the market, confers a universal public entitlement on all women. Regardless (Addams insists) of educational status, social particularity, class, or (she implies) race, the public identity of woman as understood through social housekeeping is universal to the gender. As a member of this generic gender group, then, every woman is entitled to the municipal vote.

Six years after publishing this argument, Addams makes use of the myth of white slavery to enlarge the claims of her social housekeeping proposals. In *A New Conscience* she calls for full universal female suffrage, wages for housework, minimum wage, labor protection laws, consumer protection legislation, and other economic and social protections and entitlements (see chapter 3, "Amelioration of Economic Conditions"). If the municipal context of housewifely functions justifies municipal suffrage, the vast and permeating context that is the market in women expands the social context of the female body to the limits of the public sphere. And in this context white slavery portrays, the female body is indistinguishable and universal. A generic entity created through the social order, the woman whose identity inheres in the commodified status of the female body is a gendered corollary of the abstracted "individual" endowed with citizenship in the liberal public sphere.[3]

When the white slave procurer of Addams' department store scene comprehends the saleswoman's deepest yearnings and uses them to lure her, through consumerist desire, into the market, he demonstrates the fungibility of all female bodies. Not only does he understand her at the deepest level of her subjectivity through her generic female attributes, but his understanding of her is indifferent to her current status. She is a worker who desires to be a consumer; but to herself (as he understands), she is a mother and a wife and therefore (to him) a prostitute. Mother, wife, worker, prostitute, to the superior understanding of the white slave trader, are aspects of the female body which, no matter what its current status, is always the same in its availability to be accessed in the public sphere.

In adopting white slavery, then, Addams establishes both the public context and the fungibility of all female bodies and all functions attributed to that body. And if all aspects and functions of female embodiment are indifferently public, all females are, by an extension of the logic of social housekeeping, indifferently entitled. Within the discourse of white slavery, this fungibility means that the housewife, as a public body, is as valuable a commodity as the prostitute— and, indeed, Addams makes just this argument. "Society," she complains, "ventures to capitalize a virtuous girl at much less than one who has yielded to temptation" (here she relies on the report of the Chicago Vice Commission, which estimates the Chicago prostitute's average income, "capitalized" or aggregated over twenty years, at $22,000). Addams wants to endow the "virtuous girl" with her value in exchange derived from the market in women.

The capitalized value of the average working girl is six thousand dollars, as she ordinarily earns six dollars a week, which is three hundred dollars a year, or five per cent on that sum. A girl who sells drinks in a disreputable saloon, earning . . . twenty-one dollars a week, is capitalized at a value of twenty-two thousand dollars (Chicago Vice Commission Report, cited in *A New Conscience*, 57–58).

But the Vice Commission misrepresents the true value of the "honest" woman, for it "does not record the economic value of the many later years in which the honest girl will live as wife and mother, in contrast to the premature death of the woman in the illicit trade" (57). These years of wifehood and motherhood should be compensated at their true economic value, Addams urges; and that value is to be determined "in contrast" to—in comparison to, by the standard of—the market value of the body of the prostitute. The domestic woman's entitlement to wages, then, is not figured or claimed by labor or reproduction, nor is it earned by her expertise as a consumer. Rather, her economic entitlement reflects the equivalence in context and value of all female bodies within the market in women. The body of the white slave stands as the universalizing form or equivalent of all female bodies. By virtue of white slavery's demonstration that prostitution expresses female consumerism, and Addams' extrapolation of female consumerism as a public form of domesticity, Addams asserts a single standard of value for women as female bodies.

The exchange value of the housewife's female body grounds her claim on economic and social entitlements. But, as Addams' drama of the working woman makes clear, these are no different from the entitlements earned by any and every woman: for women have economic value, not as laborers, but as female bodies. This universalization not only opens up economic entitlements, but, in the expanding public sphere of Progressivism, it also fully *politicizes* the female body—or, more precisely, what it politicizes is the body in its abstracted public identity as a sexual commodity. The management of woman's sexual accessibility, Addams argues, has become a public concern. Recently "socialized" along with other "instruments of social control" ("Law, Publicity, Litera-ture, Education and Religion"), "chastity"—the obverse of sexual accessibil-ity—"which has hitherto been a matter of individual opinion, comes to be re-garded . . . as a great basic requirement which society has learned to demand." No longer the interest and responsibility of the private sphere, chastity reflects the "conviction of social responsibility."

Addams writes:

A shifting to social grounds is . . . obviously taking place in regard to the chastity of women. Formerly all that the best woman possessed was a negative chastity which had been carefully guarded by her parents and duennas. . . . As woman, however, fulfills her civic obligations while still guarding her chastity, she will be in a position as never be-fore to uphold the "single standard," demanding that men shall add the personal virtues to their performance of public duties. (*A New Conscience*, 210–11)

If the new woman citizen will consolidate her citizenship by eradicating prosti-tution, it is, paradoxically, the very existence of widespread prostitution itself that ratifies female citizenship. The private sphere having ceased to operate as her context (as witness the massive, syndicated sexual trafficking in women's bodies), woman lacks any provisional shelter or retreat from the public sphere. The prostitute lives out the cost to woman of her public sexual embodiment, going public not only in her body but again in the widely disseminated narra-tives (such as Addams' drama of the saleswoman's painful erectness and pa-thetic fall) that recount her exploitation. Addams transforms this lack of shel-ter from the public into the possession of a lever of public entitlement, a claim on the public to respond to and compensate her accessibility. But in order for the public—which includes women—to make this response by eradicating prostitution, woman must continue to do the "job" of living out her accessibil-ity. Remaining erect at her public post, she must endure public exposure with-out falling into commodification, repeatedly fulfilling her "civic obligations while still guarding her chastity." This job earns her, not a new, self-supporting public presence, but the privilege of never having to support herself again, as the new public sphere woman helps construct becomes the protector of woman, sheltering her from the exploitative commodification of her public presence as a female body.[4]

The Female Self and Citizen

The Progressive Era . . . witnessed the birth of the modern American state. That birth . . . owed more than has been commonly conceded to the women who,

entering upon the national arena, called for a very different kind of state than
that envisioned by most male reformers.   —Rosenberg, 38

Addams' woman citizen, unlike the classical citizen of the liberal sphere, is
neither disembodied nor neuter. Endowed with needs and drives that are both
particular (to her gender) and universalizing (to her gender), she is defined by
the sexual specificity of her female body while she is abstracted from the particular, material body she inhabits. The differences of race, ethnicity, and class
that were so prominent in the Progressive Era city are elided by the "solidarity
of human interest" Addams sees in the female instincts shared among all
women—particularly the instincts to nurture, to regulate, and to protect, which
in Addams' brand of social housekeeping would bring a socialized version of
domestic propriety to the public sphere.

Just as Addams' Progressivist proposals imagine a new, gendered kind of
citizen, they also imagine a new public sphere. Revising the public sphere of
liberalism scholars trace to the differentiation of private from public, Addams,
like other Progressives, undoes the separation between public and private.[5] Describing, in her white slavery writing, how the newly commercialized ownership of woman commodifies her maternal, sexual, and domestic attributes, Addams uses the discourse of the exchange of woman to explain that the ownership
of woman gives rise to the market and the civil sphere. The fight against white
slavery, Addams urges, requires that the public's stake in woman's value, and
the public stature of exchanged woman, be acknowledged. The new public
sphere, reformed by the inclusion of woman, will be shaped by her instinctual
altruism and her procreative orientation—not merely through influence or
volunteerism, but through her contribution as a citizen.

In Addams' rhetoric, woman's status as commodity makes her a citizen. In
the fictions of Chopin and Wharton, the selfhood and social identity to which
the heroines aspire, like the citizenship Addams considers, are accessible only
through woman's status in exchange. This is a status which, while endowing
woman with value, denies her the right to own that value. As commodities in
a consumerist market, the women imagined by these authors have access to
selfhood and identity only through the mediation of owners and exchangers.
And entwined with woman's commodity status is the consumerist role in
which, the authors imagine—and white slavery writing, in particular, dramatizes—woman's traditional familial dependence and subjection extend into the
public context of the market, making her the dependent possession of many
providers.

Like male possessive selfhood—and like liberal individualism and citizenship, its civil and political corollaries—the selfhood and citizenship of the woman of exchange exist in reference to ownership rights. But these texts suggest that the feminism we have inherited from the turn of the century, the individualist feminism that defines women as selves and political equals, is distinctly gendered. Leaving her familial status, entering the liberal order, woman takes her place not as a neuter, disembodied individual, a possessive self, or an equal, but as the commodified and consumerist woman of exchange.

Introduction

1. Elizabeth Ammons was the first to read texts of this period through the exchange of women. Ammons defines Wharton's *The House of Mirth* as an "economic novel" that critiques the traffic in women. Ammons sees the novel as an exposé of the American leisure class culture of consumption and the marriage market, and she applies Thorstein Veblen's analysis of this marriage system to discuss woman's roles (Ammons 1980, 25, 26–29). In an article on *The House of Mirth,* Wai-Chee Dimock writes that the principle of exchange governs social relations in the novel, but parity in exchange is a fiction; only Lily Bart actually pays up, thus exposing the inequalities in exchange and bringing her own punishment (Dimock 1985). In her recent book, *Bordering on the Body,* Laura Doyle explores a related anthropological/race narrative she calls "the racial group mother." Doyle explains how "boundaries" between racialized groups are marked by the body of woman. In contrast to the emphasis of this study, Doyle concentrates on the reproductive iconography of woman as group marker and maker. See especially pp. 21ff.

2. "The exchange of woman," which Lévi-Strauss puts at the junction of nature and culture, was described by late-nineteenth-century anthropological writers—notably McLennan, Maine, Morgan, and Lubbock—who traced society's evolution through the stages of savagery and barbarism to its culmination in civilization. In human prehistory, their theory asserts, social disorganization is tempered by the fundamental and (in their view) naturally given differentiation of gender. Based on this difference, social groups create a variety of institutions (all featuring some element of dominance) as society moves through successive stages characterized by varying familial and material relations structured through kinship and marriage. The great culmination of social evolution comes when group marriage (which relies on matrilineal descent) is succeeded by the institutions of private property and male-dominated monogamy—that is, the ownership of woman by man, which supports the institution

of private property in general. In the twentieth century, Claude Lévi-Strauss worked this anthropological theory into a structural analysis of culture, writing that all marriage is structured as the exchange of woman and that "exchange . . . provides the means of binding men together, and of superimposing upon the natural links of kinship the . . . artificial links . . . of alliance governed by rule" (Lévi-Strauss, 480).

In her influential feminist reappraisal of Lévi-Strauss, Gayle Rubin describes the exchange of woman as key to the ways in which, on several levels, "sex and gender are organized and produced" (Rubin, 177).

3. For a discussion of Gilman's use of Spencer's anthropological evolutionism and Social Darwinism, see Magner. Both Bell's white slavery collection *Fighting the Traffic* and Regan's *Crimes of the White Slavers and the Results* open with historical overviews, reaching back to ancient times, of the sexual commodification of woman. *Woman in the Past, Present and Future,* German Socialist August Bebel's synthesis of Romantic historicism and ethnological findings, was an influential source of such accounts.

4. Locke, *Two Treatises of Government* II, Section 27; MacPherson.

5. Political theorist Carole Pateman argues that the civil sphere of liberalism inhabited by the liberal individual comes about only through an occluded "sexual contract" by which men accede to individualism through their mastery of women in the private sphere (Pateman 1988, 3–5, 112).

6. On women's employment, also see Matthaei. The "New Woman," historian Carroll Smith-Rosenberg writes, emerged in the 1880s and 1890s "rejecting conventional female roles and asserting their right to a career, to a public voice, to visible power. [New Women] laid claim to the rights and privileges customarily accorded bourgeois men." The group includes not only prominent women reformers and professionals, but "a host of less visible women who worked . . . provided these women lived economically and socially autonomous lives" (Smith-Rosenberg, 176–77).

7. Lévi-Strauss, 233, 265; for restricted exchange, see 146ff.

8. Rachel Bowlby, writing on the late-nineteenth-century identification of women as consumers, remarks on the mutually constitutive female identities of consumer and commodity: "it was above all to women that the new commerce made its appeal, urging and inviting them to procure its luxurious benefits and purchase sexually attractive images for themselves" (Bowlby, 10). On consumer culture, also see Seltzer and Ewen.

9. This "elaborate" network of overlapping markets through which a white slave passes is described in detail in (The) Research Committee of the Committee of Fourteen's *Social Evil,* in Kauffman's white slavery novel, *The House of Bondage,* and in Quale's "Thrilling Stories."

10. As part of his discussion of the fictional creation of value in turn-of-the-century culture, and of that culture's fascination with the relation between representation and its substrate, Walter Benn Michaels suggests that hysteria (a term that derives from the Greek *hystera,* meaning womb), a disease of self-alienation attributed to women and imagined to be grounded in female biology, appealed to its inventors as an analogy of the market self constructed through difference from the self (Michaels 1987, 4ff.). For a discussion of the metaphysical nature of value and its relation to the form in which it "comes into the world," see Marx, Part I, Commodities and Money, esp. Section 3, "The Form of Value or Exchange Value" (54ff.).

11. For a discussion of Gilman's racist views in general, see Lanser.

12. Analogizing woman and language, Lévi-Strauss identifies woman as both a sign and a value because she brings the extrasocial into society through sex, love, and reproduction. Thus woman protects symbolic systems from the entropy in which signs would lose their meaning. In their gloss of Lévi-Strauss, Helene Cixous and Catherine Clément comment on the cultural myth in which woman "preserves the . . . intrinsic value of origin" understood as the primitive, the natural, and the biological as opposed to the social (Lévi-Strauss, 496; Cixous and Clément, 28, 29).

13. As historian Aileen S. Kraditor explains, social housekeeping argued that women's domestic and motherly duties required them to take a hand in "public affairs" (Kraditor, 67ff.).

14. Denise Riley writes of the "changing relations of 'woman' and her variants to the concept of a general humanity" (Riley, 8–9). Catherine MacKinnon opposes the fight for "equality," arguing that gender "equality" under the law "substantively embraces masculinity, the male standard for men, and applies it to women" with prejudicial effect (MacKinnon, 71).

Chapter 1. Exchange Value and the Female Self in The Awakening

1. Stanton, 249. In this speech Stanton gave in 1892 on the occasion of her resignation from the presidency of the suffrage movement, woman's entitlement to a full complement of civil rights stems from her aloneness and existential "self-sovereignty." The female self Stanton evokes is an absolute, possessive self whose metaphorical situation is that of a lone individual "on a solitary island" or "launched on the sea of life." *The Awakening*'s original title was *A Solitary Soul;* and in Chopin's novel, as in Stanton's rhetoric, female subjectivity and women's rights are grounded in absolute and irreducible selfhood. For an account of early English feminists' commitment to absolute selfhood, see Gallagher 1988.

2. In her essay on race colonialism in *The Awakening*, Michele A. Birnbaum writes that in her "sexual liberation," Edna's emerging self-definition as a white woman is brought into being by nonwhite "others." In similar fashion, Edna's voluntary motherhood emerges in reference to the compulsory mothering performed by the black women Chopin places around the margins of Edna's social vista. The "quadroon" nanny who tends the Pontellier children by "following them with little quick steps, having assumed a fictitious animation and alacrity for the occasion" while "a fruit vender was crying his wares in the street" figures a woman who, like Adèle, assumes the mothering role under the compunctions of an economy. While Adèle's "madonna" is imbued with aesthetic value, the mothering tasks of the quadroon are part of the market scene of the street; and the quadroon brings the chattel status and compulsory maternity of recently emancipated black women into the "relations" within which Chopin's heroine is beginning to define herself (104).

3. Edna's insistence on a sense of privacy may be part of the "rightful subjectivity" Wai Chee Dimock delineates. Dimock argues that Edna makes property out of her "own thoughts and emotions" and "turn[s] her very subjectivity into a kind of ownable object." On the ground of this property right, Edna then tries to secure for herself extended "rights" (Dimock 1990, 30).

Chapter 2. Edith Wharton and the Problem of the Woman Author

1. Catherine Gallagher writes of the association between authorship and prostitution in nineteenth-century British writers, especially Eliot. Through the identification of authorship with exchange rather than production, the author comes to be seen as a nonreproducing woman (Gallagher 1986). For Wharton, however, production is itself problematic, and value is determined by relations in the sphere of exchange—particularly at the level of consumption.

2. Gilbert and Gubar argue that in the turn-of-the-century literary market, the struggle between the sexes took the form of a struggle by woman authors to take over masculine literary authority and thus attain "autonomy"—and this autonomy is dramatized in *The Touchstone*, in which Aubyn is a founder of a female literary authority and a precursor of female literary autonomy, and, as such, lives on even after death. The novella shows, they argue, that the woman author can rise above the romantic rejection her autonomy risks. In my reading it is feminization, passivity, and the failure of the sphere of private erotic appropriation, rather than the escape from gender and autonomy, which constitute Wharton's vision (admittedly ironic) of Aubyn's success and fame as an author. See *No Man's Land*, 189–94.

Chapter 3. Lily Bart at the Point of "Modification"

1. Veblen, 61. Discussing the aestheticization of the body through "fashion" and "incapacity," Seltzer quotes and paraphrases Veblen's *Theory of the Leisure Class* (Seltzer, 123).

2. Elizabeth Ammons calls *The House of Mirth* an "economic novel"—a genre she says was popular at the turn of the century. Ammons uses Veblen's analysis of this marriage system to discuss woman's roles in *The House of Mirth* which, she explains, is an exposé of the marriage economy in the American leisure class (1980, 25, 26–29).

3. Margaret McDowell argues that Lily's unfitness stems from the transition in which new money is coming into the American leisure class, bringing about a changed social and economic environment to which Lily is unable to adapt. In a similar vein, Elaine Showalter sees Wharton as "killing off" the "lady novelist" in herself when she kills the "perfect lady" who is Lily in favor of the destruction of the old leisure class and the coming of the New Woman.

4. Darwin, *The Descent of Man,* 2nd ed., 597 n. 33, quoted in Richards, 69, 70, 71. Maureen Howard argues that Wharton, through her "playful . . . use of the evolutionary metaphor in her fiction," distanced herself from the theories of Darwin and Spencer and, in particular, from the popularized adoption of these theories as "meliorist." Howard writes of Wharton's own "concern with heritage, its imprint or possible erasure," describing the "mixed" novelistic "modes" Wharton uses in *The House of Mirth,* with its melodrama, manners, and brave defiance of "heritage" (145, 146, 155). The use of Darwin by another woman novelist is the topic of Bert Bender's reading of *The Awakening* as "an extended and darkening meditation on the meaning of human life and love in the light of Darwinian thought." Bender's argument that Edna Pontellier, in thinking she is discovering herself, confronts instead her determination by "blood," suggests that Chopin and Wharton both create fictional heroines whose gendered status is imposed on them in multiple ways (459, 470).

5. Darwin, explains Cynthia Eagle Russett, concluded that "far from conferring an advantage in the struggle for existence, some traits [gained by sexual selection] appeared downright detrimental. . . . Many male birds found their movements actually impeded by the beautiful plumage with which they charmed their mates" (79).

6. Darwin, *The Descent of Man,* 222, 510; quoted in Russett, 79 and 220 n. 3.

7. Selden's "republic of the Spirit" is a consumerist utopia in which the subjectivity of the consumer, through his desire and disavowal, allows him to transcend the body to attain "freedom from material accident." Understood as what

Lily suspects it to be—a "close corporation"—this republic exists in privileged relation to women who, whether in excessive consumption or the struggle to live, remain collapsed with the corporeal that lends its form to the disembodied collectivity of the *res* (the real, feminine) remade (as and in) public (73).

8. A Tanagra statuette or figurine is a small terra-cotta statuette often representing people of fashion discovered in ancient tombs—principally in the Boetian town of Tanagra—and much prized by collectors in the late nineteenth century.

9. "Evolution is an integration of matter and concomitant dissipation of motion; during which the matter passes from an indefinite, incoherent homogeneity to a definite, coherent heterogeneity" (Spencer, *First Principles,* 1862, quoted in Gilman 1988, 223).

10. In Ruth Bernard Yeazell's Veblen-inspired reading of the novel, this moment dramatizes "The Conspicuous Wasting of Lily Bart." Other critical speculations about this moment are found in Hochman, esp. 148. Also see Dimock 1985.

11. Mrs. Haffen's "red fists" are reminiscent of the nonwhite, "sallow" shopgirls at the novel's opening. Wharton's portrayal of mass readers collapses class and racial discourses to show how a "specialized" white woman like Lily is constantly collapsed back into the raw material of the market.

12. Claire Colquitt argues that Lily, whose expression of desire is painfully repressed, identifies with the powerful expressiveness of "the writer of the letters." "After all," Colquitt writes, "Wharton constructs her plot so that the letters Lily buys are addressed to the man she herself desires and composed by the woman whose expressive sexual force and social financial power simultaneously repel and intrigue the virginal heroine. . . . In some way Lily also desires 'to be the writer of the letters'" (155).

13. Susan Gubar reads this blankness as Lily's need and opportunity to turn her body into a text. The "word" she transmits to Selden is her own dead body, finally converted into a "script" (251). Judith Fryer considers the *tableau vivant* scene the "core" of this novel which, as she writes, is about "the making up and presenting of the woman's body." Like Gubar, Fryer considers Lily an "author" who uses the "text" of her body. The action depicted in the Reynolds portrait—Joanna Leigh writing her future husband's name on a tree—underlines Lily's authorial intent.

14. Walter Benn Michaels argues that Wharton presents writing as the epitome of an activity which, by incurring the separation of intention and action, helps constitute the difference from the self that makes for selfhood (makes the self "interesting") in a risk-loving culture of speculation (Michaels 1987, 240ff.).

Judith Fryer, in contrast, sees Lily as depicting the writing woman's intention to be the author of herself, with her body serving as her text.

15. Martha Banta explains that the relation between the material object and its meaning expressed in the notion of the "type" was a question particularly associated with women, who were almost obsessively depicted as "types" in American pictorial art around the turn of the century—a development assisted by the perfection of techniques for black-and-white reproduction such as zinc cuts and photoengraving. In nineteenth-century photography, Miles Orvell explains, the "type" was "metonymic": it was a means "whereby the pictured subject, with all its concrete particularity, *stands for* a more general class of like subjects. The individuality of the subject is thus presented on its own terms while it simultaneously serves the larger purpose of representing a general category" (88).

16. Though the pleasure of *tableau vivant* does depend on the confounding of the natural and the artificial, it is not exactly an example of what Michaels calls "the love of natural things that resemble artificial ones" (1987, 159ff.). Nonetheless, like illusionistic art, it affords to the spectator what Seltzer calls "the certainty of being a subject." In Seltzer's extrapolation of this logic, the difference between brain and mind becomes the difference between eye and gaze. The observer who experiences the capacity of his own "gaze" to create illusion and thus to make representation possible knows the "certainty of being a subject" (Seltzer quotes Lacan; 141–42).

17. White, in the pictorial language familiar to Sir Joshua Reynolds, signifies the universal. In his article on Reynolds, John Barrell explains that Reynolds' artistic practice was informed by a discourse in which pictorial language was valued for its universality (as distinguished from its capacity to evoke particularity). This was part of the evolving discourse of English nationalism in which color and ornament, when associated with the local or customary, mitigated the civic universalism on which nationality identity is built (Barrell, 166, 169). Elizabeth Ammons also cites Barrell in this connection (1995, 79 and 85 n. 25).

Chapter 4. "No Girl Is Safe!"

1. Another comparable white slavery compendium is Bell, *Fighting the Traffic*. For an account of the scope of white slavery literature, see Connelly, 114–15. Reginald Kauffman's 1910 white slavery novel, *The House of Bondage*, was a best-seller. Its dramatization as one of the many white slavery plays that were drawing large audiences is discussed in an April 1914 edition of *The Journal of the Society of Sanitary and Moral Prophylaxis* (vol. 5, no. 2). The movie, vari-

ously called *A Traffic in Souls* and *The Traffic in Souls,* was produced in 1913 by "two of the best filmmakers at Universal Studios, George Loane Tucker and Walter McNamara," according to Sloan. For a discussion of this and other white slavery films, see Sloan, 78–98.

2. Frederick Grittner traces the genre back through nineteenth-century "captivity literature" (15–32). Similarly, Connelly presses the comparison between the Indian captivity narrative and white slave narrative (117, 118). On the captivity narrative in general, see David Brion Davis, "Some Themes of Counter-Subversion: An Analysis of Anti-Masonic, Anti-Catholic, and Anti-Mormon Literature, *Mississippi Valley Historical Review* 47, no. 2 (Sept. 1960): 205–24. Larry Hartsfield writes of the developing professionalization, in post–Civil War America, of crime, crime fighting, and crime writing. He describes the symbiosis among the professional thief, the detective, the police officer, and the crime author (5ff.). Laura Hapke examines the premise of antivice writing that prostitutes are innocent victims. In her "Conventions of Denial" (3) and *Girls Who Went Wrong* (chapters 1 and 5), Hapke links the conventional construction of women as sexual innocents to earlier antivice genres such as the "mysteries and miseries of the city" genre. For examples of that genre, see Pember, Crapsey, and Talmage. For a discussion of the working-class politics of the "mysteries and miseries" genre, especially in the works of George Lippard, see Denning, chapter 6. Castiglia, in his recent *Bound and Determined,* writes of the women who, as readers and writers, made the captivity narrative a popular genre. This genre's popularity among women, he argues, reflects the woman reader's fantasied escape from the confinements of home and a restrictive culture (4); yet he also argues that accounts of imprisonment are disguised protests against domestic confinement (179).

3. In April 1907, Turner published "The City of Chicago" in *McClure's.* This article exposed the businesses dealing in liquor and an organized commercial prostitution enterprise involving a "sort of loosely organized association" of foreign men, mostly "Russian Jews" (George Kibbe Turner, "The City of Chicago" in *McClure's* April 1907, quoted in Cordasco, 18). On the European anti–white slavery movement, see Cordasco, 4ff. White slavery agitation began in Britain. See, for example, William Stead's "The Maiden Tribute of Modern Babylon," *Pall Mall Gazette,* 1885, for an early expose of domestic white slavery (cited in Rosen, 116). Frederick Grittner explains that the idea that the prostitutes were slaves was a powerful tool for vice reform in British social purity campaigns of the 1870s and 1880s (6) and useful to movements such as Josephine Butler's resistance to the Contagious Disease Acts of the 1860s (a crusade against state legitimation of prostitution) (Grittner, 40). Grittner's source is Bristow, *Prostitu-*

tion and Prejudice. Bristow traces this use of "white slavery" back to 1839 in England as a reference to Jewish trafficking in women (36). On prostitution reform in Victorian England, see Walkowitz. For France, see Harsin.

4. "Over a thousand white slavers were prosecuted between 1910 and 1918 under the Mann Act and—a less reliable statistic—about seven percent of some six thousand prostitutes interviewed in one study listed white slavery or 'extreme coercion' as causes," writes Laura Hapke (1989, 118). Hapke's note 19 cites Rosen, 155, 124. Also see Connelly, 128; Cordasco, 33. Five years after passage of the Mann Act, women were explicitly included as criminally responsible under the Act. In *United States v. Holte* (1915), the U.S. Supreme Court "held that a woman who was a willing participant in her own interstate travel for the purposes of prostitution could be convicted under the [Mann] Act" (Connelly, 129).

5. For example, the so-called Rockefeller report, which resulted from a 1910 New York Grand Jury whose foreman was John D. Rockefeller Jr., reported that the traffic in women was apparently "carried on by individuals"; the Grand Jury found "no evidence of the existence in the County of New York of any organization or organizations . . . engaged as such in the traffic in women . . . nor have we found evidence of an organized traffic in women for immoral purposes" (*Presentment of the Additional Grand Jury for the January Term of the Court of General Sessions in the County of New York, in the matter of the investigation as to the alleged existence . . . of an organized traffic in women for immoral purposes,* filed June 19, 1910; reprinted in Kauffman, 469–80). Historian Ruth Rosen suspects that a certain amount of forced prostitution actually existed; Rosen cites Kathleen Barry's assertion that a significant component of the prostitution trade involved forced prostitution. According to Rosen, however, most prostitutes entered the profession as a voluntary, although often an unwanted and desperate, measure (Rosen, 112–35). See Barry for an account of the historical and contemporary (1980s) forcible traffic in women (esp. 32–38). A recent book investigating the contemporary international sex traffic is Altink, *Stolen Lives.* Altink writes about global trafficking in women who are transported out of their impoverished homelands to take jobs abroad. Having no money or passports, these women, the author claims, are basically trapped into prostitution or domestic slavery by an "international crime network" of "trafficking gangs."

6. *Current Opinion* 40 (August 1913): 113–14. Quoted in Cordasco, 38.

7. The American Social History Project, in *Who Built America?,* ed. Stephen Brier, vol. 2, describes the techniques for business monopolization perfected by emerging industrialists during the closing decades of the nineteenth century. Control of the market was achieved through mergers and takeovers of compet-

ing businesses (horizontal integration)—this is one way Rockefeller built Standard Oil. Carnegie used vertical integration, acquiring sources of raw material, buying up the means of distribution as well as owning and controlling production. On the actions taken to reform big business, especially the trust-busting of Roosevelt's administration, and the increasing government regulation of business in the Progressive Era, see *Who Built America?*, 208ff.; Peter N. Carroll and David Noble, *The Free and the Unfree: A New History of the United States* (New York: Penguin, 1977), 188ff. On the Sherman Anti-Trust Act and the Interstate Commerce Commission in particular, see Kenneth C. Davis, *Don't Know Much about History: Everything You Need to Know about American History but Never Learned* (New York: Avon Books, 1990). The 1901 merger of competing steel companies into U.S. Steel made it the first multibillion-dollar corporation in the world. This was an event Rosalind Rosenberg believes helped launch the era of Progressive reform (1992, 37).

8. Bingham had been removed from his post in 1909 as New York City Police Commissioner for too forcefully fighting the organized crime gangs that flourished under the Tammany administration; his removal was to propitiate the powerful Sullivan clan (Cordasco, 22, 28–29).

9. "Pianola" was a brand name owned by Aeolian Company for a particular device that converted a piano to a player piano. Later, the term became a generic term for a player piano. The original pianola was a pneumatic device installed alongside or inside a piano to convert it to a player piano. It was powered by foot pedals (Jim Cather, "What is a Pianola?" Online posting, Article 23963, Newsgroup: rec.music.makers.piano., 5 July 1996). In white slavery literature, the (generic) pianola is associated with cheap entertainment; for example, one of the notorious procuring sites, the ice-cream parlor, is described in a white slavery book as containing "gaudy signs," "an old mechanical piano," and a Greek proprietor (Regan, 159).

10. For an account of Tarbell's Standard Oil Series, and her mixture of admiration and accusation, see Ohmann, 279, 281. See 280ff. for Tarbell's treatment of the Standard Oil Trust's vertical and horizontal integration.

11. White slavery writer Regan reports that young Rockefeller was known to have spent $100,000 "and much of his valuable time" in getting a New York State statute amendment passed under which white slavers could be prosecuted (138).

12. The pimping system, writes historian Ruth Rosen, came about largely in response to mid-nineteenth-century criminalization, when the new "criminal status" of prostitution meant that "control of prostitution shifted from madams and prostitutes themselves to pimps and organized crime syndicates."

And, forced by criminalization out of many city neighborhoods into "red light districts," the business appeared, as well as functioned, as a consolidated, organized form of commerce. Rosen writes, "the professionalization of the police helped to create the red-light districts that sprang up in many American cities during the second half of the nineteenth century" (4, 5). Conspicuousness was heightened, as well, by the practice of brothel-raiding (made easy by localization), which drove prostitutes out into the streets (xii, xviiff., 4, 5). See also Hartsfield, 5ff., and Connelly, 198.

13. Quale's "wires" envisage the market's metaphysical network of demand by evoking the rapidly expanding electronic communications network. These new communications were featured in the plot of the 1913 white slave film, *The Traffic in Souls,* in which an in-house telephone allows the crooked city father to run his white slave ring. But technology, being neutral, comes to the aid of the crime fighters as well: a dictaphone, cleverly used by the boss's plucky secretary, enables the police to uncover the operation.

14. Laura Doyle points out the early-twentieth-century association between racial "otherness" (nonwhiteness) and archaism. Doyle's recent *Bordering on the Body* is a study of modernist responses to the anthropological discourse. Doyle writes of the ways in which, whether being contained or exchanged by their group, women are used to mark the "group boundaries" within what Doyle calls "the kin-patriarchal" or "racial patriarchal economy" (16, 27). For commentary on the racial "otherness" of the "new immigrant" in early-twentieth-century sociological and popular discourse, see Stocking, 50. On the "monogenist" view of racial difference as an evolutionary difference, see ibid., 38, 40, 63ff., 76. Anne McClintock discusses the association made in bourgeois discourse between prostitutes and Africans as sexually "atavistic and regressive" in their transgressions of the "boundaries" dividing the public and private spheres. Because they "transgressed the middle-class boundary between private and public, paid work and unpaid work," prostitutes were figured as "'white Negroes' inhabiting anachronistic space" (McClintock, 1995, 56). For a discussion of race, prostitution, and the law, see McClintock, "Screwing the System: Sexwork, Race and the Law," *Boundary II* 19, 2 (Summer 1992): 70–95.

15. For a discussion of the general derivation of the modern idea of the nation from the race, see Ernest Renan, "What Is a Nation?" in Bhaba, 8–22. Laura Doyle describes the late-eighteenth-century Anglo-European concept of the national ideal as a racial ideal (40ff.). For a discussion of anti- and post-Reconstruction white racism in Progressive nationalism, see Michaels 1995, esp. 140. Gwendolyn Mink argues that Progressive Era feminist reforms were based on the normalization of the citizen as racially white. See Mink, 92–122.

16. Ruth Frankenberg discusses the racialization of the European immigrant, including Jews, Irish, Italians, and Celts (esp. 275 n. 16). Susan S. Lanser writes of turn-of-the-century anti-Asian and anti-Semitic racist sentiments in which Jews are classed as "yellow."

17. Roe, *Panders and Their White Slaves* (New York: Fleming H. Revell, 1910), 211–12, cited in Cordasco, 34.

18. Frankenberg, 1. Also see Toni Morrison, *Playing in the Dark: Whiteness and the Literary Imagination* (Cambridge, Mass.: Harvard University Press, 1992), esp. xii.

19. In 1899, British social purity reformers successfully organized the First International Congress for the Suppression of the White Slave Traffic. Bristow writes: "the original aim of the white-slaver crusade was to prevent the movement of women across international borders for purposes of vice" (172). Donna Guy and Frederick Grittner both describe the subsequent international meetings and agreements of 1902 and 1910 in which thirteen nations agreed to establish international agencies to monitor, and finally to prosecute, persons engaged in "importing or exporting 'women and girls destined for an immoral life'" (Guy, 207; see also Grittner, 39).

20. Sexual purity was considered "white" (the White Cross was the social purity rescue department the WCTU, adopting the name of its British model, formed in 1885; the slogan "a white life for two" launched an 1890s campaign for the single sexual standard (Grittner, 48).

21. Particularly as a European traveler, Wharton would have been familiar with some of the specific white slavery conventions. White slavery was current in Britain and on the Continent from the 1870s.

22. Elizabeth Ammons argues that Wharton's gender and race agendas are in "fierce . . . conflict" (78). But Lily's whiteness, as manifested in the tableau, is a constituting attribute of the gender status that makes possible her moment of artistic triumph, as well as, in Wharton's "tragic" plot, dooming her to debasement and sacrifice. See Ammons 1995, 68–86 (78).

23. While white slavery narratives excuse their depictions of women's debasement by appealing to the urgency of social reform, Wharton claims to be using the genre for aesthetic effect: her dialectic of debasement, and the loss it makes manifest through the reader's imaginative powers, are aesthetic and moral ends in themselves. But Wharton's narrative was nearly as popular as white slavery writing, and her best-selling status might indicate that her fiction shares the qualities that made white slavery writing so popular.

24. Catherine Gallagher explains that during this period, political radicals "used the word 'slavery' to describe disenfranchisement and equated freedom

with manhood suffrage and with the freedom to assemble and to vote" (6, 7). In 1823, anti-abolitionist William Cobbett, whose focus was increasingly to attack industrial capitalism, popularized the use of "white slaves" to identify England's factory workers in an open letter to a leading abolitionist. While Cobbett popularized the term "white slave," the use of the metaphor of enslavement to characterize the situation of industrial workers was widely used in attacks on industrial capitalism and the condition of wage laborers in Britain in the 1820s, 1830s, and 1840s (9–10).

25. Bristow writes that "white slavery was first used in the context of prostitution in the 1830s by Dr. Michael Ryan, a London reformer," who identified Jews as the "white-slave dealers" who "trepan young girls into their dens of iniquity, [to] sell them to vile debaucheries." "Finally in the 1870s white slavery and its continental counterparts, traite des blanches and Madchenhandel, became firmly associated with prostitution." Bristow points out that "slavery" is not always used in this context to mean entrapment and coercion, but rather sometimes refers to state-regulated vice and the curtailment of civil freedoms of prostitutes (Bristow, 35, 36; on oppressive regulation, see Guy, 205).

26. For a discussion of the abstracted, "disembodied" citizen of classical liberalism, see Pateman 1989, 3–4.

27. Donna Guy discusses both strategies in her essay focusing on the Argentinean response to the international anti–white slave negotiations. At a time of imperialist jockeyings, during which large numbers of European women migrated to new world lands where their nationalities and civil rights were ambiguously defined, the expansion of citizenship rights to women was a way of "defining one nation's sovereignty against another's." Guy writes that Argentina responded to allegations of harboring a white slave trade by extending nationality, civil rights, and, eventually, full citizenship rights to women, taking women/prostitutes out of the category of "slaves" (201).

28. White, in the pictorial language familiar to Sir Joshua Reynolds, signifies the universal. See the preceding chapter for a discussion on John Barrell's essay on the Reynoldsian pictorial language that associated whiteness with universality (as distinguished from its capacity to evoke particularity) in the context of the evolving discourse of English nationalism (Barrell, esp. 166, 169).

Chapter 5. Papa's Girl

1. This reading of the Commissioners' report follows Carole Pateman's critique of prostitution. Pateman argues that prostitution, by ensuring that "men can buy 'the sex act,'" enables men to exercise their patriarchal right. Prostitu-

tion, in this view, upholds the "original sexual contract" of which the "marriage contract" is an important part (1988, 199).

2. Pateman argues that the subordination of women through this "contractual" entry into the "private" sphere of the family constitutes men, in contrast, as free civil individuals who enjoy the putative benefits of public contractual relations. But Pateman's general thesis—that the original contract, "the sexual contract," reveals contract in general to be a tool of subjection—argues that this privilege to which men accede through their relations to women, though it allows men to dominate women, does not make them free (7, 14ff.).

3. "The College Woman and the Family Claim," *The Commons* (September 1898): 3–7; quoted in Rosenberg 1992, 3.

4. Larry Hartsfield describes the post–Civil War emerging "professionalization" of criminals, law enforcement agents, and crime authors. Professionalization means "emphasis on formal training, special skills, and esoteric knowledge as a way of defining the self and its place in a fluid society." Hartsfield traces the symbiosis between criminals and their prosecutors in this process of professional self-definition and the narrative genres related to it (5).

5. McLennan was the first anthropologist of exchange to elaborate on bride-capture. In the transition from group marriage to individual marriage, McLennan theorized, capture was the means by which wives were acquired and valued as individual possessions (*Primitive Marriage,* 228, cited in Fee, 93).

Conclusion

1. Meyerowitz cites census figures that show that "from 1880–1930 the female labor force [in the United States] rose from 2.6 million to 10.8 million." Her source is U.S. Bureau of the Census Tenth Census 1880, Population, vol. 1, 712 and idem, *Fifteenth Census, Population,* vol. 3, pt. 1, 12 (Meyerowitz, *Women Adrift,* xvii)

2. Addams, "Why Women Should Vote," 1909; quoted in Kraditor, 69. Imagining the effects of woman's political contribution, Addams follows Geddes, who writes that women, as they bring to bear their temperamental qualities on the conduct and evolution of human society, will redirect social change toward "a cooperative society, provided that it preserved separate sex roles appropriate to male and female temperaments." But Addams imagines that women's impact would spread beyond national borders to affect the course of world history. In *Democracy and Social Ethics* (1902) and *New Ideals of Peace* (1907), she argues that the innate social conscience and nonbelligerence of women will reform the industrial rapacity and political bellicosity of the modern world (Conway, 142, 151).

3. Disembodiment, according to a feminist critical analysis of liberalism recently articulated by Carole Pateman (among others), is a precondition of accession to the status of the universalized "citizen" or abstracted individual in the civil sphere. Women, lacking the privilege of disembodiment, are barred from full participation in the public sphere of the liberal state: "women, womanhood, and women's bodies represent the private; they represent all that is excluded from the public sphere" (Patemen 1989, 3–4). For further analysis of the implied masculinity of the "neuter" disembodied citizen, see Berlant, 112, 113.

4. A judicial ratification of women's accession to social responsibility for their own sexual value came five years after passage of the Mann Act when, in *United States v. Holte* (1915), the U.S. Supreme Court ruled that "a woman who was a willing participant in her own interstate travel for the purposes of prostitution could be convicted under the [Mann] Act" (cited in Connelly, 129). Addams is imagining a polity based on a kind of social contract that begins, for women, not with the Rousseauian surrender of freedom for protection, but with an input of sexual value; but because this value is not simply "natural" like freedom, but already a construct of the public sphere, woman is included in the polity through ratification or acknowledgment of her established and ongoing contribution.

5. "'Civil Society' is distinguished from other forms of social order by the separation of the private from the public sphere; civil society is divided into two opposing realms" (Pateman 1988, 11). For an account of the protectionist and domestic ideals of Progressivism—and of women's crucial part in its development—see Paula Baker, "The Domestication of Politics: Woman and American Political Society, 1780–1920," in DuBois and Ruiz, 66–91 (see esp. 77ff. and 84 n. 5 on "policy" and "government"). See also Rosenberg, 37–39.

Primary Sources

Addams, Jane. 1910. *The Spirit of Youth and the City Streets.* New York: Macmillan.
———. 1912. *A New Conscience and an Ancient Evil.* New York: Macmillan.
———. [1910] 1960. *Twenty Years at Hull House.* New York: Signet.
Bachofen, Johann J. 1967. *Myth, Religion, and Mother Right: Selected Writings of J. J. Bachofen.* Trans. Ralph Mannheim. Princeton, N.J.: Bollinger Foundation.
Bebel, August. N.d. *Woman in the Past, Present and Future.* Trans. H. B. Adams Walther. London: Wm. Reeves.
Bell, Ernest. 1910. *Fighting the Traffic in Young Girls or War on the White Slave Trade.* New York: N.p.
Bingham, (Gen.) Theodore A. 1911. *The Girl That Disappears: The Real Facts about the White Slave Traffic.* Boston: Gorham Press.
Chandler, Lucinda. 1871. "Motherhood." *Woodhull and Claflin's Weekly,* 13 May.
Chopin, Kate. [1899] 1976. *The Awakening.* Ed. Margaret Culley. New York: Norton.
Cooper, Frederic Taber. 1901. Review of *Love Letters of an Englishwoman. Bookman* 41 (February): 560–61.
Crapsey, Edward. 1872. *The Nether Side of New York.* New York: Sheldon Publishing Co.
Darwin, Charles. [1871] 1974. *The Descent of Man, and Selection in Relation to Sex.* 2nd ed. Chicago: Rand McNally.
DuBois, Ellen Carol, ed. 1981. *Elizabeth Cady Stanton, Susan B. Anthony: Correspondence, Writing, Speeches.* New York: Schocken.
Engels, Frederick. [1884] 1942. *The Origin of the Family, Private Property, and the State in Light of the Researches of Lewis H. Morgan.* New York: International Publishers.
Geddes, Patrick, and J. Arthur Thompson. 1889. *The Evolution of Sex.* New York: Humboldt.
Gilman, Charlotte Perkins. 1899. "What Work Is." *Cosmopolitan* 27: 678–82.
———. [1898] 1988. *Women and Economics: A Study of the Economic Relation between Men and Women as a Factor in Social Evolution.* New York: Harper and Row.
Goldman, Emma. [1917] 1970. "The Traffic in Women." In *The Traffic in Women and Other Essays on Feminism,* edited by Alix Kates Shulman. Albion, Calif.: Times Change Press.
James, Henry. [1884] 1980. "The Art of Fiction." In *Anthology of American Literature,* edited by George McMichael. New York: Macmillan. 2:713–26.
Kauffman, Reginald Wright. 1910. *The House of Bondage.* New York: Grosset & Dunlap.

Lehman, Rev. F. M. 1910. *The White Slave Hell or With Christ at Midnight in the Slums of Chicago*. Slum Data Furnished by Rev. N. K. Clarkson. Chicago and Boston: Christian Witness Company.

Lewis, Dido. 1881. *Chastity, or Our Secret Sins*. New York: Canfield.

Locke, John. [1772] 1967. *Two Treatises of Government*. Ed. P. Laslett. 2nd ed. Cambridge: Cambridge University Press. II, Section 27.

MacKirdy, Mrs. Archibald (Olive Christian Malvery), and W. N. Willis. 1909. *The White Slave Market*. London: Stanley Paul & Co.

"Madeleine." 1919. *Madeleine: An Autobiography*. New York: Harper Bros.

Marx, Karl. 1906. *Capital: A Critique of Political Economy*. New York: Modern Library.

McLennan, John. 1865. *Primitive Marriage: An Inquiry into the Origins of the Form of Capture in Marriage Ceremonies*. Edinburgh: A & C Black.

Morgan, Lewis Henry. [1877–78] 1964. *Ancient Society*. Ed. Leslie A. White. Cambridge, Mass.: Harvard University Press.

Pember, Arthur. 1874. *Mysteries and Miseries of the Great Metropolis*. New York: D. Appleton and Co.

Quale, Dr. C. C. 1912. "Thrilling Stories of Eye-Opener on White Slavery." Chicago: Hamming Publishing Co.

Regan, John, comp. 1912. *Crimes of the White Slavers and the Results*. Chicago: J. Regan & Co.

(The) Research Committee of the Committee of Fourteen for the Suppression of the "Raines Law Hotels" in New York City. 1910. *The Social Evil in New York City*. New York: Andrew H. Kellogg Co.

Roe, Clifford. 1911. *The Great War on White Slavery, or Fighting for the Protection of Our Girls*. Chicago: B. S. Steadwell.

Schreiner, Olive. 1911. *Woman and Labor*. New York: Frederick A. Stokes.

Spencer, Herbert. 1880. *First Principles*. 4th ed. New York: P. F. Collier.

———. 1880. *Principles of Sociology*. New York: D. Appleton.

Stanton, Elizabeth Cady. [1892] 1981. "The Solitude of Self." In *Elizabeth Cady Stanton, Susan B. Anthony: Correspondence, Writing, Speeches*, edited by Ellen Carol DuBois. New York: Schocken.

Stead, William. 1885. "The Maiden Tribute of Modern Babylon." *Pall Mall Gazette*.

Talmage, Reverend Thomas DeWitt. 1878. *The Night Sides of City Life*. Philadelphia: National Pub. Co.

Tarbell, Ida. 1912. *The Business of Being a Woman*. New York: Macmillan.

———. 1925. *The History of the Standard Oil Company*. New York: Macmillan.

Veblen, Thorstein. [1899] 1953. *The Theory of the Leisure Class: An Economic Study of Institutions*. New York: Macmillan.

Wharton, Edith. 1901. "More Love Letters of an Englishwoman." *Bookman* 41 (February): 562–66.

———. 1902. "George Eliot [by Leslie Stephen]." *Bookman* 15 (May): 247–51.

———. [1900] 1970. *The Touchstone*. In *Madame de Treymes and Three Novellas*. New York: Macmillan. 3–101.

———. [1905] 1964. *The House of Mirth*. New York: Signet.

———. 1903. "The Vice of Reading." *North American Review* 187 (October): 513–21.

———. [1924] 1966. *The Writing of Fiction*. New York: Octagon Books.

————. [1933] 1983. *A Backward Glance.* New York: Charles Scribner's Sons.

————. 1968. *The Collected Short Stories.* Vol. 2. Ed. R. W. B. Lewis. New York: Charles Scribner's Sons.

Wharton, Edith, and Ogden Codman, Jr. 1897. *The Decoration of Houses.* New York: Charles Scribner's Sons.

Woods, Robert A., and Albert J. Kennedy, eds. 1913. *Young Working Girls: A Summary of Evidence from Two Thousand Social Workers.* Boston: Houghton Mifflin.

Wright, Henry C. 1853. *Marriage and Parentage.* Boston: Marsh.

Secondary Sources

Altink, Sietske. 1996. *Stolen Lives: Trading Women into Sex and Slavery.* Binghamton, N.Y.: Haworth Press.

American Social History Project, The. 1992. *Who Built America? Working People and the Nation's Economy, Politics, Culture, and Society.* Vol. 2, *From the Gilded Age to the Present.* Ed. Stephen Brier. New York: Pantheon Books.

Ammons, Elizabeth. 1980. *Edith Wharton's Argument with America.* Athens: University of Georgia Press.

————. 1992. *Conflicting Stories: American Women Writers at the Turn into the Twentieth Century.* New York and Oxford: Oxford University Press.

————. 1995. "Edith Wharton and Race." In *The Cambridge Companion to Edith Wharton,* edited by Millicent Bell. Cambridge and New York: Cambridge University Press. 68–86.

Armstrong, Nancy. 1987. *Desire and Domestic Fiction: A Political History of the Novel.* New York: Oxford University Press.

Baker, Paula. 1990. "The Domestication of Politics: Women and American Political Society, 1780–1920." In *Unequal Sisters: A Multi-Cultural Reader in U.S. Women's History,* edited by Ellen Carol DuBois and Vicki L. Ruiz. New York and London: Routledge. 66–91.

Banta, Martha. 1987. *Imagining American Women: Ideas and Ideals in Cultural History.* New York: Columbia University Press.

Barrell, John. 1991. "Sir Joshua Reynolds and the Englishness of English Art." In *Nation and Narration,* edited by Homi K. Bhaba. London and New York: Routledge. 154–76.

Barry, Kathleen. 1984. *Female Sexual Slavery.* New York: New York University Press.

Bell, Millicent, ed. 1995. *The Cambridge Companion to Edith Wharton.* Cambridge and New York: Cambridge University Press.

Bender, Bert. 1991. "The Teeth of Desire: *The Awakening* and *The Descent of Man.*" *American Literature* 63, no. 3 (September): 459–73.

Berlant, Lauren. 1991. "National Brands/National Body." In *Comparative American Identities: Race, Sex and Nationality in the Modern Text,* edited by Hortense J. Spillers. Series: Essays from the English Institute. New York: Routledge and Kegan Paul. 110–40.

Bhaba, Homi K., ed. 1991. *Nation and Narration.* London and New York: Routledge.

Birnbaum, Michele A. 1995. "'Alien Hands': Kate Chopin and the Colonization of Race." In *Subjects and Citizens: Nation, Race and Gender from Oroonoko to Anita Hill,* edited by Michael Moon and Cathy N. Davidson. Durham, N.C.: Duke University Press. 319–41.

Bledstein, Burton. 1978. *The Culture of Professionalism: The Middle Class and the Development of Higher Education in America.* New York: Norton.

Bowlby, Rachel. 1985. *Just Looking: Consumer Culture in Dreiser, Gissing, and Zola.* New York: Methuen.

Bristow, Edward J. 1982. *Prostitution and Prejudice: The Jewish Fight Against White Slavery, 1870–1939.* Oxford: Clarendon Press.

Brown, Gillian. 1990. *Domestic Individualism: Imagining Self in Nineteenth-Century America.* Berkeley: University of California Press.

Castiglia, Christopher. 1996. *Bound and Determined: Captivity, Culture-Crossing, and White Womanhood from Mary Rowlandson to Patty Hearst.* Chicago: University of Chicago Press.

Cixous, Hélène, and Catherine Clément. 1986. *The Newly Born Woman.* Trans. Betsy Wing. Minneapolis: University of Minnesota Press.

Colquitt, Clare. 1991. "Succumbing to the 'Literary Style.'" *Women's Studies* 20, no. 2: 153–62.

Connelly, Mark. 1980. *The Response to Prostitution in the Progressive Era.* Chapel Hill: University of North Carolina Press.

Conway, Jill. 1972. "Stereotypes of Femininity in a Theory of Sexual Evolution." In *Suffer and Be Still,* edited by Martha Vicinus. Bloomington: Indiana University Press. 140–54.

Cordasco, Francesco, with Thomas Monroe Pitkin. 1981. *The White Slave Trade and the Immigrants.* Detroit: Blaine Ethridge.

Culver, Stuart. 1984. "Representing the Author: Henry James, Intellectual Property and the Work of Writing." In *Henry James: Fiction as History,* edited by Ian Bell. London: Vision Press. 114–36.

Denning, Michael. 1987. *Mechanic Accents: Dime Novels and Working-Class Culture in America.* London and New York: Verso.

Dimock, Wai Chee. 1985. "Debasing Exchange: Edith Wharton's *The House of Mirth.*" *PMLA* 100, no. 5 (October): 783–92.

———. 1990. "Rightful Subjectivity." *Yale Journal of Criticism* 4, no. 1 (Fall): 25–51.

Dobb, Maurice. 1973. *Theories of Value and Distribution.* Cambridge: Cambridge University Press.

Doyle, Laura. 1994. *Bordering on the Body: The Racial Matrix of Modern Fiction and Culture.* New York: Oxford University Press.

Eagleton, Terry. 1982. *The Rape of Clarissa: Writing, Sexuality and Class Struggle in Samuel Richardson.* Oxford: Basil Blackwell.

Ewen, Stuart. 1976. *Captains of Consciousness: Advertising and the Social Roots of the Consumer Culture.* New York: McGraw-Hill.

Fee, Elizabeth. 1974. "The Sexual Politics of Victorian Social Anthropology." In *Clio's Consciousness Raised: New Perspectives on the History of Women,* edited by Mary S. Hartman and Lois Banner. New York: Harper and Row. 86–102.

Foucault, Michel. 1979. *Discipline and Punish: The Birth of the Prison.* New York: Vintage Books.

Frankel, Noralee, and Nancy S. Dye, eds. 1991. *Gender, Class, Race, and Reform in the Progressive Era.* Lexington: University Press of Kentucky.

Frankenberg, Ruth. 1993. *White Women, Race Matters: The Social Construction of Whiteness.* Minneapolis: University of Minnesota Press.

Fryer, Judith. 1992. "Reading Mrs. Lloyd." In *Edith Wharton: New Critical Essays,* edited by Alfred Bendixen and Annette Zilversmit. New York: Garland. 27–56.

Gallagher, Catherine. 1985. *The Industrial Reformation of English Fiction, 1832–1967.* Chicago and London: University of Chicago Press.

———. 1986. "George Eliot and *Daniel Deronda:* The Prostitute and the Jewish Question." In *Sex, Politics, and Science in the Nineteenth-Century Novel: Selected Papers from the English Institute, 1983–84,* edited by Ruth Yeazell. Baltimore: Johns Hopkins University Press. 39–62.

———. 1988. "Embracing the Absolute: The Politics of the Female Subject in Seventeenth-Century England." *Genders* 1 (Spring): 24–39.

Gilbert, Sandra M., and Susan Gubar. 1987. *No Man's Land: The Place of the Woman Writer in the Twentieth Century.* Vol. 1, *The War of the Words.* New Haven, Conn.: Yale University Press.

Gordon, Linda. 1976. *Woman's Body, Woman's Right: A Social History of Birth Control in America.* New York: Grossman.

———., ed. 1990. *Women, the State, and Welfare.* Madison: University of Wisconsin Press.

Grittner, Frederick. 1990. *White Slavery: Myth, Ideology, and American Law.* New York: Garland.

Gubar, Susan. 1981. "'The Blank Page' and the Issues of Female Creativity." *Critical Inquiry* 8 (Winter): 251.

Guy, Donna J. 1992. "'White Slavery,' Citizenship and Nationality in Argentina." In *Nationalisms and Sexualities,* edited by Andrew Parker et al. New York: Routledge. 201–17

Hapke, Laura. 1982. "Conventions of Denial: Prostitution in the Late Nineteenth-Century American Anti-Vice Narrative." *Michigan Occasional Paper* 24 (Winter): 3.

———. 1989. *Girls Who Went Wrong: Prostitutes in American Fiction, 1885–1917.* Bowling Green, Ohio: Bowling Green State University Press.

Harsin, Jill. 1985. *Policing Prostitution in Nineteenth-Century Paris.* Princeton, N.J.: Princeton University Press.

Hartsfield, Larry. 1985. *The American Response to Professional Crime, 1870–1917.* Westport, Conn.: Greenwood Press.

Hartsock, Nancy. 1983. *Money, Sex and Power: Toward a Feminist Historical Materialism.* New York: Longman.

Hayden, Dolores. 1981. *The Grand Domestic Revolution: A History of Feminist Designs for American Homes, Neighborhoods, and Cities.* Cambridge, Mass.: MIT Press.

Hochman, Barbara. 1991. "The Rewards of Representation: Edith Wharton, Lily Bart and the Writer/Reader Interchange." *Novel* 24 (Winter): 147–61.

Howard, Maureen. 1995. "The Bachelor and the Baby." In *The Cambridge Companion to Edith Wharton,* edited by Millicent Bell. Cambridge: Cambridge University Press. 137–56.

Irigaray, Luce. 1974. "Le marché des femmes." *Speculum de l'autre femme.* Paris: Editions de Minuit.

———. 1977. "Si les marchandises parlaient." *Ce sex qui n'en est pas un.* Paris: Editions de Minuit.

Kaplan, Amy. 1988. *The Social Construction of American Realism.* Chicago and London: University of Chicago Press.

Koven, Seth, and Sonya Michel, eds. 1993. *Mothers of a New World: Maternalist Politics and the Origins of Welfare States.* New York and London: Routledge.

Kraditor, Aileen S. 1981. *The Ideas of the Woman Suffrage Movement, 1890–1920.* New York: Norton.

Lanser, Susan S. 1989. "'The Yellow Wallpaper' and the Politics of Color in America." *Feminist Studies* 15, no. 30 (Fall): 415–41.

Larsen, Magali Sarfatt. 1977. *The Rise of Professionalism.* Berkeley: University of California Press.

Leach, William. 1981. *True Love and Perfect Union: The Feminist Reform of Sex and Society.* London: Routledge and Kegan Paul.

Lévi-Strauss, Claude. 1967. *The Elementary Structures of Kinship.* Rev. ed. Boston: Beacon Press.

MacKinnon, Catherine A. 1987. *Feminism Unmodified: Discourses on Life and Law.* Cambridge, Mass.: Harvard University Press.

MacPherson, C. B. 1962. *The Political Theory of Possessive Individualism: Hobbes to Locke.* Oxford: Clarendon Press.

Magner, Lois N. 1992. "Darwinism and the Woman Question: The Evolving Views of Charlotte Perkins Gilman." In *Critical Essays on Charlotte Perkins Gilman,* edited by Joanne B. Karpinski. New York: G. K. Hall. 115–28.

Matthaei, Julie A. 1982. *An Economic History of Women in America: Women's Work, the Sexual Division of Labor, and the Development of Capitalism.* New York: Schocken.

McClintock, Anne. 1995. *Imperial Leather: Race, Gender and Sexuality in the Colonial Context.* New York and London: Routledge.

McDowell, Margaret. 1976. *Edith Wharton.* Boston: Twayne.

Meyerowitz, Joanne J. 1988. *Women Adrift: Independent Wage Earners in Chicago, 1880–1930.* Chicago: University of Chicago Press.

Michaels, Walter Benn. 1987. *The Gold Standard and the Logic of Naturalism.* Berkeley: University of California Press.

———. 1995. *Our America: Nativism, Modernism, and Pluralism.* Durham, N.C., and London: Duke University Press.

Mink, Gwendolyn. 1990. "The Lady and the Tramp: Gender, Race, and the Origins of the American Welfare State." In *Women, the State, and Welfare,* edited by Linda Gordon. Madison: University of Wisconsin Press. 92–122.

Ohmann, Richard. 1996. *Selling Culture: Magazines, Markets, and Class at the Turn of the Century.* London and New York: Verso.

Orvell, Miles. 1989. *The Real Thing: Imitation and Authenticity in American Culture, 1880–1940.* Chapel Hill and London: University of North Carolina Press.

Parker, Andrew, et al., eds. 1992. *Nationalisms and Sexualities.* New York: Routledge.

Pateman, Carole. 1988. *The Sexual Contract.* Stanford, Calif.: Stanford University Press.

———. 1989. *The Disorder of Women.* Stanford, Calif.: Stanford University Press.

Peiss, Kathy. 1986. *Cheap Amusements: Working Women and Leisure in Turn-of-the-Century New York.* Philadelphia: Temple University Press.

Richards, Evelleen. 1983. "Darwin and the Descent of Woman." In *The Wider Domain of Evolutionary Thought,* edited by David Oldroyd and Ian Langham. Dordrecht, Holland: D. Reidel Publishing Co. 57–112.

Riley, Denise. 1988. *"Am I That Name?" Feminism and the Category of "Women" in History.* Minneapolis: University of Minnesota Press.

Rosen, Ruth. 1982. *The Lost Sisterhood: Prostitution in America, 1900–1918.* Baltimore: Johns Hopkins University Press.

Rosenberg, Rosalind. 1982. *Beyond Separate Spheres: Intellectual Roots of Modern Feminism.* New Haven, Conn.: Yale University Press.

———. 1992. *Divided Lives: American Women in the Twentieth Century.* New York: Hill and Wang.

Rubin, Gayle. 1975. "The Traffic in Women." In *Toward an Anthropology of Women,* edited by Rayna R. Reiter. New York: Monthly Review Press. 157–210.

Russett, Cynthia Eagle. 1989. *Sexual Science: The Victorian Construction of Womanhood.* Cambridge, Mass.: Harvard University Press.

Sacks, Karen. 1975. "Engels Revisited: Women, the Organization of Production, and Private Property." In *Toward an Anthropology of Women.* Ed. Rayna R. Reiter. New York: Monthly Review Press. 211–34.

Sanchez-Eppler, Karen. 1993. *Touching Liberty: Abolition, Feminism, and the Politics of the Body.* Berkeley: University of California Press.

Sedgwick, Eve Kosofsky. 1985. *Between Men: English Literature and Male Homosocial Desire.* New York: Columbia University Press.

Seltzer, Mark. 1992. *Bodies and Machines.* New York and London: Routledge.

Shell, Marc. 1978. *The Economy of Literature.* Baltimore: Johns Hopkins University Press.

Showalter, Elaine. 1985. "The Death of the Lady (Novelist): Wharton's *House of Mirth.*" *Representations* 9 (Winter).

Sloan, Kay. 1988. *The Loud Silents: Origins of the Social Problem Film.* Urbana and Chicago: University of Illinois Press.

Smith-Rosenberg, Carroll. 1985. *Disorderly Conduct: Visions of Gender in Victorian America.* New York: Oxford University Press.

Stocking, George W. 1968. *Race, Culture and Evolution: Essays in the History of Anthropology.* Chicago: University of Chicago Press.

Stoler, Ann Laura. 1995. *Race and the Education of Desire: Foucault's History of Sexuality and the Colonial Order of Things.* Durham, N.C., and London: Duke University Press.

Walkowitz, Judith K. 1980. *Prostitution and Victorian Society: Women, Class, and the State.* Cambridge: Cambridge University Press.

Welter, Barbara. 1976. *Dimity Convictions.* Athens: Ohio University Press.

Wiegman, Robyn. 1995. *American Anatomies: Theorizing Race and Gender.* Durham, N.C., and London: Duke University Press.

Yeazell, Ruth Bernard. 1992. "The Conspicuous Wasting of Lily Bart." *English Literary History* 59, no. 3: 713–34.

Addams, Jane, 2, 7, 16, 86, 111–15, 127–38, 154 n. 2; *A New Conscience and an Ancient Evil*, 127–31, 135–36; *New Ideals of Peace*, 154 n. 2

aesthetics, 44, 64, 65; and architecture, 64; of the body, 54–60, 63–64, 70–71; and male preferences, 64; value, 54, 59. *See also* art; beauty

alien, 94; and exchange, 83. *See also* race; whiteness

Altink, Sietske, 149 n. 5

America. *See* United States

Amhigh, Mrs. Ophelia (superintendant), 82–84, 91

Ammons, Elizabeth, 141 n. 1, 145 n. 2, 147 n. 17

anthropological theory, 3, 4, 8, 90, 126, 151 n. 14. *See also* barbarism

Armstrong, Nancy, 6

Arobin (gambler), 32–34

art, 62; and visual appropriation, 24

"Art of Fiction, The" (James), 37

artifacts, 61

artist, the, 61–62

Asiatic, 95

Aubyn, Margaret (author), 42, 48–52, 62, 66

Australia, 94

author, 37–40; and authorial self, 38–39, 43; as commodity, 2, 40, 43; and consumption, 38; and market, 39, 66; and marriage, 47; modification of, 40, 42, 47, 65; and possession, 51; and private/public, 52; and value, 40, 43, 50, 53, 62; and women's professional

autonomy, 50, 144 n. 2. *See also* authorship

authorship, 36–37, 67; and femininity, 52; and prostitution, 40, 144 n. 1; and public/private, 40. *See also* author

Awakening, The (Chopin), 2, 21, 143 n. 1, 144 n. 2, 145 n. 4

Backward Glance, A (Wharton), 36, 39, 40, 55

Baker, Paula, 4, 155 n. 5

Banta, Martha, 147 n. 15

barbarism, 9, 89; anthropological accounts of, 89; and exchange, 89–90; and kinship networks, 90; and ownership, 9; and tribal chief, 89–91. *See also* anthropological theory; big business; family; immigration; marriage; patriarchy

Barrell, John, 147 n. 17

Bart, Lily (heroine), 29, 36, 44, 53–60, 63–71, 96–99, 102

beauty, 54–55, 58–59, 64; and value, 26, 44. *See also* aesthetics; body

Bebel, August, 142 n. 3

Bell, Rev. Ernest, 1, 78, 82, 85–90, 93, 107–8, 115, 117, 129, 142 n. 3, 147 n. 1; *Fighting the Traffic in Young Girls*, 134 n. 14

Bender, Bert, 145 n. 4

Berry, Walter (Wharton's co-editor), 39

big business, 2, 5–6, 78, 82, 85; and industrial expansion, 4; and monopoly, 149 n. 7; and trust, 88. *See also* Standard Trust Oil

Bingham, Chief Theodore, 79–80, 85–86

Birnbaum, Michele A., 144 n. 2

blacks, 92, 95, 103; and slavery, 95, 102–3

body, 22, 60–61; and beauty, 55; as commodity, 56, 64; and consumerism, 58; as exchange value, 25–26, 30, 63; and medical education market, 79; and paintings, 69. *See also* female body

Bookman, 42

Bordering on the Body (Doyle), 141 n. 1, 151 n. 14

Bowlby, Rachel, 142 n. 8

Brier, Stephen, 149 n. 7

Bristow, Edward, 149 n. 3, 152 n. 19, 153 n. 25

British Empire, 94, 101

British nationalism, 96. *See also* nationalism

British reform movement, 94, 101, 152 n. 19. *See also* reform

brothel, 5, 104; commercialization of, 5, 104–7, 124; madam, 89; raids, 107, 151 n. 12. *See also* white slavery

"Brother Cutting Up His Own Sister" (Quale), 76, 93, 97

Brown, Gillian, 8

Butler, Josephine, 148 n. 3

capitalism. *See* commodification; consumerism; value

captivity narrative, 76, 148 n. 2

Carnegie, Andrew, 82, 150 n. 7

Castiglia, Christopher, 148 n. 2

Chandler, Lucinda, 22

Chicago, 75–76

Chicago Sunday Record-Herald, 134

Chicago Vice Commission, 136

Chopin, Kate, 2, 16–17, 21–22, 24, 26, 29, 138, 143 n. 1, 144 n. 2, 145 n. 4; *The Awakening,* 2, 21, 143 n. 1, 144 n. 2, 145 n. 4

citizenship, 100–101, 102, 135, 138–39; and disembodiment, 155 n. 3; and prostitution, 137

Civil War, 102–3

Cixous, Helene, 143 n. 12

Clement, Catherine, 143 n. 12

clothing, 41, 68–70, 107–9, 114–17, 131–33; as value, 33

Cobbett, William, 153 n. 24

Cogman, Ogden, 44, 64

colonial discourses, 94; and white slavery literature, 94–95

Colquitt, Claire, 146 n. 12

commodification: and femaleness, 6–7, 11; of motherhood, 13; of woman, 10. *See also* consumerism; value

Connelly, Mark, 77–78, 88–89, 90

consumerism, 2; and daughter, 112, 114; and evolution, 11, 130; and femininity, 11, 56; and forced prostitution, 129; and materialism, 12, 133; and mechanical readers, 42, 45, 49–50; and mechanical writer, 44; and wife, 9, 10; and women, 108, 134, 136. *See also* commodification; value

consumption. *See* consumerism.

Contagious Disease Acts of the 1860s, 148 n. 3

contraceptive technology, 23, 24

contract, 108–10, 117, 154 n. 2. *See also* marriage

Conway, Jill, 130

Cooper, Frederic Taber, 43–44

Cordasco, Francesco, 77–78

Creole, 30, 32

Crimes of the White Slavers and the Results (Regan), 142 n. 3

Crittendon, Charles, 109–10, 118–19

Crittendon Mission, 109

Culver, Stuart, 39

Darwin, Charles, 57, 59, 64, 145 nn. 4, 5; and evolutionary theories, 8; and sexual selection, 11, 12, 57

daughter: and consumerism, 112, 114; as family possession, 41, 111–12, 114. *See also* family; possession

Davis, David Brion, 148 n. 2

debasement: of author and book, 39; in the marketplace, 37; as professionalism, 37; and redemption, 36

Decoration of Houses, The (Wharton), 39, 44, 64
Democracy and Social Ethics (Addams), 154 n. 2
Descent of Man, and Selection in Relation to Sex, The (Darwin), 57
detective story, 122
Dimock, Wai-Chee, 141 n. 1, 144 n. 3
domestic ideology, 8, 16, 133; and barbarism, 8; and consumerism, 7–8; and femininity, 44–45; and possession, 56; and separate spheres, 7; and sexual commodity, 118. *See also* family; marriage; social housekeeping
Doyle, Laura, 141 n. 1, 151 n. 14

Eastern Europe, 90, 92. *See also* immigrants
economic novel, 145 n. 2
Elementary Structures of Kinship, The (Lévi-Strauss), 80
Eliot, George, 144 n. 1
European discourses, 88–95
European white slavery, 101. *See also* white slavery
evolution, stages in civilization, 8–11; and differentiation, 63; and femininity, 10–11; and sexual selection, 11–12, 57. *See also* anthropological theory; Darwin, Charles
Ewen, Stuart, 117
exchange of woman, 1, 4, 6, 8, 10, 16, 80–81, 91, 126, 141 n. 2; and altruism, 10; and body, 7; and capitalism, 2; as critique of consumer culture, 8; and maternity, 14; network of, 83, 93; and whiteness, 94. *See also* exchange value; value
exchange value, 6; and body, 25; and domestic woman, 136; and femaleness, 6; of women's bodies, 127. *See also* exchange of woman; value
exogamy, 33, 80, 86. *See also* marriage

familial possession, 84, 86; of property, 84; of women, 115. *See also* possession

family: and affinity, 92; traditional, 111–12, 114–15, 120; values, 105; and white slavery, 118. *See also* marriage; patriarchy
Fee, Elizabeth, 3–4
female body, 41, 56, 71, 75, 79, 81, 129, 132–34, 137–38; and disembodiment, 155 n. 3; and embodiment, 135; and hands, 56; as item of trade, 127; sister, 80, 93; as subject of representation, 69–70; and value forms, 65. *See also* body
femininity. *See* female body
feminist reform ideology: contraceptive technology, 23; female citizenship, 127; social housekeeping, 134. *See also* reform
feminist reformers, 24
femme couverte, 26–27
femme seule, 26–27
Fighting the Traffic (Bell), 142 n. 3, 147 n. 1
Frankenberg, Ruth, 94, 152 n. 16
Fryer, Judith, 146 n. 13

Gallagher, Catherine, 101, 144 n. 1, 152 n. 24
Geddes, Patrick, 130
Gilbert, Sandra M., 50, 144 n. 2
Gilman, Charlotte Perkins, 2, 3, 7, 10–16, 21, 24, 58, 129–31
Girl That Disappears, The (Bingham), 79
Glennard, Stephen, 47–53
Gordon, Linda, 23
Great War on White Slavery, or Fighting for the Protection of Our Girls, The (Roe), 76
Greater Inclination, The (Wharton), 39
Grittner, Frederick, 93, 148 nn. 2, 3, 152 n. 19
Gryce, Percy, 65
Gubar, Susan, 50, 144 n. 2, 146 n. 13
Guy, Donna, 101, 152 n. 19, 153 n. 27

Hapke, Laura, 79, 148 n. 2, 149 n. 4
Hartsfield, Larry, 154 n. 4

History of the Standard Oil Company
    (Tarbell), 85
House of Bondage, The (Kauffman),
    142 n. 9, 147 n. 1
House of Mirth, The (Wharton), 29,
    36–40, 44, 54, 60, 66, 96, 101, 141 n. 1,
    145 nn. 2, 4

Illinois Training School for Girls, 82
immigrant, 111, 151 n. 14. *See also* immi-
    gration
immigration, 90–92, 94–95; and U.S.
    Immigration Commission Report,
    88; and white slavery literature, 78.
    See also immigrant
incest, 80–81, 100. *See also* family
Indians, 90
Italians, 92

James, Henry, 37–38, 53
Jews, 78, 92, 96

Kaplan, Amy, 45
Kauffman, Reginald, 142 n. 9, 147 n. 1
Kentucky, 27
kinship. *See* barbarism; family; Lévi-
    Strauss, Claude; marriage; patriarchy
Kraditor, Aileen S., 134, 143 n. 13

Lanser, Susan S., 152 n. 16
law enforcement narrative, 123–24,
    154 n. 4
Leach, William, 22–23
Lévi-Strauss, Claude, 1, 5, 16, 80, 100,
    141 n. 1, 142 n. 2, 143 n. 12
Lewis, Dido, 23
Lippard, George, 148 n. 2
literary documents, love letters, 48–49,
    66-67
literary market, 42, 50, 52, 67–68; and
    debasement, 40, 52; and value, 40,
    42, 45. *See also* author; authorship
literary professionalism, 45- 46; and
    private/public selves, 46. *See also* au-
    thor; authorship
Locke, John, 3

London, England, 94
Louisiana, 26
Love Letters of an English Woman, 42–43

MacKinnon, 143 n. 14
MacKirdy, Mrs. Archibald, 94–95
MacPherson, C. B., 3
Madeleine, 126–27
Mann Act, 76, 93, 149 n. 4, 155 n. 4
market. *See* literary market; value
marriage, 56, 92, 126; bourgeois, 6;
    and childhood, 120; contract, 110;
    and divorce, 46–47; false, 119–29; and
    fidelity, 31; market, 32; monogamous,
    10; and prostitution, 124–25. *See also*
    patriarchy
Married Womenís Property Acts, 27
Marx, Karl, 143 n. 10
maternalism, 133; as exchange value, 14.
    See also motherhood
matriolatry, 12 -13, 15
Matthaei, Julie A., 142 n. 6
McClintock, Anne, 151 n. 14
McClure's magazine, 76
McDowell, Margaret, 145 n. 3
McLennan, John, 3, 154 n. 5
Mediterranean, 78
melodrama, 7, 99, 152 n. 23
Meyerowitz, Joanne, 154 n. 1
Michaels, Walter Benn, 29, 69, 143 n. 10,
    146 n. 14, 147 n. 16, 151 n.15
Mink, Gwendolyn, 151 n. 15
"More Love Letters of an English-
    woman" (Wharton), 43
Morrison, Toni, 152 n. 18
motherhood, 14, 29–30; and economic
    exchange, 13; modern version, 14;
    mother-woman, 28–30; natural,
    13; and race, 12; and reform, 15;
    and sacrifice, 14–16, 35; and sexual
    commodification, 15; voluntary,
    28; and work, 133. *See also* social
    housekeeping
muckraking, 76, 148 n. 3
mysteries and miseries (genre), 76,
    148 n. 2

Napoleonic Code, 26
nationalism, 78, 90, 93, 94–95, 101–3
New Conscience and an Ancient Evil, A
    (Addams), 127–31, 135–36
New Ideals of Peace (Addams), 154 n. 2
New Woman, 4
New York City, 85
New York Vice Commission, 104–5,
    123, 124

Orvell, Miles, 147 n. 15
"Other Two, The" (Wharton), 46
ownership. *See* possession

Pateman, Carole, 110, 142 n. 5, 153 n. 1,
    154 n. 2, 155 n. 3
patriarch, 119, 125–26
patriarchy: and kinship, 151 n. 14; pa-
    triarchal authority, 116, 117, 124;
    patriarchal family, 117; patriarchal
    possessiveness, 115; and white slav-
    ery, 126
Pontellier, Edna, 21, 22, 24–35
Pontellier, Léonce, 21, 22, 24–25, 27,
    31–33
possession, 31, 108; of authorship, 44;
    and capitalism, 3; of commodities,
    132; and monogamy, 1; and self, 31;
    and sexuality, 32. *See also* property
    system
potlatch, 32–33
private sphere, 31–32; and market,
    42, 47; and professionalism, 45; and
    property, 41. *See also* public sphere;
    self-ownership
"Procuring Country Girls for City Re-
    sorts" (Roe), 95
Progressive Era, 77–78, 85–86, 90,
    92, 128–29, 134, 138, 150 n. 7, 155 n. 5;
    market, 5
Progressive nationalism, 92
Progressive nativism, 151 n. 15
Progressivism, 90, 136
property system, 2–4, 8–9; and body,
    22, 24–25; and hands, 24–26; and
    white slave, 3

prostitute: display of, 86; protection of,
    110; street vs. brothel, 109
prostitution, 1, 3, 6, 79; "commercial-
    ized," 77, 149 n. 5; criminalization
    of, 150 n. 12; and reform, 76, 148 n. 3,
    149 nn. 4, 5
public sphere, 32, 128–29, 133, 135, 137–
    38, 155 n. 4; and private self, 53, 138.
    See also private sphere

Quale, Dr. C. C., 76, 79–81, 83–84, 86–
    89, 100, 126, 142 n. 9

race, 56–57, 90–92, 94–95, 96, 100–101,
    144 n. 2; and nation, 151 n. 15; and
    racial difference, 151 n. 14
Ramon, Amanda, 115–21
Ramon, Estelle, 1–7, 119–22, 125–26
Ramon, John, 115–21, 126
Ratignolle, Adele, 25–31, 34
reader: mechanical, 38; and owner-
    ship of woman, 93, 97–98, 100; and
    readership, 42; and reading public,
    37; and reform, 84. *See also* consum-
    erism; literary market
reform, 78; and anti–white slavery cru-
    saders, 123, 125; and commercialism,
    128; and family, 105, 129; and mar-
    riage, 27
Regan, John, 5, 142 n. 3, 150 n. 11
Renan, Ernest, 151 n. 15
representation, 69; as a value form, 68
Republic of the Spirit (Selden), 53, 70,
    145 n. 7
Reynolds, Sir Joshua, 67–69, 96–97, 101
Richards, Evelleen, 57
Riley, Denise, 143 n. 14
Rockefeller, John D., Jr., 85, 86, 89,
    149 n. 5, 150 n. 7
Rockefeller Commission, 86
Roe, Clifford, 76–81, 85–89, 93–95,
    102–3, 107, 123–27
roman à clef, 62
Roosevelt administration, 150 n. 7
Rosedale, Sim, 96
Rosen, Ruth, 149 n. 5, 150 n. 12, 151 n. 12

Rubin, Gayle, 16, 142 n. 2
Russett, Cynthia Eagle, 145 n. 5

Schreiner, Olive, 8
Scott, David, 120
Scott, William, 119–22, 125–27
Scribner's Magazine, 37, 39, 47
Selden, Lawrence, 54–59, 63–67, 70–71,
  96, 98–99, 102, 145 n. 7
selfhood. *See* self-ownership
self-ownership, 21–22, 24; and motherhood, 24; and prostitution, 110; and
  public, 41; and reproduction, 23;
  sacrifice of, 3–4; and selfhood, 34–
  35, 39, 41, 67, 139; and sex, 22, 27–28;
  and voluntary motherhood, 23,
  27–28
Seltzer, Mark, 54, 58, 145 n. 1, 147 n. 16
sexuality, 34; and markets, 79; and
  value, 32
Shearer, Reverend J. G., 78, 102
Sherman Anti-Trust Act, 150 n. 7
Showalter, Elaine, 145 n. 3
Sinclair, Paul, 89, 123–25
Sloan, Kay, 148 n. 1
Smith-Rosenberg, Carroll, 142 n. 6
social housekeeping, 16, 135. *See also*
  Addams, Jane; reform
Spectator, 48, 50
speculation: and aesthetic pleasure, 55,
  56, 58; and pregnancy, 29; and white-
  ness, 102
Spencer, Herbert, 3, 8, 10, 63
Standard Oil Trust, 85, 150 n. 7
Stanton, Elizabeth Cady, 22, 27, 35,
  143 n. 1
Stead, William, 148 n. 3
Stocking, George, 151 n. 14
Stolen Lives (Altink), 149 n. 5
Sutherland, Principal D. F., 115, 119–
  22, 125

tableau vivant, 68, 96, 98
Tanagra, 62, 68; powder, 63; statu-
  ettes, 61
Tarbell, Ida, 85, 89

Theory of the Leisure Class (Veblen),
  8, 10
"Thrilling Stories of Eye-Opener
  on White Slavery" (Quale), 76, 79,
  142 n. 9
Touchstone, The (Wharton), 42, 47–48,
  51–52, 65
Traffic in Souls, The, 76, 87, 151 n. 13
tragedy (literary), 7, 36, 55, 99
Trenor, Gus, 99
Trent, Alexa, 47–48
trompe l'oeil, 69
"True Story of Estelle Ramon of Ken-
  tucky, The" (Sutherland), 1, 7, 115
True Womanhood, 7
Turner, George Kibbe, 76, 85, 148 n. 3

Unionist abolitionism, 102–3
United States, 1, 76, 78, 88–89, 93
United States v. Holte (1915), 149 n. 4,
  155 n. 4

value: and aesthetics, 71; and book,
  37–38, 53; bride as, 33; and child, 121;
  clothing, 108; of daughter, 84; and
  erotics, 31, 34; in exchange, 3, 6; and
  female body, 24, 55; of love letters,
  49–51, 67; and reproduction, 30; and
  selfhood, 24; and sexual exchange,
  3, 6, 24, 127; of sister, 81–82, 86; and
  wealth, 50–51; of woman, 7, 83, 84,
  136
Van Alstyne, Ned, 70
Veblen, Thorstein, 8-9, 10, 24–25, 40, 45,
  55, 89–90, 109, 114, 116
Vice Commissions, 77, 149 n. 5
"Vice of Reading, The" (Wharton), 37,
  39, 42–43, 45, 49–50, 64–65
voluntary motherhood, 21, 23, 29,
  144 n. 2. *See also* motherhood

Ward, Lester, 59
Waythorn, Alice, 46–47
Welter, Barbara, 7
Wharton, Edith, 2-3, 6-7, 16- 17, 29, 36–
  47, 50–58, 60–62, 64–65, 69, 96–99,

101, 138, 141 n. 1, 145 n. 4, 146 n. 14, 152 nn. 21, 23
"white slave," 94, 100–102, 153 n. 24
White Slave Hell, The, 103
White Slave Market, The (MacKirdy), 94–95
White Slave Traffic Act, 76–77
white slavery, 76, 77; and abolitionism, 103; and class, 6, 91; and commercialization, 77, 82, 85; and daughters, 83–84; and exchange network, 93; and immigration, 88; and materialism, 130; organization of, 2, 84, 86–89; and race, 5; reform, 123–25; symbolic economy of, 86, 87; U.S. vs. European, 78, 88, 93, 95; and women's consumerism, 129
white slavery literature, 1–3, 75–77, 81; and alienness, 91; and brother narratives, 80–81, 86, 100; and commercialization, 7, 85; and debasement of female body, 97–99; as detective literature, 76, 122; and exchange of female body, 100; and exchange system, 91; and market value of women, 127; and narrative conventions, 76; and reform, 5; and symbolic economy, 92
whiteness, 94, 96–98, 100–102; and economic value, 95, 102; and female body, 96

Who Built America? (Brier), 82, 149 n. 7
"Why Women Should Vote" (Addams), 134
wife, 1, 9; as personal property, 22; and prostitution, 118–19, 136. *See also* family; marriage; patriarchy
Willis, W. N., 94–95
woman: as commodity, 4–5, 7; and consumerism, 9, 10; and contractual relations, 109; and nonproductivity, 9; as property, 9; and public/private, 1, 46; as sexual commodity, 2, 10, 29, 30; as surplus wealth, 25; woman as type, 68
Woman Past, Present, and Future (Bebel), 142 n. 3
woman question, the, 4, 6
women: as commodities, 2, 7, 12, 133; and consumerism, 9, 129–30; and economic production, 11; and evolutionary modification, 11; as objects of exchange, 3, 15; as property, 2, 3; and property rights, 27; and self-speculation, 29
Women and Economics (Gilman), 2, 3, 10, 129
work, 64; and consumerism, 131; ethics, 8; and women, 131–33, 154 n. 1
World War I, 1
Wright, Henry C., 23
Writing of Fiction, The (Wharton), 61

Library of Congress Cataloging-in-Publication Data

Stange, Margit.
    Personal property : wives, white slaves, and the market in
women / Margit Stange.
        p.   cm.
    Includes bibliographical references and index.
    ISBN 0-8018-5626-4 (alk. paper)
    1. American fiction—Women authors—History and
criticism.   2. Wharton, Edith, 1862–1937—Characters—
Women.   3. Women and literature—United States—History.
4. Women—United States—Economic conditions.   5. Chopin,
Kate, 1851–1904. Awakening.   6. Prostitution—United States—
History.   7. Married women in literature.   8. Prostitution in
literature.   9. Property in literature.   I. Title.
    PS374.W6S74   1998
813.009'9287—dc21   97-29656
                                                          CIP